COP WORLD

COP WORLD

Inside an American Police Force

JAMES McCLURE

PANTHEON BOOKS, NEW YORK

All rights reserved under International and Pan-American Copyright
Conventions. Published in the United States by Pantheon Books, a division of
Random House, Inc., New York, and simultaneously in Canada by Random
House of Canada Limited, Toronto.
Originally published in Great Britain by Macmillan London Ltd.

Library of Congress Cataloging in Publication Data

McClure, James, 1939–
Cop World.
1. Police—California—San Diego.   2. Police
patrol—California—San Diego.   I. Title.
HV1848.S3M37 1985   363.2' 09794' 98   84-25431
ISBN 0-394-51007-0

Manufactured in the United States of America

First American Edition

For my twin brother

Contents

COP WORLD

A very brief briefing

Every police department is the child of its city. Before attempting to gain any insight into one, it helps to know a little about the other.

This city is the seaport of San Diego, which lies roughly a hundred miles south of Los Angeles and only fourteen miles north of the Mexican border.

It has an interesting history, full of small surprises.

Spain's first exploratory voyage into the Pacific was led by Juan Rodriquez Cabrillo, a former crossbowman who had taken part in the destruction of the Aztec empire under Cortez.

Fleeing a storm on the way north from Guatemala, his two ships made for what looked like a large island, and found sanctuary in calm waters that he dubbed the Bay of San Miguel. There, on 25 September 1542, Cabrillo became the first European to set foot on the west coast of, latterly, the United States of America, and the 'large island' was named after a fabulous isle in *The Deeds of Esplandian*, an immensely popular epic of those times, written by Garcia de Montalvo.

'It is a mysterious place of uncommon beauty and unparalleled wealth,' ran de Montalvo's description of the isle. 'All about its shores are steep mountains and rugged cliffs. . . . The rivers that empty into the sea from the interior are full of gold. . . . But most mysterious and beautiful of all is the woman for whom this island is named . . . Calafia.'

And the name of her island was of course, California.

Cabrillo died suddenly not long after. Sixty years went by before the next Spanish explorer, Sebastian Vizcaino, sailed into the Bay of San Miguel, which he promptly renamed in honor of his flagship. San Diego, Vizcaino reported back, would make an ideal settlement, but it took another 167 years or so, and a nasty rumor about the Russians, before anything further happened.

This rumor reached King Carlos III of Spain in 1769. Russia, he was told, having set up outposts in Alaska, now had its eye on the west coast and was beginning to expand southward. Carlos immediately issued orders, and within months both a mission and a *presidio*, or military headquarters, had been established at San Diego, overlooking the bay.

Spanish rule then continued until San Diego became part of Mexico in 1821, and it was for a time the capital of Alta and Baja (Upper and Lower) California, although it was to remain essentially an adobe village for two decades or more. The whaling and hide industries flourished, and immigrants began arriving. Some came by sea from New England; others were led there in overland parties by Kit Carson and other legendary mountain men; all were to have their effect on the predominantly Spanish culture. But a far more abrupt change followed when President James Polk declared war on Mexico in 1846.

It wasn't battle and bloodshed that did this – San Diego was taken without any resistance – but the belated arrival of the Mormon Battalion after hostilities had ceased. Despite the fact the Mormons had just completed the longest infantry march in history, covering two thousand miles from Council Bluffs in Iowa, they instantly set about putting to rights what struck them as a squalid pueblo, and asked nothing in return.

They made a brick kiln and used the bricks to construct the first brick building in California, to line drinking wells, and to repair houses, which they also gave a coat of whitewash. They opened a bakery and a blacksmith's forge, started a coal mine, and cleared away the accumulated garbage and filth of almost half a century. Then back they marched to Salt Lake, blazing a trail through San Bernardino and Las Vegas that was to become the route taken by Interstate 15, and leaving behind them the basis for a tradition of innovation and civic pride.

In 1867, a redoubtable innovator, San Francisco financier Alonzo E. Honzo, bought one thousand acres along the shoreline at twenty-six cents an acre, and then offered free plots of land to both merchants and families. This shifted the center of the population down from Presidio Hill, and when there was a gold strike in the county two years later, the so-called 'Founder of San Diego' was able to note with satisfaction that the settlement had an established economy.

San Diego was incorporated as a city in 1872 – the council-manager form of local government was adopted in 1931 – and as the decade ended, the Californian Southern Railroad reached the port, followed soon afterwards by the Santa Fe. Ready access from the East brought a land boom, and in just two years, between 1885 and 1887, the city's population rose six times from 5000 to 30,000.

It has never stopped rising. The 1950s saw a surge from 334,387 to over half a million, and at the start of the 1980s the figure was topping 850,000, to make it, in terms of population, California's second-largest city. Anglo-Americans predominate (76 percent), followed by the Mexican American (15 percent) and Black American (9 percent) communities, with other ethnic groups, such as Vietnamese refugees and a handful of American Indians, making up the balance.

Physically, San Diego is in fact the second-largest city in the whole of the western United States, covering an area of 392 square miles, and has about ten inches of rain a year, falling mainly in the winter months.

The city's most important feature is the landlocked, deepwater bay, extending over twenty-two square miles, that has been described as one of the great natural harbors of the world. Shipping using the Panama Canal makes San Diego a first port of call, there is a large commercial fishing fleet, and the bay is a major base for U.S. Navy, Marine Corps and Coast Guard operations.

Industrially, San Diego is highly diversified to include, among a great number of other things, clothing manufacture, fish canning, aerospace and electronics. San Diego County is one of America's leading agricultural areas, and so it also acts as the chief distribution center in southern California for citrus, avocado and truck-farming crops.

Tourism plays a large part in the city's economy, too, and as a resort with more than seventy miles of beach, it draws close on half a million visitors a year. Disneyland is not far away, the bullring at Tijuana is only a step across the border, and then

11

there are San Diego's own attractions, such as Sea World, Balboa Park, the three-masted Star of India, and one of the world's most famous zoos. Yet, facts and figures aside, San Diego cannot be called a big city, in that it never feels in the least overwhelming. The downtown area, for example, when approached from almost any direction, gives the impression of having scarcely more than a dozen tall buildings.

Another striking thing about San Diego is that people appear, rather like Juan Rodriquez Cabrillo, disinclined to take the place simply at face value, but hint instead at myths and legends just a scratch beneath the surface. Some San Diegans refer to it as 'Camelot by the Sea', and seem to be only half-joking.

Is that because this city, spread out lazily between encircling mountains and the sea, can be so beautiful it doesn't look quite real at times? It could be. Even the less fanciful, with both feet on the ground, seem to find ways of conceding a sense of underlying unreality. Like the well-traveled tourist, quoted in a local guide book, who was heard to remark that had Walt Disney designed and built Spain, he would have ended up with San Diego.

All too real, however, if less obvious to someone just passing through, are aspects of its ugly side: murder, rape, child abuse, armed robbery, suicide.

Law enforcement within the city limits is primarily the responsibility of the City of San Diego Police Department. If its 1300 sworn officers no longer look quite like other American police officers, and don't conduct themselves quite as others do, that is because the San Diego PD now spells COP with capital letters.

It stands for the Community Oriented Policing program, a succession of sweeping changes, largely initiated over the past few years, which is still gathering momentum and could well make the department a legend in its own right some day.

But, paradoxically, one of the main functions of COP is to debunk myths, and in particular those that threaten a realistic working relationship between the department and its public. Some, chiefly those associated with the Wild West and with knights in shining armor, still haven't been entirely overcome, and probably never will be. But, through COP, which has already done so much to alter that basic policing archetype, Macho Man, ways are being found to modify them.

Every job tends to create a world of its own, and this is very true of police work, which then goes on to set up worlds within worlds, known as divisions or precincts or districts.

Central Division, San Diego, is the smallest in the city, taking in only about thirty square miles, but this is because its officers have to deal with more than a quarter of the total crime workload.

The division has three beat areas, each again as different as a separate country, and these are referred to in workaday conversation as 'downtown, the Heights, and Hillcrest'. Time adds a further dimension, affecting how each police officer regards his or her working world. Second Watch, which begins in the early afternoon, is perhaps the most balanced of the three eight-hour shifts, combining as it does night and day.

Worlds such as these are not only unique, in that they reflect the particular societies they are superimposed upon, but they are more often than not exclusive worlds, and not open to the public. In San Diego, however, in this, as in so many other ways, things are very different.

Part I

Ride-along

1

Way up, two hundred and more feet above the bay, a glitter of cars is gathering on the giddy curve of the bridge to Coronado.

'We have a jumper . . .'

Something pale is clinging to the parapet of the bridge, only the minutest speck at this distance.

'A male jumper . . . ,' says the police radio.

If he should suddenly let go, to drop flailing, making a thin forlorn cry like the hungry gulls around him, that lapping blue water, dainty with sailboats, is going to turn to solid glass for an instant. He'll burst wide and open.

Then see those gulls dive.

'Usually, if he's going to go, he goes pretty fast,' remarks a young police officer to his ride-along, as they draw up on the outskirts of downtown to watch.

The ride-along, nondescript in shirt, slacks and loafers, simply nods. Second Watch has barely begun, and he is still adjusting to being in the patrol unit with Officer Lee Easton, who joined the San Diego Police Department just on a year ago.

Lee Easton is twenty-three, fair-haired, six-feet-two tall, weighs two hundred, has a small neat mustache under flared nostrils, and could rival Hutch's good looks, although his own are more masculine. If he has a particular trait, then it is one of appearing far more detached than he actually feels.

I had a jumper my second day out – near Thanksgiving. He had taken some drugs epileptics take, and between the drugs and the holidays, he started to feel sorry for himself, so he got up on this archway above the top of a twelve-story arcade.

When I originally got the call, it was for a drunk – I guess because someone had seen him stagger back and forth – and that's what I thought it was, until he said he was going to jump. There was no way anyone could have gotten to him. He was on a ledge, swaying because of the wind and the drugs – all I could do was try to stand up there in the wind and talk to him. You try to at least do something.

I talked to him for almost twenty minutes. He started crying two different times, his emotions fluctuated. They'd go to where he felt real sad and wanted to come down, and then he'd turn round

17

and say, 'No, it's not worth living for.' The only real hold I had on
him was: 'Hey, your mother's going to find out!'
    '*No*,' he'd say, 'no, I don't want her to find out.' And I'd say,
'Well, if you jump, I'm going to have to send her a letter and tell
her you jumped. That you killed yourself.' All this. Then he'd say,
'No, don't! Because my sister blew her brains out with a forty-five,
and I don't want my mom to go through the same trouble again.'

The blowfly glitter on that long bleached rib-bone of a bridge is
starting to disperse, shooed away by the police units now
arriving. And the jumper, in the droll words of someone on
the radio, is still hanging in there.
    'If you can get to the guy safely, without worrying about
yourself, okay,' Easton tells his ride-along. 'If you think he's
big enough to pull you with him, don't waste your time. But
it's rare they'll jump, if you can bargain with them, talk to
them for a really long time.'
    'Mmm-hm. Bargain, how?'
    'All they want is sympathy, you know. He wants somebody
to come up and tell him how they care for him, and how
they're going to help him and everything. It makes him feel
like, "Hey, I'm wanted! I exist! I'm *alive* . . ."'

> You could hear the big pop sound. My gut and everything just
> turned around and I really felt for the guy – whereas now, I don't
> think it would hit me as hard. You kind of build up to where you
> don't let your emotions out, and being as new as I was, I hadn't
> gotten to that point yet. But I've still of course, in the back of my
> mind, that big *blap*. Sounded like a shotgun.
>   It was only a split-second after wanting to come down, my guy
> goes, 'Lee, turn away. I don't want you to see it.'
>   I shall never forget that – so he did have part of his mind, as he
> was swaying back and forth. And I kept on saying, 'No, don't!
> Don't! I'm NOT going to turn away!'
>   He just turned round and did a dive. People who saw him said it
> was a perfect dive.

Nothing moves up on the bridge. The afternoon remains as
pretty as a picture postcard. That huge Pacific sky, blue
enough to dip a pen in; that sunbaked butter-cookie tract of
land beneath; linking them, those long flamingo legs of
concrete, wading the bay to Coronado. And the jumper, just a
tiny white flaw in the printing.
    The ride-along begins to fidget. Jumpers are far from
uncommon in San Diego, and besides, they show you them

on TV, flying through the air and everything. You don't have
to wait. Sometimes, when folk in the crowd below become
impatient, they'll shout, 'Jump, baby, jump!'

> After that jumper I had, they showed a little cartoon – I think it
> was in one of the papers. They had a guy jumping and a big splat
> on the ground, and guys holding up scores like they do in the
> Olympics.

2

A tendency for the public at large to take a different view of
things is part of what prompts the San Diego PD to carry
ride-alongs in its patrol units.

Norm Stamper, chief architect of COP, and Special Adviser
to the Chief of Police, recalls, 'The original COP program in '74
had two objectives.

'One was to get the officers to become very much more
knowledgeable about their beats, taking a look at everything
from socio-economic data to the networks of leadership and
communication within the community – and, most important-
ly from our perspective, the crime, the trends, patterns, the
victims.

'We also encouraged these officers, as a second objective, to
come up with new ways of doing business in San Diego. One
of these new ideas was the ride-along.

'They said, "Look, if we can get that fifteen-year-old kid in
the car with us, the one who's causing us problems – and who
is an influential community leader, of one description – and let
him see what police work is all about, try to educate him, be
educated *by* him about the community, we'll probably make
some progress."

'There were tremendous problems getting the administration of that time to accept it, but we had many officers using
this strategy for closing the gap between cops and kids.'

Now an everyday aspect of police work in the city, the
program is open to anyone who shows an interest, provided
the shift is spent in the area where the ride-along either lives or
works. The belief is that whether the ride-along is a teacher,
community worker, inquisitive teenager or self-styled 'ordin-

ary citizen', the exchange of insights and information, plus the shared experience, can only increase mutual understanding.

Two things, other than departmental approval of the idea, are necessary to run such a program.

Firstly, there has to be somewhere for the ride-along to sit. This isn't a problem in San Diego, where all patrol units carry only one officer, except in special circumstances.

Secondly, the administration has to be very confident that its officers will maintain professional standards at all times, irrespective of stress and of the fact many of them are young and inexperienced.

It isn't enough simply to insure that every ride-along signs an indemnity waiver before setting off. What about the ride-along, say, who would be outraged to hear a racial slur used in a heated moment? And it's perfectly possible, of course, for a ride-along to pass unnoticed at a scene where there are several units involved.

Patrol units carrying ride-alongs continue to work normally in San Diego, answering any call that comes their way, from family fights to liquor store hold-ups, and as yet no ride-along has been harmed. In fact, on more than one occasion, officers in difficulties have been saved from serious injury by ride-alongs using the radio to bring help. Ride-alongs are shown how to work the radio, and how to turn the unit into a yelping beacon with the help of its siren and flashing lights, before venturing on to the streets – just as they are also asked to note their exact whereabouts every time the officer makes a stop.

And this, say opponents of the one-man car system, which was introduced as more cost effective, only goes to show what a dumb idea it was, if officer safety is still a consideration. There are damned few ride-alongs abroad at two o'clock in the morning.

3

Lee Easton has been patrolling on his own for seven months now, and as COP is the only approach he knows to the job, he seems to accept the ride-along program without demur. He is also close enough to the community he serves to make another point about the program's value.

> I've had all kinds of ride-alongs. I had a sixteen-year-old girl, and I went and started talking to a transvestite. I was asking things like: 'How long have you been doing it?' 'What are your average prices?' 'Have you ever been beat up or cut?' Then the girl ride-along asked her things, too. These people are willing to talk – it's a big kick for them to tell someone their side of the story.

As for working alone, that is something else that Easton simply accepts, although, like all patrol officers, he is very aware of the dangers he faces.

> Most of my squad like it downtown – there's more security. If you're working out in the Heights, it may take three minutes, five even, for another unit to get to you. There, a lot of the time you're in some awkward street, they're trying to find where you're at in the map book, and you could be in a real big dangerous situation. Downtown, no matter where you are, if you call for cover, within a minute you'll have at least one unit to help you – sometimes, in fifteen seconds, you'll have two or three units! Just like that.
>
> For the first two days, it was kind of hectic, because here you have laws you don't enforce in other areas – drinking in public, jaywalking, all this – but now I love working downtown. Almost every corner, there's something to look at. There's a lot of people around that're actually bums, but I'll stop and speak to them, find out what their problems are. It's a shame, a lot of them aren't that bad. They could do much more with their lives.

4

The jumper hasn't budged.

'What's he waitin' for?' grumbles the ride-along.

Easton starts up the unit and turns away toward the center of downtown. 'All these guys want the TV cameras,' he says. 'The media's also attention. Right after the jumper I had was all over TV, I knew right away somebody else would do it. A couple of days later, a guy goes up on the same archway for two hours.'

'He jump?'

'Came down.'

'Yeah?' grunts the ride-along. Then he reaches out to stroke

21

the barrel of the 12-gauge shotgun locked to the dashboard in front of him. 'Where we goin'?' he asks.

'The Plaza. See that girl over there?'

Crossing an open expanse diagonally, scuffling along nowhere obvious, is a slight figure in a filthy dress and a pair of flappy old tennis shoes, her bowed face hidden by a tangle of long hair.

'Yeah, gross,' says the ride-along.

'It's illegal,' Easton tells him, 'to take anything out of city trash cans. That way it stops people from rummaging round and throwing trash about. Keeps trash where trash belongs.'

'Huh?' queries the ride-along, perplexed.

Easton makes a right, turning up toward Broadway. 'So these people were eating out of trash cans on my beat,' he says. 'The first time, I warned them. I said, "Don't eat out of trash cans! Tidy up the mess around it!" Second time I caught them, I had a longer talk, and afterwards I started thinking about it. These guys eat out of trash cans behind the restaurants, where actually some of the good food's thrown away, and they – '

'Jeez! Like . . . ?'

'Oh, fresh fruit, lettuces, all this,' explains Easton. 'And when I caught them, they were cleaning up around the trash cans, and it was a lot dirtier before they got there. So the third time, I said: "Hey, I'm not going to harass you – I'm goin' to let you keep eatin' it. All I want you to do is watch what you get out of there, and keep cleaning up like I saw you do the other day."' Easton shrugs. 'So there are a couple of areas that were really dirty, and now they're clean – and these guys are watching what they get to eat a little bit more. One of them's that twenty-four-year-old girl back there, not bad looking.'

The ride-along twists round in his seat, trying for another look at her through the rear window.

'It's a shame,' says Easton, 'because she could do a lot more for herself. But I guess she doesn't want to turn to prostitution or anything.'

And there is a hint of admiration in his voice that seems to confuse the ride-along, who probably can't conceive a lower form of American life than a garbage-eater.

He casts a searching glance at Easton. 'You like bein' a cop?' he asks.

'Everyone loves it. Every conversation goes towards it. When you go in a place and say, "I'm a police officer", it isn't like you're a janitor or a dishwasher. It's more like "Are you *really*?" It's respect and I like respect. I think everybody does – even the guy in the gutter wants respect.'

'Always wanted to be one?'

'I went into the army to save up a lot of money and see Europe,' says Easton, briefly scrutinizing two ragpickers on a vacant lot. 'My brother was already in the army, and he suggested I either go in the firefighters or in the military police. That military police, I really enjoyed it. I was in the service for three years, over in Germany.'

'Uh-huh – and then?'

'When I got out, I went to work for a stereo company for a little bit, as well as just bumming around, spending my money, getting used to being back. So then I went for a test to see how I'd do in the police department, and I came out in a high category. I said, "Hey, that's for you."'

The ride-along nods. 'Musta been a big help, bein' a cop before,' he says.

'Wasn't a big help at the academy,' says Easton, smiling, 'But out on the streets it is. Most new cops have trouble just getting out and walking up and just talking to everybody, but I was used to dealing with people.'

'And how about when you're off duty? What kinda – '

'Oh, I like athletics, weights – I like all sports. I try to get down to the beach a lot.' Then, in almost the same breath, Easton runs a check on the license plate two cars ahead of him. 'Ten-four,' he says, getting a 'no wants' reply from Communications.

Seconds later, he pulls over to the curb.

'Hey,' says the ride-along, 'why're we – ?'

Opening his car door, and removing a baton from its crude holster in the door panel, Easton motions at a sprawled figure on a bus bench, a few yards farther on.

'Watch the hands,' he instructs the ride-along. 'If I'm out and talking to somebody, and somebody else walks up, watch the hands. A guy isn't going to use his feet to shoot you.'

5

Others are watching the arrival of the patrol unit. Some do so casually; some covertly, warily. What they see has been carefully calculated.

The car is a modest-sized, four-door white sedan – in this case, a Dodge Aspen – with a toffee-brown interior. It has a strong metal grille separating its front and rear seats, a very plain light bar on the roof, an adjustable spotlight, a radio aerial, and the front bumper is protected by push-bars, which are used to clear away wrecks at traffic accidents. The city's crest is displayed on the front doors, above TO PROTECT AND SERVE in large gold lettering, and then along the front fenders and across the trunk, more gold spells out SAN DIEGO POLICE. The overall effect is muted, urbane.

Bill Kolender, who rose from the ranks in San Diego to take over as Chief of Police in 1977, believes that the 'black and white', America's traditional police car, has a popular image far too menacing and melodramatic to be compatible with community-oriented policing. Further evidence of COP thinking – which actually began, albeit in a small way, long before anyone put a name to it – is apparent in the dress and equipment of every patrol officer.

As Easton approaches the bus bench, its occupants are confronted by a uniform in keeping with both the physical and social climates of southern California: a short-sleeved, open-necked shirt in pale khaki, worn over a white sweat shirt (and armored vest), a pair of tan trousers with knife-edged creases; black shoes and a black gunbelt. Other law enforcement agencies favor a similar look, but there are significant differences in detail.

Easton wears only his badge and no other insignia. Chief Kolender has no time for what he calls 'Boy Scout' patches, regarding them not simply as superfluous, but also as 'alienators' between police and public. For the same reason, the trousers do not have colored stripes down their seams.

Then there is the badge itself. Tradition has it that patrol officers wear silver badges and detectives get to carry gold ones. Every officer has a gold badge in the San Diego PD, where being a detective is not a rank but an assignment. Silver badges are used instead to distinguish the unpaid part-timers who make up the Police Reserve.

Above his other shirt pocket, Easton has a brass name tag. For every five years he completes with the department, he'll rate a small symbol under his name – hence the term 'starships', applied to veterans with several of these stars in a row.

And now to what Easton does not have with him.

He is bare-headed, for instance. Chief Kolender, who wants his officers to be seen as individuals and not as 'robots', says: 'What is more individualistic than somebody's hair style? Why hide it?' By the same token, he holds that there are times when the community is best served by 'dehumanizing' an officer's appearance.

San Diego patrol officers are in fact issued with the same sort of protective helmets worn by motorcycle officers in Traffic, only this headgear remains, under normal circumstances, locked in the trunks of their units. Things were once very different.

> *Two-star officer*: I can remember how I must have intimidated the hell out of kids, when I got out of my black-and-white unit with my macho helmet on, my long-sleeved shirt and my neck-tie and my gun and my Mace and my combat boots.
>
> You stood there and you looked like you just wanted to *kill* this poor little bastard, and he's afraid. He's afraid even to tell you where he lives! For fear that one day he may wake up and you'll be out there, waitin' for him.
>
> Up until '71, we were required to wear a helmet, chin strap on all the time, even when you went into somebody's home to listen to their problems – you did not walk around the station patio without the old chin strap on! That in itself was macho, 'cos we all went out and bought these big chin cups and, wow, you were right *on*. They even wore sap gloves in those days – now they're outlawed, *very* outlawed. You can't carry any form of sap.

And the restrictions go further, as one of the recruits indicates: 'We're not supposed to wear black gloves or mirror sunglasses, ski glasses. They say they'd make us much too intimidating.'

So what are patrol officers allowed? Regular sunglasses and, in addition to the shotguns in their cars, the three weapons carried on their gunbelts: a canister of Mace; a light

25

wooden baton with no strap, resembling a length of broomstick; and, of course, a revolver.

The latter can be either the very basic Smith and Wesson with a 6" barrel on issue, or the officer's own choice of make and model, privately purchased. The most popular alternative is perhaps a .357 magnum, but whatever the handgun selected, it must likewise be able to fire conventional round-nosed .38 Special ammunition.

This is the only type of bullet permitted patrol officers by the San Diego PD, which rejects any suggestion there is a need for the devastating 'dumdum' effect of the hollow-points that some law enforcement agencies advocate. It is an outlook that has been summed up as, 'A hit is a hit, but overkill is a whole different attitude.'

And creating the appropriate COP attitude lies at the heart of all these measures, which have a double edge in that they take into account not only the impact of 'externals' on the public, but on the police officers themselves.

6

Few of the older patrol officers in San Diego need convincing that, in some ways, their job has become harder – nor that people can be strongly influenced by appearances.

> When at night I'm driving down the street and I see a car with a light bar on it, even being an eleven-year veteran of the police department, it still causes me to look at my speedo and check I'm doin' everything right. If it's one of ours, maybe I'll have a little game with him, drive a little faster. But if it's a black-and-white California Highway Patrol unit, *no* fun and games are to be played! Because they don't know me, and here's this big souped-up unit, the guy's got a hat on and all the patches and the point four-four magnum, and his command appearance tells me he's *not* to be played with, y'know. He may be just as nice as some of the officers we have, maybe nicer, but I just have that respect.

It seems rare, however, for anyone in the San Diego PD to lament that 'respect' is no longer an automatic right, conferred by a similar 'command appearance', and there could be a twofold explanation for this.

'A lot of guys couldn't handle the anti-macho thing and quit,' says a survivor of the changes, which once contributed to a high attrition rate. 'I guess they felt too exposed. It was scary for them to go into situations with kind of the minimum. Plus, a lot weren't into community oriented. "Who needs to stand around rappin' with a bunch of fuckin' assholes and scumbags, f'chrissake?" – that kind of remark. We still get guys like that, but mostly they don't stick around too long.'

And then there is the other side of that same coin: 'I like the challenge,' says another officer. 'Sure, it's scary sometimes, but . . . Oh, it's you have to be more professional, be real good at your job. And I like the feeling, the pride it gives me – y'know, it's a different kind of macho, more subtle. It really takes balls to do it this way.'

7

Lee Easton, quietly and without fuss, approaches the youth sprawled on the bus bench, gets him to his feet, handcuffs his hands behind his back, and returns with him to the unit, all without any overt hostility among the onlookers.

Once the prisoner has been locked in the back, the staid interior of the unit becomes disreputable with the fumes of cheap liquor. The ride-along wrinkles his nose, but seems excited by this. He turns to peer through the grille behind him, and now there is an overlay of a second, foetid sort of smell. It hints at only urine, feces, stale sweat and vomit, but probably confirms the trite yet compelling impression that he faces a caged and potentially dangerous animal. Especially when the prisoner, growing resentful of his gaze, snarls an obscenity and lunges forward, making the ride-along jerk back.

Unmoved, Easton clicks a pen and prepares for some form filling. 'Okay, so what's your name?' he says.

Last name, middle name, first name . . . The prisoner's personal details emerge in a grudging incantation, right down to the last digit of his Social Security number. He is also expected, despite his state of obvious self-neglect, to know his correct weight, and gives it to the nearest pound. The ride-along glances back and forth, between the shower-fresh, seemingly favored, personable young officer and the dissipated ancient in an unbuttoned red shirt, soiled jeans and cowboy boots, who turns out to be only nineteen.

After Easton has run a check on the radio to make sure his prisoner isn't wanted on warrant, he puts aside his clipboard and sets the unit in motion.

'I'm going to jail?' the prisoner asks.

'How much money you got?' says Easton, having adopted a street accent.

'Oh, a dollar.'

'How are you going to eat dinner tonight?'

The prisoner frowns. '*Dinner?*' he repeats, as though suddenly tossed a word in an alien tongue.

The unit stops for a red light. 'How long have you been in San Diego?' asks Easton, watching the late Saturday traffic.

'About two and a half weeks.'

'And all you've been doin' is just drink?'

A pause. 'Not really.'

'Why did you leave New York?'

'To go to school.' The prisoner edges forward, trying to catch Easton's expression. 'I'm going to detox?'

Easton shrugs. 'I'm still debatin',' he says. 'I can't have you sleepin' on my benches.'

'I plan to get a hotel room.'

Easton says nothing, just looks thoughtful.

Whenever you go in the jail, the atmosphere is so negative you almost get depressed. Drunks aren't usually going to be there long, so they're mostly in one big tank and they're watched a lot. But if you're in there any length of time, over the weekend, then you're in with a bunch of guys who've been through prison, and a lot of them get together and take advantage of younger guys like him. Someone like him would probably end up getting raped within the first couple of nights.

'Hey,' says the prisoner, his tone very aggrieved, 'why didn't you arrest those other guys next to me?'

'They weren't passed out. How would you like a family to come by and see a bunch of guys laying there?'

'I didn't hurt nobody.'

'You're hurting yourself – that's somebody!'

Incredulous, the prisoner says, 'I can get *arrested* for that?'

The green shows.

Then, as the unit gathers momentum, thrusting the young drunk back into his seat, Easton remarks lightly: 'Oh, I'm feeling good today – I'll take you to detox. You're going to stay the four hours? You're not going to make me look bad?'

'No, *sir*.'

'And if they call me back because you won't stay, I'll put you in jail, all right?'

'I'll stay.'

So it's down to the wide deserted corner of 12th and Island Avenue, beyond which, there in the distance, soars the bridge to Coronado. Doesn't look as if the jumper has jumped yet.

8

'Detox' is obviously short for something like 'detoxification unit', but the sign above the doorway actually reads: *Inebriate Reception Center – open to public 6 a.m.–7 p.m. – agency referrals 24 hours*. It looks like an abandoned supermarket: glass front, plenty of floorspace, a few doors opening off on the left and at the back. Yellow paintwork mostly, with the bottom five feet of the walls in brown.

Moving warily, the ride-along follows Easton and the prisoner to a small desk against the wall, about halfway down the room. The only other furniture is a sturdy table and a scatter of stacking chairs over on the right, unless you count the mattresses arranged on the floor, the Dr Pepper dispenser, the pay phone, the snacks and cigarette machines.

'Hi, how're you doing?' says a jovial Mexican behind the desk, flashing great teeth and good jewelry. 'You guys are sure bringin' 'em in today!' He looks like he loves it, like he's holding a party. 'Take a seat,' he says to the prisoner, but Easton has to remove the handcuffs first.

The ride-along reads the hand-lettered notice on the wall behind:

THIS IS OUR HOUSE
THESE ARE THE RULES OF OUR HOUSE
SWEARING IS NOT ALLOWED IN OUR HOUSE
FIGHTING IS NOT ALLOWED IN OUR HOUSE

29

DRINKING IS NOT ALLOWED IN OUR HOUSE
STEALING IS NOT ALLOWED IN OUR HOUSE
DIRTYING FLOORS IS NOT ALLOWED IN OUR HOUSE
THE USE OR SALE OF DRUGS IS NOT ALLOWED IN OUR HOUSE
DESTROYING PROPERTY IS NOT ALLOWED IN OUR HOUSE
EASY DOES IT

Avoiding anyone's eye, the ride-along then takes a look around the rest of the room. There are about three grown women and twenty grown men in it, but it's more like a kindergarten class, seen in slow motion. Some sit at the table, spilling their cold drinks, making a mess with their potato chips, squabbling peevishly, having difficulty with simple words or repeating the same little phrases over and over, pleased with the way they sound: 'Life sucks, man; sucks, man; life sucks, man; lemme tell ya, life . . .' On and on. Others move around, none too steadily. One like a toddler, liable to drop abruptly on his butt. Another, in a series of dignified lurches, each pause a triumph of balance. The rest are on the mattresses, either good as gold and out cold, or stirring restlessly, in need of a diaper change. One bald inebriate, curled in a foetal position, thumb in toothless mouth, is staring at the childlike artwork taped up on the wall.

'Gotta cigarette, sir?'

Flinching, the ride-along turns to find a giant red-nosed, white-bearded drunk looming over him benignly, like Santa Claus trying his hand at role reversal. 'I – um, don't smoke,' the ride-along says feebly. The drunk stares at the Marlboro pack peeking from his shirt pocket. Stares very sadly. Then, in a chill, North Pole moment, he changes mood. His fists bunch and he grates, 'Gotta cigarette, *mister* . . . ?' In two seconds flat, at least five house rules, including the one about not dirtying the floor, look due to be broken.

But before the ride-along can fumble for his pack, a tiny woman dives between them, clucking and scolding like a bantam hen, which sends the drunk, humbled and apologetic, into the far corner. She laughs, delighted with herself, and this attracts Easton's attention.

'This is Rosa,' says Easton, making the introduction. 'You talk to her – she'll tell you about this place. We used to bring her here, right?'

'Right!' agrees Rosa, giggling. She looks faintly Oriental and maybe around fifty. 'Every night the cops bring me here. Now, every day you see me working here. I was drinking for forty years.'

'Is that right? For *forty*?'

She nods. 'No more. I try to help others.'

'How come? I mean, why'd you drink so much?'

'I was afraid.'

'Of what?'

'I was afraid of the streets, afraid to walk in the streets; all these crazy people around, waiting to hurt you. Afraid of many things. When I was drunk, I was not afraid.'

'Oh, I get it.' The ride-along glances around him. 'This place, it doesn't scare you?'

She giggles again, probably not understanding the question, but wanting to be friendly.

The ride-along mumbles, wanting to be friendly too. 'Well, um, so you're okay now. That's great.'

'I'm not afraid, the whole block knows me. When I walk home at night, everyone knows me, knows Rosa. They know me from here, from the detox.'

Suddenly it's time to go, and Easton is at his elbow, car keys in hand.

'That all?' says the ride-along, surprised.

'That's it,' says Easton, giving the Mexican a parting wave. 'Tony'll take care of him.'

'And if he stays the four hours, he can split? No charges?'

'Nothing.'

On their way out, they stand aside briefly to allow a grumpy old woman, hugging a parcel tied with about a mile of string, to weave her way into the detox, escorted by a tall officer who winks at them.

'Hey, what was that pin that cop was wearing?' asks the ride-along. 'Y'know, on his shirt near where his name was.'

'Oh, he's in the SWAT team,' explains Easton, reaching for the radio mike to ten-eight himself back in service.

'In SWAT?' echoes the ride-along. 'I thought those guys went around in the dark military-style uniforms and the caps and only handled the big stuff.'

Just for the moment, however, Easton is too preoccupied to

reply. Communications is giving him the address of a four-fifteen call.

9

SWAT – Special Weapons and Tactics.

San Diego's best known SWAT alert is probably the one which occurred on a Monday morning in January 1979, when Brenda Spencer, a sixteen-year-old, shot dead the principal of a school and its caretaker, also injuring eight pupils and a police officer – an outburst of mayhem later celebrated in odious taste by the Boomtown Rats with their hit single, *I Don't Like Mondays*. The incident ended without further bloodshed once SWAT took control, winning time for hostage negotiators to talk Spencer into giving herself up.

Other departments have SWAT teams, and many of those teams live up to the televised image of SWAT teams: in a phrase, shoot first and ask questions later – if you ask questions at all. The San Diego Police Department does not train its SWAT officers that way.

So began a series of short television documentaries by News Center 39 which the ride-along must have missed. The series was a model of crisp, comprehensive reportage, and if somewhat partisan, being locally produced, it nonetheless had plenty of hard fact to offer. If he liked, the ride-along could always ask to see the copy kept in the department's video section.

[These] officers of SWAT do not sit around the station, drinking coffee and waiting for the Code Ten call – the SWAT alert – to be sounded. SWAT is a function of the police department's Patrol Division. The officers are all on the street, working their beats, handling other calls. Only when the Code Ten is sounded do they begin readying themselves for the possibility they might have to go into a barricaded house or store to bring out a suspect or rescue a hostage.

At a stroke, this does away with the most common criticism levelled at the SWAT concept on both sides of the Atlantic: that it creates an elite, out of touch with both the people and the rest of the police force.

But that isn't all that makes San Diego's approach unlike that of other departments.

> *[At a SWAT alert] the field commander is the non-SWAT officer in total command. He decides what will be done. SWAT decides how it will be done – and they do it.*

Such a division of responsibility would kill stone dead the lead role in *SWAT*, the television series based on the LAPD, but in the real world it undoubtedly helps to preserve life. Any field commander is bound to think twice before ordering men to do something he isn't going to do himself. Moreover, he is under no pressure to prove that *his* SWAT team can match any bunch of actors when it comes to spectacular heroics.

> *In SWAT we emphasize lowering the risk level to the lowest possible level we can, both for the officer and for the individual that may be a suspect.*

There are several ways of doing this. One is to concentrate on special tactics rather than on weaponry. Another is to take great care over who gets to wear the dark blue paramilitary uniform, an honor that carries no extra pay – apart from overtime.

> *Only patrol officers are accepted as SWAT candidates. If they qualify for SWAT, and it takes a lot more than just applying, they must be willing to remain on patrol status. They must be willing to rearrange their work shifts so there will always be SWAT officers working, no matter what shift, day or night, weekday or weekend, just in case.*

> *They are intelligent, educated men, many of them have college degrees, many are either working on their masters degrees or already have them.*

> *The officer candidate must undergo a battery of interviews to insure that he does not fly off the handle in a high-pressure life-and-death situation. Cowboys are not wanted, there are no John Waynes in this outfit – too many other people's lives are at stake.*

> *'We're not looking for someone who is overly aggressive or overly excitable [says the SWAT lieutenant]. I think I can sum it up that if a San Diego police officer that is in SWAT has to take a life, he would be remorseful, tearful, and very very upset about it. That's what we're looking for.'*

Turning to the 'special weapons' here the selection is limited, in comparison with those of other departments, but considered quite adequate. The three firearms are: the 12-gauge shotgun, for short-range, close-contact situations; the M-16 automatic rifle, which can be fired in single shot; and, for long-distance sniping, the .308 rifle with telescopic sights.

> *Chemical agents are a major part of the SWAT arsenal, especially CS gas – commonly known as 'tear gas'. The gas is used fairly freely if it's needed.*

It's effective, it disables the suspect, and it's infinitely preferable to a bullet.

San Diego SWAT team has never been involved in a fire fight – unlike a lot of other SWAT teams have – and hope they never will be.

But if the ride-along gets to see the video tape, what he will be most likely to remember is this part of the introduction to the series:

The San Diego Police Department SWAT team was formed in 1970. Since the team came into existence, they have performed over a hundred SWAT missions. They have never had an officer killed. They have never had an officer wounded. They have applied a peaceful solution to almost all those hundred missions.

In those nine years, SWAT has fired only five shots. Those shots were all fired the same day – the same day SWAT officers killed the only man ever to die in a SWAT action, Millham Augustine Ossaba.

10

'Was I pleased to see you guys . . . ,' confides a young waitress to the ride-along. 'Twice before you got here, I thought: this is *it*. This is where he gets to throw her through the window!'

The ride-along smiles reassuringly, and does nothing to correct her assumption that he's also some form of police officer, working in plain clothes maybe.

'Your partner,' she whispers, nervously twisting a strand of her blonde hair, 'he'll be able to handle it?'

'Lee's the best,' says the ride-along.

'Oh, okay.'

From the sound of it, the subject of the four-fifteen call is still very angry, back there in the kitchen of the diner. Apparently, he'd come busting in, shouting abuse at another waitress, who had once been his lover, and had looked so dangerous that customers had fled.

Now, as the ride-along waits, he is probably thinking about kitchens as he has never thought of them before: as horrific armories, almost medieval in their supplies of long sharp knives, cleavers, skewers and boiling oil. If anything goes suddenly and horribly wrong, it could be his moral duty to jump to Easton's assistance.

'I think they're coming out,' says the blonde waitress, backing off a couple of tables.

After a moment's hesitation, the ride-along stands his ground, and wins an admiring smile from her, making him look twice as resolute.

It is over in seconds. Easton shepherds a lanky, seething man out on to the sidewalk, says something to him, and off the man goes, thrusting his fists deep into his pockets.

'For a four-fifteen, that wasn't much,' remarks Easton making an entry in his log, back in the unit.

'What made him so mad?' asks the ride-along.

'She owes him thirty dollars, so he keeps coming back and harassing her and embarrassing her in front of all her customers. I said to him, "Hey, if you want to do something, get hold of her when she's not working, or take her to court. But you can't come to her place of business and start harassing, otherwise we have to arrest you and put you in jail." So he's mellowed out.'

'Uh-huh. Okay if I smoke?'

'Go right ahead.'

Something seems to have happened to the ride-along. Small things, things you never see on a cop show, are making him nervous, aware of what a fine line there is between small things turning to big things. It was also plain he liked being mistaken in the heat of the moment for a police officer, and has begun to hold himself slightly differently.

Easton makes for the Plaza where several units are parked on the south side. The small square doesn't look like much. Some threadbare lawn, litter, a fountain in the middle, palm trees, pay phones, underground restrooms and park benches, but, in its way, it's the focal point of San Diego. Bus lines stand along the sidewalks, only feet away from some of the lowest low life the city has to offer, and a Hare Krishna combo is in full wail, competing with a chain-smoking woman evangelist, who shouts about what Jesus has done for her, in between quick puffs and splutters. As always, the cops are watching the low life with the casual, proprietorial air of zoo keepers. It's not difficult to imagine them saying, 'Don't get too close to the bars, lady – Hey, you in the beanie, don't feed 'em!'

One of the pay phones starts to ring.

The ride-along watches a youth in a purple tank-top show

35

his pet boa constrictor to some friends. The chicks look really turned on by it. The pay phone is still ringing, and one of the other officers, a huge man built like an all-in wrestler, goes to answer it, while his companion strolls across to exchange a few words with Easton. They agree things have been very quiet so far. An officer from another unit joins them.

Then the officer on the phone hangs up, and approaches Easton's unit, grinning. 'The phone was ringing,' he says, speaking with a slight speech impediment, 'and I picked it up, and he said "Hello, Michael?" I said, "Mike isn't here – you mean Mike Kritzinger?" He said, "Yeah, he's one of the hustlers there, right?" I said, "Yeah, I know him," so he said, "You're a hustler too?" And I said, "Yeah."'

Everyone laughs.

'So he said, "Well, how would you like to make a little money?"' the officer goes on. 'I said, "I could use some money – how much do you want to spend?" He said, "Well, what do you look like?"'

Another big laugh.

'And I had to describe myself. He said, "What do you like to do?" I said, "What do *you* like to do?" He said, "Well, I like to fuck and get fucked." I said, "How much money did you say you had again?" "Thirty bucks." So I made an arrangement to meet him in twenty minutes in front of the Grant, and I'm going to go and pinch him for soliciting.'

The biggest laugh of all.

'You watch out,' one officer warns. 'You might defect!'

'Yeah,' agrees another, 'if he's good lookin'!'

Happily, the group splits up, and the others go back to their units.

The U.S. Grant Hotel isn't far, just the other side of the Plaza on Broadway: a grand hotel in the old tradition that stands as a bastion of respectability. North of it, banks and fine buildings and discreet signwriting; south of it, the Palace Pawnbrokers and funky bars and bright colors publicizing *Apache Girls Go-go*, *Salazar's Taco Shop*, *The Sandwich Factory* – *100 different sandwiches*. Immediately to the ride-along's right, boasting by far the biggest sign on the Plaza, the *Cabrillo* movie theater announces it's *open all nite* and promises *madly raunchy comedy*.

36

11

Without warning, some sadly raunchy comedy erupts on the grass right opposite the Cabrillo. A slack-lipped, watery-eyed little old drunk is caught trying to slip a hand into the pants of a sleeping girl, asprawl near the fountain.

'Okay, take it easy now, take it easy!' says the arresting officer. 'You're – '

'What I do? I do nothing!'

'Hey, don't give me that, you – '

'I drop a quarter, that's all! I drop a fuckin' quarter, I put my hand down to – '

'What quarter? Where?'

'You not touch me!'

A curious indignation, considering his own blatant intentions of a moment ago, but now he's struggling wildly, blaspheming in Spanish. So, with the help of another officer, he's carried kicking from the Plaza, pat-searched, handcuffed, and then forced into the back of a unit, where he carries on raising hell, spitting and bellowing.

'You know what's funny?' says Easton, putting away his paperwork. 'When you try to treat some of these people like human beings, they turn around and make you seem like an asshole for trying to be nice. You have to handcuff them, throw them around, treat them like animals – then all of a sudden, they'll come back with, "Oh, *look* how you're treatin' me!" ' He laughs.

The ride-along nods, then sneaks a glance at his wristwatch before looking across at the Grant. But the unit is moving.

'Where's the action?' he asks, cocking an ear at the radio.

'Three black males fighting on the sidewalk,' says Easton. 'They're calling for cover units.'

The three-block dash ends outside a pancake parlor, where a short officer is closing the door on a black youth in the back of his unit. 'Code Four,' he says to Easton, which is jargon for 'no further help needed'. 'The other two split. He had this.' It's a knife with a sixteen-inch blade.

'Did he stab anybody?'

'No, just had it in his hand.'

37

Other units come hurrying up, and the short officer raises the four fingers of his right hand to them. 'Code Four,' he repeats, 'but thanks, guys.' They drive on.

'Victim?' says Easton.

'No victim. So what is it? PC four-seventeen?'

A ticklish one. Easton opens the trunk of his unit and takes out an enormously fat book, containing the California Penal Code. It is just one of several texts carried by patrol officers in an attempt to keep track of ever more complicated legislation.

'Oh, boy . . .' murmurs the ride-along.

All that excitement, that surge of adrenalin, only for these two to end up with their noses in a book. It's unreal.

In the end, it's decided that the Watch Commander down at the station should have the answer, and the unit is on its way again. Twice, on the short return journey to the Plaza, Easton gives verbal warnings to pedestrians crossing against the lights, and a jaywalker is left clutching a ticket.

As the Plaza comes into view, the ride-along tries to spot the officer who was planning a pinch for soliciting outside the U.S. Grant, but Easton's attention is once again on his bus benches. This time the prisoner is a paunchy, bespectacled man, almost a match for Sergeant Bilko. He smells like a ripe cheese and wheezes a lot.

'What was that?' queries Easton, as he drives off.

'I said,' says the prisoner, 'I don't want to be in jail.'

'Hey, I wouldn't want to be in jail neither! It goes on your record, and you have to spend twice as long.'

'Can I smoke?'

'No, you can't. But you'll be out in just a couple of minutes – we're going to detox. How long have you been living in the downtown area?'

'About thirty years.'

'About *thirty* years? What kind of job you got?'

'I've got no job.'

'Would you consider yourself an alcoholic?'

'Been one for years.'

'How old are you?'

'Fifty years old.'

'You know, since you're young, and besides a little excess weight – '

'I'm not young,' interrupts the drunk.

38

'Fifty years is young. Why aren't you out workin'?'
'I can't do no work.'
'But you don't look as bad as a lot of guys you hang around with! There are guys worse off than you, aren't they?'
'Shit,' the drunk says softly, subsiding.

12

All those reference works, carried around in the trunks of patrol units, are seen as a regrettable sign of the times by Captain Bob Walker, Area Commander of Central Division who feels that, in some ways, the quality of police work is no longer what it once was in San Diego.

Years ago we covered every call and we did more at each call. Nowadays, when somebody calls in and says, 'During the night, somebody stole my battery,' there's not going to be any follow-up on that: we've filed a report and their insurance company is happy. At least fifty-five percent of our reports are taken right there at Communications, strictly for insurance purposes. Even with a lot of the reports that the officers do go out and take personally, if it doesn't appear it's going to be a fruitful investigation, we send people a postcard saying, 'If you learn anything more, let us know.' It's kinda sad in a way. We've had to cut back our services, and a lot of that is due to complexity.

The job has become more and more complex over the years. When I came on, you could memorize a few sections out of the vehicle code, the muni' code, and the penal code, and then go out and do your job. That lasted for years. Then they started changing the law constantly. The penal code now comes out every one or two years, and it's gotten so thick because they don't bother to research the whole code to find conflicts in there – they just throw in new laws. Everybody who is elected to office seems to think he has to write a new law, and a lot of them are just ridiculous. We've had to put a legislative analyst up there in Sacramento, just to take a look at all these new bills coming out, and we try to fight those that seem inappropriate. And then of course, they come out with new court decisions, and we make training bulletins of them – you can't even carry those volumes of changes around. Just our department instructions are three inches thick! You can't digest all that and keep it digested.

I've heard people say, 'Don't call it a game.' Believe me, it *is* a game – and you have to play it according to every little rule, every last decision handed down by the courts. Nowadays, when you go to trial, it isn't whether the crook did what you said he did, it's whether or not you played the game right in catching him.

13

Darkness comes. The ride-along and Easton eat at McDonald's. They wear a groove carrying drunks down to the detox. The radio is never silent for more than a minute, but all the urgent calls are on the Heights, or up at Hillcrest.

'It can be quiet for a long time,' remarks Easton, 'then boom, boom, boom! There isn't any Middlesville.'

He uses his spotlight to stop jaywalkers in their tracks, and the loudspeaker in his light bar to admonish them to cross streets only at intersections. A young mother, caught ignoring a DON'T WALK sign, hurriedly drags her small son back onto the sidewalk.

'I don't write tickets for something like that,' Easton says to the ride-along. 'It's really petty and she knows she did wrong. You know there's something called "attitude tickets"?'

The ride-along shakes his head.

'Say you stop somebody, and you say to yourself you're going to warn this guy. You walk up to the car and you say, "Sir, you just went through the red light. I'd appreciate it if you'd watch it, as it could save your life or somebody else's." And the guy goes, "I'm so sorry, I wasn't paying attention. I won't do it again . . ." – well, that's it. But if the guy goes, "What the hell you stop me for? You guys are always harassin' me! I didn't do nothin'!" – you write him a ticket.

'Well, you could say that's bad, because you do it because of the way he acted. But obviously he doesn't care what you say to him, so the only way you're going to get the point through to him *is* by giving a ticket.'

'I'll remember that,' says the ride-along, smiling. 'I guess a lot of it is petty – this not drinkin' in public downtown and stuff.'

'See,' says Easton, pointing to a huddle of winos, frozen like statues until the unit has gone by, 'they keep their bottles in paper bags – that's funny, because they think that hides it!

We'll go round the block and come back for them.' Then he nods. 'In some ways, it is really petty, the arrests you make for drinking downtown – but there's good reasoning behind it.

'Drunks get upset over almost anything, and if they get in a fight, they'll use the bottle – or the beer can, which can also hurt. People just don't realize, and they say, "You guys are just mean – you want to harass us." But it's mainly to keep it off the streets, keep it in the bars where it belongs.'

Keeping things where they belong is important to Easton, the ride-along has learned, just as is the concept of the decent average American family, and what it should not be expected to tolerate in society. Easton also begins many of his sentences with either 'It's funny' or 'It's a shame', and never seems bored by all the drunks he picks up. Although once, when a young sailor started to mouth off in the back, he had been quick to say coldly: 'Okay, it's your choice. You wanna get raped or go to detox?' And the sailor had been quiet after that.

Halfway round the block, Communications comes through with a message, and Easton changes course.

'Where now?' asks the ride-along, who is still finding it difficult to catch everything on the radio.

'Front counter, down at the station.'

'What for?'

'They'll tell me when I get there.'

14

The so-called 'front counter' down at the station on West Market is the small public inquiries office just to the left of the arched main entrance, now sealed off by iron gates that close at five o'clock.

Easton takes a look through the front counter door.

The situation appears mildly chaotic. A lot of people seem to be doing a lot of talking and very little listening. At the center of it stands a black mother of about nineteen, holding the hands of two frightened-looking small boys, and declaiming loudly and indignantly at the desk officer. Backing her up are three other black people, a woman and two well-dressed men, who seem to be her friends.

Then the desk officer sees Easton, and comes outside to speak to him out of earshot. 'No visible means of support – okay? They want to come and drop the kids off.'

'They do?' says Easton, glancing back at the boys, who are aged about two and four.

'They've been the rounds of all these places,' the desk officer goes on, 'Salvation Army, all that stuff. I tried to find out why, and what brought her out here to California. "I just wanted to come out here," she said. So I said, "Well, why have you come such a long distance with just a little bit of money, and not be able to take care of your children?" She goes, "No, um . . ." Well, something doesn't make sense. She's got these friends here.'

Another officer chips in: 'She's getting a check. I said to that guy over there, "If you're a friend, and she gets paid the check, why can't she take care of the kids?" They just want to shove everything off on the county.'

'Well, if they just want to shove everything off on the county,' says the desk officer, 'I think we've got to take a good hard look at the whole problem. You'll notice, as soon as we said they'll be made a ward of the court, they said, "That's okay, we'll take care of the kids." But clearly she's no means of visible support, and so . . .'

Easton raises his eyebrows inquiringly.

'Take her and the kids up to Hillcrest Receiving, okay?' decides the desk officer.

The two small boys don't weep, don't protest, don't say anything. They just sit on either side of their mother on the back seat of the unit and shiver, although the temperature, according to an illuminated display downtown, is still touching the seventies. Nor does the mother say anything. She simply sits and stares at her chewed painted fingernails.

'What's your name?' Easton asks in a friendly tone, as the unit leaves the commercial area.

No response.

'Hey, I'm not out to hurt you, lady!'

'Why are you doing this?'

'I just came there and they told me you wanted your kids to be taken into Hillcrest Receiving. I don't know you, I don't know how you feel about your kids. I don't know any of that – that's why I'm asking, okay?'

'I want to know why you guys are doing this.'

'Ma'am, I wasn't there. I'm just the officer who was called in because I'm the one who has the vehicle. I'm not clear on the situation. That's what I want to get clear in my mind.'

The unit moves steadily on up the slope, through a prosperous-looking neighborhood: apartment buildings, houses, office blocks, lots and lots of doctors' shingles, which is why it has been dubbed Pill Hill. The streets are wide and clean, the vegetation is lush.

'What's your name, ma'am?'

No response.

Easton checks his rear-view mirror. 'For kids to be taken into Hillcrest Receiving Center,' he says, 'they either have to be lost; or it has to be shown the mother is not taking good care of them; or that she is incapable, due to finances or whatever.'

No response.

'So, if you're not financially capable to take care of them, we're taking them there and letting the center know that's the reason.'

Not a sound.

The ride-along listens to the radio, to the calls going out for cover units in the Heights, and now, ironically, for the nearest unit to respond to a stabbing just off the Plaza.

'At least,' says Easton, breaking a prolonged silence, 'you'll know your kids are being well taken care of.'

They have arrived. The ride-along sees a long, pleasantly designed modern building with plenty of parking, greenery, and no hint of an austere institution. The bigger of the two boys starts crying.

15

Somewhat confused, the ride-along watches the comings and goings in the reception area of Hillcrest Receiving Center, very aware of the weight of the youngest black boy on his lap.

It is a bright, brisk place, staffed by preoccupied-looking people – people not letting their emotions out, as Officer Lee Easton would probably put it. He is seated on the next chair along, holding the other child and talking to a lady doctor.

43

Nobody seems to have a clear idea of what is happening, apart from the fact the children need care and protection. The mother has vanished, led away by some sort of social worker, presumably, although the man had the blank cold face of a B-movie executioner. Perhaps he has had to do a lot of severing, to watch a lot of pain.

'You okay?' the ride-along asks the boy on his knee. 'Don't worry – everything will be fine!'

His words go ignored. The two brothers are staring at each other, closed off in a just-you-and-me world.

Then a motherly woman enters the lobby and whispers something to the doctor, who nods, warms up a smile, and reaches out a hand to the older boy, inviting him to accompany her. He doesn't want to go, so Easton has to hand him over bodily. A moment later, Easton has gone too, murmuring about having paper work to see to, and the ride-along is left alone.

It's a bad moment. The child on his lap makes a sudden attempt to get away, upset by the shrill sobs coming from the doctor's examination room, and is grabbed only just in time.

'Hey, you like gum?' asks the ride-along, digging deep in his shirt pocket behind the Marlboro pack. 'Oh, shhhh . . .' No gum.

But the child has switched off again, and sits there inscrutable, shivering, yet very warm. The sobbing from the examination room, counterpointed by a kindly, soothing sound, dies away too.

A long time goes by. The ride-along looks at the childish artwork taped to the wall, glances at the kindergarten selection of books on the little table, and then back at the little boy on his knee, so somber and frighteningly adult.

'Here,' says the ride-along, placing a picture book in the child's hands. 'You take a look at that. Isn't that a cute rabbit?'

The boy doesn't look at the cute rabbit. He looks at the door through which his brother disappeared. He never looks the other way, toward the door where his mother did the same.

'Hey, what's your name?' asks the ride-along. 'I know, it's Tommy.'

Not a blink. The ride-along's expression is becoming drawn. His left hand, cupped in support on the far side of the tiny rib-cage, feels a heart beating wildly.

'Okay, so it's not Tommy,' he says. 'How about Jimmy?'

Easton walks by, cool and detached, carrying some forms. 'How're you doing?' he asks.

'Oh fine!' says the ride-along, acting cheerful.

The child's eyes shift from the door. They follow Easton down to a table where he sits to do some writing. Shocked, the ride-along realizes that the sudden extra warmth, felt on his knee, is wet.

Motionless, he and his charge remain seated. More minutes drag by. Easton finishes filling in the forms and checks a few details.

Then abruptly, it's all over.

The doctor comes out of her examination room, and reaches for the younger brother, who clings to the ride-along, making it necessary to prise them gently apart.

16

The unit is halfway down Pill Hill before the ride-along says, his voice uneven, 'Phew, doing that to those kids was . . .'

'It's a shame,' remarks Easton. 'Did you see her friends were up there, waiting for the mother? They had a car.'

'When you think of all the other kids in that place too, broken homes and stuff.'

Easton nods.

'How much has being a cop changed you?' asks the ride-along. 'Y'know, the way you see the world?'

'Oh, it really hasn't changed that much. There's good people and bad people wherever you go, and in this work you tend to run mostly into the bad. But you realize, "Hey, stop! Those are just the few." Some people let it get to them, they start getting ulcers and all the rest of it. It doesn't really affect me. I think it's the way I laugh at stuff, take it as ordinary.'

Entering the downtown area, Easton spots two hookers on a street corner, and pauses briefly to tell them to move south of Broadway, down where they belong. Then he makes a right and heads in the direction of the station on West Market.

'You're through for the night?' the ride-along asks.

'It was quiet,' says Easton.

'Some of those drunks were great.'

Easton laughs. 'Drink for twenty-thirty years, live in the gutters for five-ten years, and they're sixty-five, seventy years old and they're still kickin'!' Again, there's that hint of admiration in his voice. 'Not much we can do – they obviously have to flop somewhere. You're not going to solve it.'

'I guess mostly being a cop is sort of trying to clean up the world.'

'Yeah, a lot of police work is trying to clean it up,' agrees Easton, knuckling a yawn. 'I don't know how it works. I think maybe you're from a broken family, and you want to go out and do some good, be better than your family was. I like it because it's one job you can come on and make your own decisions, be a person who says, "Hey, this should be done, that should be done!" And you have the authority. I think most cops like the fact that, hey, they're in the upper seat, y'know. They like to be on top of things, instead of always being looked down upon – "I don't want to be like my dad who ran away; I want to be a cop, somebody who's respected." They just want to go out and be on the good side or something.'

The ride-along lapses into silence. He looks tired and it's a long time since he last did any fidgeting. 'Hey, what happened to the jumper?' he murmurs.

'Oh, he jumped,' says Easton, motioning at the radio. 'You came in your car?'

'Right. It's parked out front of the station. Say, can I buy you a beer?'

'No, that's okay,' says Easton.

That broken home theory. It was in the academy: one of the instructors brought it up, and almost everybody was going, 'Hey, that's me too!' Most guys I talk to, their parents were divorced. Divorce wasn't so common when most police officers were growing up: we grew up when it was still looked down upon. Nowadays, it's nothing to get divorced. You're out and you meet a girl that's divorced, and you say, 'Hey, really?' Nobody cares. Mine was a broken family. I grew up with two brothers and a dad since I was about four years old.

Part II

Ten-eight from the station . . .

1

The San Diego Police Department has its headquarters and main station outside the busy area of downtown, right beside the bay where one end of Market Street meets Pacific Highway. It shares the south-east corner with State Registered Landmark No. 57, Dead Man's Point, and for a police station, the place does seem strangely quiet.

This isn't all that could disconcert someone more accustomed to the sort of police station featured, say, in *Hill Street Blues*, where the overall impression is one of pandemonium set in crowded, squalid surroundings. There is plenty of open space all around, nothing squalid in view, and at a glance, 801 West Market might itself be taken for some form of historic site.

Because, give or take a few details, the long, low building, with its red-tiled watch tower rising high above an arched gateway, looks very like a white-washed Mexican fort, and that is in fact the basis of its design. Tall palm trees bracket the gateway, which leads through an 'outer wall' of offices, and more palms grow in the large patio that lies beyond, enclosed on its remaining three sides by a vehicle repair shop, a coffee shop, press bureau, records department, other offices and an armory.

Back in 1939, when the building was opened to serve only about a fifth of the number it does today, the patio had a fountain, special seating, and a palm tree placed decoratively out in the middle of the stone paving, encircled by a small flowerbed. All these have since been removed, however, to allow more space for vehicles. This is where prisoners are brought, to wait in parked cars while the arresting officers see the watch commander, who examines the charges before anyone is fingerprinted, photographed and taken off to jail. The department once had its own jail – currently refurbished to house the video section, among other things – but it can no longer afford to run one, and so has become entirely dependent on the Sheriff's Department of San Diego County for holding facilities.

And this, in turn, is why the station is so strangely quiet,

49

having no equivalent of the sort of noisy, noisome room usually presided over by a desk sergeant, trying to cope with a confusion of prisoners and their escorts. Very occasionally, a prisoner will be taken to the watch commander's office, which is one of the most lavishly appointed in the station, but the great majority see only the tiny, drab room over at Records where fingerprints and mug-shots are taken by a civilian ID clerk.

It is one of the curious 'blindspots' of COP that what happens to a prisoner after arrest can seem at odds with its own high ideals, and there is no need to look beyond the patio for evidence of this. Many prisoners are compelled to spend lengthy periods there, handcuffed in units with the windows left rolled up, despite sweltering temperatures. The distress this causes is often extreme, yet most officers appear genuinely surprised when the point is raised.

Hey, that's right – I've seen people sit out there for forty-five minutes in handcuffs. There is a paradox, there really is. But what the hell, I'm not the one who's in handcuffs – what a terrible thing to say.

2

Just stepping out of the coffee shop doorway and on to the patio is a tall, lean, solemn-faced man of fifty-one, wearing a short-sleeved blue shirt, necktie, and a holster clipped to his trouser waistband. Capt. Walker, area commander of Central Division, has been described by a colleague as a 'true Westerner', and although this isn't technically accurate, that is the immediate impression he conveys: it's partly his stance, partly his walk, and in large measure, it's his understated toughness and directness of manner. He was in fact born in Pasadena, California.

I came from a broken home, and I went to thirty-six different grammar schools between Pasadena, Los Angeles and Santa Barbara, and I lived with relatives and in foster homes. I was kicked from pillar to post. I went to one high school though, here in San Diego, and I consider it my home. I went from school to the air force. I was a flying crew chief on B-29s – '48 to '52, Korea – and I was on Guam for twenty-six months. We flew air weather, typhoons. When I left the air force, I worked at a few jobs, nothing real steady: Standard stations, termite control, Safeways; for the gas and electricity company, digging ditches and laying lines, and in what they called the 'trouble department', answering telephones. I wanted something steady and this job just sounded attractive to me. I joined the department on June the 16th, twenty-seven years ago.

As he crosses the patio, Capt. Walker is stopped by an officer in Internal Affairs with some information to pass on. He has worked Internal Affairs himself, investigating fellow officers, and has had experience in almost every other field, come to that, from being a motorcycle sergeant in Traffic to a lieutenant in Homicide. It is really simpler to stick to the exceptions: 'I've never worked in Communications,' he says, 'and I only worked a day or two in the jail when we had it.'

He goes through the door in the left-hand wall of the arched gateway, entering a long hallway, carpeted in pale green, that leads down to Chief Kolender's suite of offices at the far end. His own office is one of the first rooms off to the right, and he shares it with his aide and the patrol lieutenant of whichever shift is on duty. There is only just enough space for the three desks, a couple of extra seats, and the odd filing cabinet.

It's early afternoon, and Lieutenant Tom Mailer of First Watch, a cheery, balding man, who frequently wears a red nose and lectures on Clownology at the University of California, San Diego, is in process of handing over to Lieutenant Rae Chassam of Second Watch, known in some circles as the man who nearly killed Tinkerbell.

3

Up in the locker room above the coffee shop, patrol officers of Second Watch are getting ready for 'squad conference' or 'line-up', the briefing that begins every shift.

The locker room is very orderly but bleak, without so much as a pin-up on its walls. What color there is, lies in the language and off-duty clothing of the officers now changing out of beach shirts, satin running shorts, jeans and tee-shirts, and into their uniforms.

'So I said to the deputy at the jail,' says a young officer, down one row of lockers, ' "What're you gonna do with this scumbag? Put him in the rubber room?" And the deputy said, "Hell, we ain't got no rubber room – where'd you get that idea?" '

Hoots of disbelief from his buddies.

'Hey, listen, guys! This happened. "Maybe," the deputy says, "what you have in mind, son, is our Attitude Adjustment Module." '

A big laugh, followed by someone asking who has stunk up the place with foot powder.

Almost everyone is putting on body armor. It is about half an inch thick, and comes with a comforting printed claim by its manufacturer: *This vest will contain .44 MAG. 240 GR (6" BBL) – U.S.A. 9 mm 124 GR. FMJ – .357 MAG. 125 GR. (6" BBL) – .22 MAG. (6" BBL) – .38 CAL. – 00 BUCKSHOT*. Even so, the armor does have its limitations, and it certainly isn't proof against nightmares of the sort every patrol officer gets to hear about.

> A traffic stop. These two guys had been smoking PCP, and they were stopped by an officer on my squad. They escaped from the car and took a shot at him. Apparently the first bullet hit him in the chest – he had a bullet-proof vest – and spun him round. There's this open spot down your side, between the front and back panels of the vest, and four bullets went in there. Then they shot him in the face.

That officer was twenty-six when he died. Most of the men in the locker room are as young if not younger than that. In fact 60 percent of those patrolling Central Division are probationary officers – or rookies, as they're more commonly known – with less than two years' service.

Not that being of tender years is mandatory among probationers, for recently included in their number was the gray-haired, bespectacled barndoor of a man – standing six-five, and weighing two-fifty – now changing back into his civilian clothes after a shift on First Watch, working the Plaza. He has three sons of his own over twenty, as well as four other children.

> I had a dental laboratory for about twenty years – twisting wire and putting plastic on it, and I was just bored. I started in the Reserve and I was working about forty hours a week, so I thought I might as well join. Nobody says much to my face, but I'm sure there's

"What's a big old fart like him doing here?" I see it in the street, too: they call me "Gramps". But I think I can deal with people pretty good. In three years, I've never shot anybody, never Maced anybody, never hit anybody with my baton – I haven't even hit anybody with my hand. Of course, I don't just run up there and be an ass-kicker like some of the young guys I see. I'm forty-seven. I think maturity makes a lot of difference.

There is also an eighteen-year-old getting changed. He will be patrolling alone in a van as a CSO (Community Service Officer), checking on parking violations and on the alert for anything suspicious up in the Balboa Park area. Being a CSO is a form of apprenticeship that takes a steady nerve: nobody under twenty-one may carry a handgun in California, so he will be going out unarmed except for a Mace canister.

4

Squad conference is held without ceremony in a room off the vehicle repair shop. The noticeboard on the way in is pinned with a variety of material, from hand-lettered advertisements for used surfboards to mug-shots of wanted persons known to be armed and dangerous. Today there is also a Polaroid color print of an innocent-looking belt buckle that slips out to become the hilt of a hidden dagger. *Be Warned*, says the caption.

The room is divided up into small cramped areas by folding partitions, the idea being that each squad, seated at a table with its sergeant at the head, is able to have a degree of privacy. Voices are kept down to conversational level, and there is an element of a family discussion about the way the briefings are conducted. Officers describe their previous shift's work, pool information on suspects, and sometimes come in for criticism from their peers, as well as from their supervisors. The sergeants pass on various items of information, regularly devote time to in-service training, and give orders related to any particular problems to be faced on the shift.

At one of the tables, Sergeant Eduardo Juarez, thirty-one, an animated, slightly-built Mexican American, is preparing his squad for what could prove a trouble-filled night in the barrio by passing on what he has gleaned about current street gang activity.

Over at an adjoining table, twenty-eight-year-old Sergeant Dave Shepherd, a soft-spoken SWAT officer with a reserved, precise manner, is briefing his Hillcrest squad on the main foreseeable problem this shift: the Gay Pride Day parade, which will culminate with a pop concert in Balboa Park – 1400 acres set aside for recreation on the long slope above downtown San Diego.

Such an event can intensify the activities of muggers, child molesters and flashers, and it's on this note that Sergeant Shepherd winds up his squad conference with a reference to an uncommonly athletic offender who has begun to plague the park. 'He's black, about six feet tall, with an Afro hairstyle,' the squad is told. 'You won't be able to miss him. He'll be the guy who'll be playing with himself *and* running from you at about a hundred miles an hour – all at the same time!'

5

Back out on the patio, members of the Hillcrest squad cross over to the armory to check out their 12-gauge shotguns, cut round the corner to pick up their 'handie-talkie' radios, and then, having also collected their briefcases, they drift down, in ones and twos, to the long line of units waiting on the dusty 'back lot', which is actually to one side of the station.

Clack-clack, clack-clack . . . Shotguns are loaded and locked into either a bracket in the trunk or into another mounted on the dashboard.

Then comes another distinctive sound of this unhurried hiatus between line-up and the start of the shift proper, when many officers appear preoccupied with 'psyching' themselves up for the moment they turn out on to West Market. There is a plaintive yelp and wail as each siren is tested.

Unit 532 William is ready to roll.

It backs out, coasts round the corner, passes the gas pumps, and then makes a right, stopping on West Market with the red-tiled watch tower directly behind it.

The officer at the wheel reaches for his handmike. Seconds from now, he will use the radio code that places him 'in service' and supposedly ready for anything.

A jumper, a lost child, some crazy sonofabitch running loose with a grievance and an M16 rifle.

Or even, since his unit is headed for Balboa Park, something funny and freakish, because the weirdest things are apt to happen up there.

'Five-thirty-two William,' he says, contacting Communications as he presses down on the accelerator. 'Ten-eight from the station . . .'

6

Three floors below street level, in a bombproof, carefully guarded bunker beneath the city operations building downtown, an operator is taking a call and asking the caller to try and calm down a little.

Nowhere could appear much calmer than the Communications Room, which otherwise largely resembles a NASA command post during a moonshot. Incoming calls are handled by two rows of operators seated at computer consoles in a brightly lit, spacious room with an immensely high ceiling. The furniture and the decor – including a display of paintings made by a party of young visitors – further mitigate any sense of being 'boxed in' deep under the ground, and the potted vegetation seems to be thriving.

'Oh, okay,' says the operator, 'and after he left your store, he took off which way?'

'Down Broadway toward Third.'

The operator finishes typing up the details on her computer screen, designates it a Priority Three call, and touches a button.

This sends the information into the computer. It identifies the beat, decides how many units may be required, and then relays its data to another screen in the adjacent dispatch area, which is partitioned off by tinted glass and lit dimly to prevent eye-strain.

Here, the dispatch operator has only to tap her keyboard a

couple of times for the computer to show her what units are available, and roughly where they are located, before the final choice becomes a matter for her personal discretion. At the same time, all this information is being displayed on one of the screens monitored by a police supervisor.

'Five-Thirty-Five,' says the dispatch operator, having made up her mind about the best unit to send.

'Ten-four!'

The one slightly unsettling thing about the Communications Room is that it exists in a limbo of electronics, artificial light and air conditioning. It has no apparent time of day, no hint of weather or season, and for the most part, the voices heard within its walls are disembodied.

7

The desert sun cuts a sharp shadow, dazzles in a burnished badge, as Sergeant Eduardo Juarez makes his own turn out on to Market Street, some twenty minutes later. He never crosses the invisible line from 'plain citizen to cop' without an acute sense of transition.

> My personality changes. Well, I look at the gun and at the uniform, and I say, 'My God . . .' It's something, y'know, you can't get over.
>
> Sometimes, when I get to walk the street, people look at me and I picture these people saying, 'Oh, here comes the town sheriff, walking down the street with a gun.' And all of a sudden – I can just see it, y'know! – some big bad guy is gonna come out of some bar and say, 'Okay, Sheriff, *draw*.'

Heading east toward the barrio, the Mexican area of the Heights, Sergeant Juarez stops off at a service station to buy a couple of bottles of chilled Perrier water to take with him. He has just returned to his unit, which has SUPERVISOR painted on its sides, when a beefy fair-haired man in shorts, sandals and a tee-shirt, approaches him.

'Hi!' says the man, very friendly. 'Say, can you help me? I need some place to eat.' And he points to a station wagon over by the gas pumps. 'Wife and kids all hungry as hell, but we don't know a good spot. We're on our way through to LA.'

Sergeant Juarez takes the man's map and shows him a place he could try. 'You from out of state?' he asks.

'New York City! And, hey, you know what? I'm the same as you – I'm a cop there.'

'Is that right, sir?' says Sergeant Juarez, handing the map back. 'Enjoy your meal.'

Sergeant Juarez gets into his unit and finds somewhere to balance his bottles of Perrier. A shadow falls over him. The man has returned with a tape recorder.

'You're a Mexican – right, Sergeant? You can speak it?'

'Sure, I can speak it.'

'I got a tape here, my father-in-law made it at a party, and there's a song on it, Mexican. I'd really like to know what the words are!'

He plays a little of it, and Sergeant Juarez translates the main theme. Effusive with thanks, the man returns to his station wagon and climbs into it, turning up the tape for his family.

There is a heat shimmer over Market Street, and already those bottles of Perrier look tempting. Sergeant Juarez opens one, and has just taken a swallow, when the shadow falls across him again.

'I've a hundred dollars in here,' says the big beefy man, holding out a plastic flask of talc powder, 'and I can't get the damn things out!' He laughs. 'Well, I hid them in here. What guy's going to steal one of these?'

'A hundred dollars?'

'Can you help me? You gotta knife?'

Sergeant Juarez considers his request. 'I've got a knife,' he says, glancing across at the woman and children in the station wagon. 'Just . . .'

'Oh, okay.'

The man waits while Sergeant Juarez gets out of his unit, and has a good look round, before handing over the penknife. As it's taken from him, Sergeant Juarez turns slightly to hide the fact he is unsnapping the strap that keeps his .357 magnum in its holster. His right hand remains poised above it.

Laughing, getting talc powder over his shorts and legs, the man slits open the container, extracts a roll of notes, and hands back the knife, being once again effusive in his thanks.

He is watched until he has returned to the station wagon and driven off, with all the kids waving.

Then Sergeant Juarez gets back into his unit, has a little more Perrier, and rejoins the traffic on Market, heading east.

> I distrust people. We had an officer writing a report on Ocean Beach a couple of years ago, and some guy comes up, no reason, and just shoots him in the head. Shot him! It went right through his vocal cords. This guy at the gas station may be a decent citizen, but for all I know, he may be a bad guy. He claimed to be a New York cop – ha, ha, that's one reason I suspected him! Y'know, he approaches the car, and when he comes up and starts talking nicely, I think: 'Why's he being so nice?' When he came back again with the tape, I wondered: 'Is he trying to distract me or something?' Then, when he came up and asked for a knife, I unsnapped – I didn't know whether he was just being a nice guy or a mentally retarded person. There's no question about it: a knife could do more damage than a bullet. It can cut your arteries and you die. I've seen more people dead with knifewounds than gunshots.

Sergeant Juarez never ceases to keep a check on everything happening around him, his eyes seldom alight anywhere for more than an instant, and at times his apparent agitation could be matched only by somebody smelling smoke in a gelignite factory. Yet he seems to thrive like this, and is no less alert off duty, as though eager for every scrap of detail life can offer.

The unit travels up into the Heights. 'This is no ghetto,' a recent recruit from back east has been heard to remark, 'Jesus Christ, it *sparkles*.' Perhaps not quite, but simply to look at it, the Mexican barrio would be the envy of many people, and not just those living in dirty, overcrowded big-city surroundings. It has wide streets, grass verges, plenty of other greenery, exotic flowering creepers, garden gates and fences, few large apartment blocks, a great variety of small houses, lush parks, playgrounds, modern school buildings, and up on Twenty-sixth Street, the shiny-bright facilities of Community Hospital. On the surface, then, despite being classified as 'low income', it's not altogether a poor neighborhood for children to grow up in, but in fact the barrio is a place of fear – escalating at times to stark terror.

Seven Mexican youths are lounging on the next street corner on the right. To some, they might look ridiculous, in women's hairnets worn with white shirts and black pants. But to the people of the barrio, those hairnets, worn to make an inverted 'V' on the forehead, signify members of a neighborhood gang, given to killing, raping and robbing almost at whim. There are about forty-five such gangs in San Diego, with a total membership of roughly three thousand; between them, they average about a dozen murders a year. Most prominent in the barrio is the Logan Heights gang, followed by the Sherman and the Lomas, each fanatically defensive of its territory to the extent that interlopers can perish for daring to cross a borderline. Lethal and unpredictable, often under the influence of drugs, gang members are generally given a wide berth.

Sergeant Juarez slows down and stops beside the group on the corner. 'Hey, guys, Immigration's coming!' he calls out, grinning. 'Haul ass, boyos! They're goin' to get you too! Waaah, you better run!'

The gang members laugh and approach the unit to talk to him in bantering Spanish. He notices that one of them has a new tattoo in the crook of an arm, and asks to be allowed to admire it properly. The gang member holds his arm out proudly. The tattoo is of a peacock, and under it are the words *MI LOCA VIDA*, which indicates 'someone who gets high'. The 'eyes' in the peacock's tail are useful for hiding the puncture marks left by a hypodermic needle, and this is the reason for the design being so popular. Sergeant Juarez teases him about the price he paid for the tattoo, and asks a few casual questions about how things are going generally. He also notes the description of a portly, rather uneasy youth who is new to him – another Chino, to go by the tattoo on his wrist. The conversation drifts to the car-hop that Sergeant Juarez is helping to organize, and there are grumbles about '*placas*' who allegedly harass the gang without provocation.

'*La Placa*' – or, the Badge – is the barrio name for the police.

'And you weren't doin' nothing?' says Sergeant Juarez, laughing and switching back to English.

'Nothing! These *placas* come and they – '

'Hey, crazy guys, I got to go!' interrupts Sergeant Juarez, reaching for his microphone to acknowledge a call. 'Remember what I tell you – haul ass, *locos*!'

This remark delights the gang members, who usually

reserve the word '*loco*' for someone to be specially admired for his psychopathic and utterly ruthless behavior – a basic qualification for most of their leaders.

Still smiling, Sergeant Juarez accelerates on up to Golden Hill Park, where trouble is brewing between some Shermans and members of the Lomas Luckies. Gang matters are meat and drink to him, and that short stop he has just made was a useful updating.

> If an officer came by who was unknown to them, they could turn on him. But I've been out here for a long time, and I tease and joke with them in their own cultural way. Some are not illegal aliens, but there's lots of them here in the barrio. You can go down the border over there, and you will see hundreds of people lining up on the other side, just waiting for darkness, and then they rush. The only time we turn somebody over to Border Patrol is if they're involved in illegal activity – it's department policy we don't enforce immigration laws.
>
> I talk to anybody I see – the guy could be the next victim you meet, the next witness, the next informer. If you get along with them, good guys or bad guys, they're going to tell you what's going to happen. I *make* them like me. Some that hang round with the gangs 'have something' – I don't know what it is. Anyway, you know they don't belong there, and you wish you could save them. I try, but it doesn't always work. My biggest problem is that I'm an idealist.

8

Up at Balboa Park, the Gay Pride Day rally and pop concert is reaching its climax beyond an archway inscribed, quaintly enough, the Organ Pavilion. Officer Frank Cobb, who answers to 'Five-thirty-two William' on the radio, has had little to do since his arrival here, other than to stand by his unit, keeping an eye on the throngs of people attracted by the music.

Two middle-aged Mexican women, dressed like tourists, come up to Cobb, and one of them raises her sunglasses to ask politely, 'Plees, concert? What ees thees?'

'It's like . . . homosexuals? Know what that means? It's a homosexual group.'

'Men *and* weemen?'

'Men and women.'

'*Dios mio!*' gasps the woman, grabbing her companion's hand, and they both run off giggling, very shocked.

Cobb enjoys the moment. Tall, broad-shouldered, he isn't a man who smiles a great deal, tending to a grave demeanor for someone of thirty-two. Although he thinks his is 'the best job in the world', he makes no attempt to glamorize it, nor to emphasize the dangers involved.

It's not really any more dangerous probably than being a pipe-fitter for National Steel, building ships or something. I've heard of a lot more guys falling off those damn cranes down there, than I've heard of police officers getting hurt.

The last chorus of *We Are Not Afraid Any More* dies away, and one of the Gay Pride Day organizers takes the microphone to declare the rally over, congratulating everyone on what a success it has been. There is cheering, and then the crowd begins to break up. A white youth, of about nineteen, comes over and stands beside Cobb, mirroring his posture as happy couples, arms around each other, stream past out of the pavilion.

'Makes ya wanna puke, right?' he says to Cobb.

Cobb ignores him, although he does have his own personal views on the gay community.

If they want to go home and play their little games and that, it's fine with me – but if they start taking juveniles into the bushes, that's a different situation. I bring two daughters up to this park. One time I was taking my nine-year-old to the bathroom, and two guys walked out. That was pretty bad. I arrested them; if they'd started a fight, they would have been sorry. There's also a vast amount of crime that takes place *against* homosexuals, particularly at night: robberies, rapes, a lot of things that aren't reported. I've been around here for about five years, and they'll come up to me and say 'Oh man, you wouldn't *believe* what happened to me last night! I got rolled by *six* of the most *savage* asses you've ever seen!' But as soon as I ask them to sign a piece of paper, it's, 'Oh no, I just wanted you to know about it.'

During the height of summer, there is in fact a special plainclothes squad that is responsible for policing an area called 'The Flowerbed', where gays bask on their 'blankies', two by two. Around the station, this squad is known as the Pink Berets.

'Officer!' someone calls out.

Cobb turns, and up comes a male homosexual to complain

of having been attacked and robbed of his wallet. Barely three minutes have gone by since the end of the rally, and already the radio is carrying reports of muggers, amateur and professional, moving in on what they consider easy pickings.

'They pinned me down, kicked me and then walked off,' says this victim, using a colored handkerchief that he had been wearing in a certain pocket to indicate his own particular predilection.

'Can you describe them, sir?' asks Cobb, with a civility that makes none of the more subtle distinctions between male and female.

'Blond, military cut – both navy guys.'

'One was blond – the other guy?'

'I don't remember him too well. He was not the one who held me down – he pulled out a gun. Oh, and there were like six other guys as well.'

It takes another minute or so to get together enough of a description to radio to other officers in the park. Only then does the victim disclose that he saw where his attackers went, down into Gold Gulch. Cobb puts out a call for assistance. Among the officers who respond is a policewoman, which is enough to make many San Diego policemen groan inwardly, and then say: 'They don't have the size, the strength, for patrol situations.' Frank Cobb, however, is less dismissive in his attitude.

> When things go really bad, it can be a liability to be with a female officer. But I had a female partner who was only five-three and about one hundred and ten, and I'd take her as a partner over virtually anybody in this department. Because she had enough guts that if it got to the stage there was a major fight going on, and she couldn't handle it, she'd start blowing people's brains out. I'd hate to see that ever happen, but I knew she had that kind of intestinal fortitude. And when it really gets down to the nitty-gritty, I'm more worried about intestinal fortitude than about size. I mean, Christ, you can take a baton and hit a guy on the kneecap and totally incapacitate him – and you don't have to be too damn tall to hit most people in the kneecap!

Just about this moment, again on the radio, someone reports what may have been a sighting of the Hundred-mph Flasher.

9

Yawning, Officer Kay Pruitt continues to patrol her down-town beat, traveling north on 2nd Street past the Plaza. Pruitt always yawns a lot behind the wheel of her unit, so much so it becomes embarrassing when she has a ride-along, and she has to apologize for it. No, she isn't bored; it's some form of reaction, she thinks.

So far on this shift, though, things have been fairly quiet. She has had to see someone who reported his truck stolen five hours earlier, and do her best to placate him. She has had to remove an unwanted guest from a bedroom in a fleabag hotel. She has also had to remove a very smelly man, with his trousers half down, after he became wedged between a lavatory pedestal and the wall in the 'Right Spot', which boasts '60 Beers In Stock From Around The World' – from the look of him, he'd just drunk his way to Bombay and back.

> I always feel dirty at the end of a shift. I can't wait to get out of the uniform and take a shower, and I'm one of these people that, y'know, washes their uniform every day. If I get it dirty at the beginning of the shift, it really bothers me. It's *uuuuurgh*, it's irritating. I wash my hands a lot during a shift.

Kay Pruitt is twenty-three, and wears her long, light-brown hair up in a style reminiscent of Grecian statues of the Golden Age; her profile and proportions likewise echo a classical beauty, which could make her, in the eyes of the average male chauvinist, very much out of place in a police uniform. But were the more imaginative of them to reflect for a moment, they might well reconcile her appearance with that of Diana, for Pruitt is, first and foremost, a huntress.

> The looking, the watching, that's a big part of it – that's what I like about it. Some of the girls say they find discrimination, but I'm the only female in the squad I'm on, and I don't have any problems with the guys. I can get as gross and as nasty as them if I need to. Sometimes you have to do it to prove you're one of them, yet you can't try proving it too hard or they get back and say, 'Here's a female trying to act like us.' It's sort of a gray, touchy area. I realize that I'm not as strong as some guys, but I have ways to compensate for it – sometimes my being female can be an advantage.

And sometimes not, when it comes to a physical disadvantage that none of the male officers ever talk about. Pruitt does not wear her bullet-proof vest. She wore it once, and the over-voluptuous effect it created made her feel ridiculous. Now, like many other female officers, she keeps her armor in the trunk of her unit for when she gets 'a really heavy call', preferring otherwise to take the sort of chances that her male colleagues are spared – if nothing else, the vest gives them all an instant Charles Atlas course.

Perhaps a heightened sense of vulnerability is what makes Pruitt more conscious of the handgun she wears on her hip.

> I've a magnum. In Oceanside, we carried .375 hollowpoints – I'd like to be still doing that. With .38 ammunition, it's a little unpredictable; you can hit some people with that stuff, and it won't even affect them.

Pruitt started out with the idea of being a lawyer, then discovered how much it cost to train and turned to law enforcement, beginning as a clerk in her hometown department in the Midwest before moving to Oceanside.

> The reason I switched to San Diego was that I want eventually to work in semi-intelligence, and Oceanside wasn't that big enough a department – I think they had about one hundred and five officers. I feel very comfortable on this squad. It's critical who trained you: there are some who're really paranoid; I'm safety-conscious, but I don't overdo it.

There are, however, limits to how much violence Pruitt feels she can tolerate in a society, as she discovered on a visit to Los Angeles.

> I couldn't believe it. The LAPD have this station that's in such a bad area they have stone walls around it. Where they park their cars is completely covered and enclosed, and they have a guard who opens this big metal gate – they go woooing out at about fifty miles per hour so they won't get shot at. And their cars – I just couldn't believe it! – have got these bullet holes where people shot at them. To work in an atmosphere like that is something I can't do, wouldn't want to do.

Pruitt uses her loudspeaker a good deal, startling jaywalkers into jumping back on to the sidewalk, and when one anticipates her warning, she booms out: 'Good idea!' A bumper sticker makes her laugh – A WOMAN'S BODY IS

SEXPLOITATION – and say, 'Hey, that's cute!' Then she slows down and shouts out, 'You know what blocking the sidewalk is?' And as the group of prostitutes disperses, she adds, 'Very good, girls – you're gettin' better!'

> Spitting on the sidewalk, blocking it, are tools to use against people who're always a problem. You can't just arbitrarily walk up to someone and say, 'Hey, do this – do that!' I never arrest anybody for spitting, but I'll use it as a reason to talk to them.

10

Reluctantly, Frank Cobb abandons the search in Gold Gulch. Just for a few minutes there, while stalking the sound of beery voices in a glade, it had been like a flashback to the childhood excitement of Cowboys and Indians: watching out for twigs that might snap, not letting pebbles shower down a slippery slope, and then the satisfaction of suddenly appearing from nowhere, making a party of eight young seamen blink at finding themselves totally surrounded. But the victim had been unable to identify any of them as his attackers, and there the matter had rested.

'Thanks, guys,' says Cobb, and leads the other officers back up the gulch wall to the Organ Pavilion.

A gut feeling tells him he has found the right suspects, but without more than that to go on, his hands are tied. Neither is there any point in speculating whether the victim hadn't lied, out of fear perhaps, when he'd failed to recognize anyone. An officer who starts mulling over his daily frustrations is only going to get an ulcer for a reward, in Cobb's view, and he does his best to avoid that kind of thinking.

> One night in the park we got a call about a car prowler, and then we started getting calls of a homicide in progress in a canyon. I started creeping around, and I heard somebody screaming: 'Oh, my God, somebody help me! He's killing me!' I finally find this guy; he's a seventeen-year-old and he's got this nineteen-year-old sitting on top of him in the middle of this huge cactus patch at the bottom of the canyon. The nineteen-year-old's going *bam, bam, bam*, right in this guy's face. What'd happened, the seventeen-year-old had literally hacked his way into the other guy's *beautiful*

van to get the radio, and the nineteen-year-old had taken off after him. He tackled him, right on the lip of the canyon, and then rode him facedown through about thirty feet of cactus. Then he turns him over and beats him, turns him the other way in the cactus and jumps up and down on him – and this must have been going on for fifteen minutes before we got there. When the kid went to court, he was just a *scab* from his head to his toes, and he still had cactus spines in him, both sides. The judge decided he'd had sufficient punishment, and she released him on his own recognizances. I guarantee he never broke into somebody's van again! And every time I get down on this job, I just think about that.

There is another message on the radio, as Cobb emerges from the eucalyptus trees above Gold Gulch, to the effect that a black flasher has been reported by a child's mother near the House of Hospitality, a piece of baroque Spanish architecture just beyond the Organ Pavilion.

Cobb hastens that way, accompanied by a couple of other officers, and by the youth who has strong views on homosexuals. They enter the building, bringing nervous glances from a wedding party posing for pictures in the garden of the Cafe del Rey Moro, and take a good look round, search the restrooms. Nothing.

'Makes you wanna puke,' says the youth.

But this time he is frozen out so successfully that he falls back, and keeps his distance when Cobb returns to his unit, there to log his sortie down into Gold Gulch. Two frustrations in a row have begun to give the afternoon an edgy feeling.

The unit's radio has a little more on the black flasher. He is about six-two, Afro hairstyle, wearing a black tank-top, blue shorts, and running shoes.

There was a flasher molesting kids too. He had the misfortune to flash and molest a Hell's Angel's three-year-old daughter. We had a report the guy was in custody, but when we got there I said, 'What's happened to the guy? Where is he?' The Hell's Angels said, 'Oh, he staggered off a while ago.' I said, 'He got away from you?' 'No,' they said, 'we let him go.' *'You let him go?'* And they just pointed to a big red spot, and they said that was where they'd stuck his dick over the wall and hit it with a baseball bat. God, can you *imagine* that?

66

11

Like Laurel and Hardy, the two males on the corner of Sixth and Broadway are a contrast in physical types, and from a distance, their antics seem as comic.

But it's a double-act that passersby are avoiding, and when Kay Pruitt drives up and jumps out, the reason for this becomes obvious. The huge, wildly indignant black man in a blue business suit is being held at knife-point by a tiny, wizened Hispanic, whose eyes are bulging like goose eggs.

As she approaches them, baton in hand, they turn to her, each demanding that the other is arrested. She takes away the weapon, and finds it is only a penknife.

'I protect myself!' says the tiny man. 'This guy is crazy!'

'*He's* the one that's crazy!' says the huge man. 'He tried to stick me with that knife!'

'Ma'am, listen,' says the tiny man. 'I'm walking down the street, I stop here for the light, and this guy looks at me, he makes a face, then he hits me! Hits me for nothin'!'

'Me? You're a liar!'

'Knocks me right over. Then he tries to do it again, and I protect myself. He shows his teeth and then he hits you!'

'Are you going to arrest him?' asks the huge man, balling his fists and grimacing.

But he is the one arrested, before he quite takes in what's happening. Pruitt, over whom he looms, is practiced in surprise tactics, combining feminine guile with a throwaway sense of humor.

> A lot of times I'll crack jokes, just to get people to do what I want them to do, or I'll ask really stupid questions. Instead of getting them all mad at me, because I'm touching them and searching them for weapons, I'll ask if they've got any bazookas or cannons in their pockets. They look at you like, 'Are you *crazy*?' – but they forget what you're actually doing. It works, it really works.

She also has a slightly detached manner when dealing with street people, and this probably helps too, by providing an unsettling counterpoint to her patter.

'You're puttin' me in no car!' warns the huge man. 'Oh, handcuffs – *damn.*'

Emboldened, now he feels safe, the tiny man darts forward. 'You get your mind together! Going round, botherin' people for no cause at all.'

A bad moment for Pruitt, who has to restrain her large prisoner. 'You're the victim so far,' she sharply reminds the tiny man, 'but you'll become the suspect if you keep interfering in my duty!'

'Okay, ma'am,' he says, backing off.

The prisoner is put into the back of the unit, and Pruitt spends five minutes with the tiny man, getting down his details and having him go over the incident again. Then she gets into her seat in the unit and does the same thing with the huge man, whose name is Gideon T. Hammersmith. He is very resentful of her questioning, and begins muttering something about J. F. Kennedy.

'Hey, I'm speaking to you,' says Pruitt.

'I don't want to speak with you.'

'That's too bad. You know what I'm going to charge you with?'

'I don't care if you charge me with homicide!'

'Oh, I'm sure you fit the description of a couple.'

Hammersmith twists in his seat, taking a look at the tiny man, who is watching from across the street. Then he gives a big sigh.

'It doesn't always happen this way,' murmurs Pruitt, filling in a form. 'Sometimes we're right and you're wrong.'

'What happens? I am on the street and a person with a knife attacks me and the person with the knife walks away!'

'Well, you haven't said anything to make me change my mind. That knife wasn't an illegal weapon.'

'You ain't no judge,' says Hammersmith. 'I'll tell the judge.'

'Okay, you tell the judge, right? Make sure you tell him – don't forget.'

Hammersmith grunts. 'Why you talkin' all that backward talk? Why don't you talk *white*, lady?'

'Just don't forget.'

'Can't you talk any whiter than that?'

'I don't think I can talk any whiter, because I've never been black, okay?'

'The police department let the individual with the knife go and now I'm being – '

68

'You forgot one big part there,' cuts in Pruitt, still writing. 'You forgot the part where you hit him.'

'He hit *me*! He was strugglin' round with the knife! He – '

'Okay, let's be quiet, because I can't think – all right?'

Hammersmith falls silent for a second or two. 'You got a smoke, lady?'

'I chew my fingernails instead,' says Pruitt. 'Besides, we're not allowed to smoke – it's bad for our image.'

'*Image?*' echoes Hammersmith.

'Yeah, we've got to look professional, y'know.'

'You're talking about your *image* and I 'most get *knifed* on the street and I'm being incarcerated! Oh, wow . . .' Hammersmith shakes his head and chuckles. 'America the beautiful!'

'It used to be, yeah.'

'No,' says Hammersmith, 'America is still pretty – it's just the people that are *in* America.'

Half an hour later, after calling at the station to see the watch commander, Pruitt and her prisoner are back downtown. Ahead of them is the county jail, a tall bare building with six floors of barred windows, beneath which metal sills have been added to prevent prisoners from spitting on pedestrians below. Pruitt makes a right and takes the unit below street level, down a ramp that leads to a steel door in a concrete wall. Another unit is already parked beside the steel door, which means she'll have to wait.

Watched by Pruitt, Hammersmith, and a security camera up near the ceiling, the officer in the other unit gets out and presses a bell. After a short delay, the steel door slides aside, allowing access to a small admitting area. On the left, set into the wall, are rows of safes into which arresting officers have to place their weapons upon entry, and before the sheriff's deputies will allow anyone to go a step farther. Facing the door, are bars through which the prisoner's possessions must be passed for searching. To the right, there is another sliding door, leading into a pen where a deputy, wearing disposable plastic gloves, will carry out a body search.

As the other officer advances toward the jail entrance, escorting his prisoner, he says with a wink, 'If you listen carefully, you may hear his asshole slam shut.'

The sliding door closes. Pruitt sits tapping her fingers on the steering wheel. Hammersmith remains quiet, breathing heavily. Finally, it's their turn.

The admitting area is very noisy, especially once the outer door has slid shut again: clangs, shouts, phones ringing, unarmed deputies beyond the bars, bustling this way and that. Pruitt gives Hammersmith a pat search, while he stands with his hands high against the second sliding door, and once the deputies are satisfied he is no more than an ordinary risk, the door opens and he steps through it.

The paper work is completed.

Pruitt, smiling slightly, retrieves her Mace and her magnum from a safe, and waits again to be let out. That is twice, within the last twenty-four hours or so, that she has brought Gideon T. Hammersmith to the county jail, both times for making allegedly unprovoked attacks on strangers at street corners.

12

Sergeant Eduardo Juarez has himself just left the county jail, having been there to help with gang members arrested for fighting up in Golden Hill Park. Supervisors don't as a rule become involved in arrests, but it had been, as one onlooker remarked, quite a fight.

> There have been a few instances when I've felt bad about putting a guy in jail. I remember one guy in particular. He had been looking for work, and the following morning he was going to start work in this building I found him sleeping behind. I did a warrant check and he came back with a warrant. The man cried on the way to jail; I put him behind bars, and there were tears. He said, 'How am I going to contact this person who gave me the job?' I felt awful, awful – still to this day I feel bad. If I'd had the money that night, I'd have bailed him out myself.
>
> I go in there to interview people, and it's not a nice feeling. I don't know how people can survive in there. I could not handle being a deputy.

One night long ago, when the police department still had its own jail, Sergeant Juarez's father was booked into it, and this had a profound effect on his son.

> I was born one thousand five hundred miles away in the interior

of Mexico, and I came here when I was about fourteen. There was this officer who used to talk to the kids in the barrio, and sometimes he stopped the bad kids from doing things. One day I walked by when he was with some people, and I liked the way he talked to them *and* in Spanish. I thought, 'God, what a nice man . . .' I watched him constantly after that, just like some of the kids watch me now, and I became interested in the job – but I still wanted to get a degree and be a teacher.

Then my dad was arrested one time for drunk driving and I had to get him out of jail – my parents don't speak any English – and he was really impressed with the way he'd been treated. I looked at all the cops walking round, and there was a certain glamor to it. Then, in my senior year at high school, a Mexican officer gave a talk and afterwards I was sold on the idea. I worked as a salesman in a store, picked up three years in police science part-time, and then came on when I was twenty-two.

There were maybe only nine or ten Mexican officers in the whole department – now there are fifty-five – but I wanted a challenge. I didn't have any problems although, nine years ago, the academy was a bit on the paramilitary side. Oh, I had problems with report writing, but I applied myself, and I had to learn to be more aggressive.

That officer from the barrio took me under his wing. What a man . . . He worked Homicide for a long time, and he's the sort of investigator people call up and say, 'Hey, I want to turn myself in, but I'll only turn myself in to you.'

Back in the barrio, Sergeant Juarez passes the street where his parents have their home, and then starts up the slope toward Golden Hill Park.

I don't live in the barrio any more, but I say to the people, 'I'm as much part of the community as you are, because I work here, provide a service for you.' To my squad, I say, 'Learn as much about the community as you can and treat them like everybody else.' We're going to start coming here on a Sunday to have breakfast at a church and see what they do there, the youth clubs and activities. We'll be in plain clothes and the people will see us as people.

He reaches an intersection where the fronts of the houses, on the street either side of him, have been covered in spray-can graffiti. It is a strange sight to come across suddenly, but none of the householders dare do anything for the graffiti is the work of rival gangs, demarcating a frontier between one gang territory and another.

Sergeant Juarez turns down the street and travels slowly,

71

running an expert eye over the 'Olde English Script' that the gangs have adopted. Some of the graffiti is chillingly clear in its meaning: *WE KILL FOR $$$$$$*. Other parts of it require his specialist knowledge to interpret correctly. The 'date' *1913*, for instance, scattered all the way down one side, is not an historic allusion, he says, but stands for 'Sherman' and 'marijuana' – S and M being the 19th and 13th letters of the alphabet. SHERMAN RIFA is also very common.

> Sherman Rifa, Lomas Rifa, Logan Rifa – 'rifa' means that they are *Number One*: 'We are the strongest, the baddest, the ones on top, so watch out!' – they all say the same thing. Traditionally they feud over stuff like this. See where the name up there is crossed out? He's going to fight who did that, if he finds out. They write their gang nicknames up here, and sometimes their real names. Someone from another gang has put *'putos'* there – it means fags, homosexuals. Sherman won't like it!

By constantly checking on gang graffiti, Sergeant Juarez is able to keep abreast of new membership, more obscure provocations, and of trends generally, all of which assists him do his job more effectively. He also passes on anything of special interest to the Gang Detail, the intelligence unit of which he was a founder member. Many of the people in the barrio are still not used to seeing him back in uniform, as he is reminded by the next person he stops to talk to, after making a quick U-turn.

'I nearly didn't recognize you,' says the teenage girl in pink pants and a lacey blouse.

She would call herself a Chicano. This abbreviation for 'Mexicano' was once a derogatory term for Mexican immigrants, but since 1960 young Mexican Americans have used it to distinguish an ethnic group to which they are proud to belong.

'You nearly didn't recognize me? Why not?'

'I saw you go by too quickly.'

Which they both know isn't true, so they laugh.

'You're mad at me,' says Sergeant Juarez, 'because at the park I harass your friends?'

'No, man, it's because you embarrass me.'

'How do I embarrass you?'

'You say "hello" to me up there.'

'My feelings are hurt,' he says, and even his mustache

seems to join his large expressive eyes in a look of utter desolation.

'But you're not supposed to be dressed in that uniform.'

'Why not? I am still the same person.'

'That uniform makes you a different person – you think you are more bad now.'

'Oh no, I've always been bad!'

She giggles. 'I don't really like policemen,' she says, touching her hair. 'I've been harassed too many times. I know a lot of *placas*, y'know, and yesterday this guy – I thought he knew me, was just playing – stopped me just for nothing.'

'I feel very unhappy,' says Sergeant Juarez, shaking his head. 'Who's going to be my favorite Sherman girl now?'

'You must be talking about my sister!' she says, with another giggle. 'You'll come by again soon?'

'Soon,' he promises.

Three blocks farther on, several gang members are sunning themselves on the porch of a wooden house on a corner. A short time ago, they were involved in an incident at this house, in which a patrol officer was shot in the leg.

Sergeant Juarez stops his unit at the foot of the short garden path, and engages in one of his jokey, teasing exchanges. It produces a few laughs, but it takes his parting shot to make them grin and jeer as though they warm to him, whatever their differences.

'*La Placa Rifa!*' Sergeant Juarez shouts out, as he drives off.

The Badge rules.

13

There is a sudden stir among the sunbathers and picnicking families on the lawns outside the House of Hospitality in Balboa Park. Heads jerk up, mothers scramble to their feet, children are grabbed and made to look away.

Meep, meep!!!

Like the Roadrunner in the Warner Brothers' cartoon, the Hundred-mph Flasher has broken cover, and is now moving at an unbelievable speed – across the grass and around the fountains – considering what he's also doing at one and the same time.

And in turn, like the coyote, Frank Cobb and his fellow officers set off in hot pursuit, inhibited by the need to avoid knocking anybody down.

In units and on foot, the chase continues, until the flasher reaches Florida Canyon and vanishes over its brim.

When his pursuers reach the same spot, and look down into a shallow valley carpeted by tumbleweed, it seems certain that he must still be there, somewhere, lying low. The canyon is surrounded, and a search of the valley floor begins.

Soon everyone is drenched in sweat as they pick their way over the rough ground; the temperature must be close to a hundred, and not a whisper of a breeze blowing.

And as crowds gather along the edge of the canyon to watch the hunt, a bridal party arrives at a pavilion overlooking the scene. This pavilion, which suggests the Tea House of the August Moon at a distance, is a popular choice among young couples who like to combine romanticism with a love of the open air.

The San Diego Police Department cannot afford its own helicopter, but it does have an arrangement with the Sheriff's Office, whereby it can borrow the use of one when necessary. It isn't long before such a helicopter appears, and makes its first sweep of Florida Canyon.

The clattering of rotors, as the helicopter passes the ceremony at the pavilion, is almost deafening, and there is a wash of turbulence of the sort that plays havoc with bridal veils and bouquets. Then back the other way clatters the helicopter, and sends a decided shiver through the petals of the celebrated rose-garden behind the pavilion.

While Frank Cobb continues to quarter the canyon on foot, examining every possible hiding place he comes across, and remaining very good humored. He makes a special point of trying to avoid ever becoming emotionally involved.

It causes you to change your perspective, to narrow and fixate, but you should be worrying about everything that's going on around you, not just the suspect. You never know who your enemies are. If you fixate on one thing, you're taking your life in your hands unnecessarily. It's like closing one eye when you're shooting – you can't afford to blind yourself.

Finally, the search works itself up to an anti-climax, and it has to be admitted that, somehow or other, the Hundred-mph Flasher has done it again, and the helicopter withdraws.

Frank Cobb, his shirt and pants sticking to him uncomfortably, makes his way back up the side of the canyon, and takes a shortcut through the rose-garden, heading for his unit.

'You, officer!' bawls out a furious matron, her new hat awry, advancing on him from the pavilion. 'Do you know what you just did? To that poor girl? The wedding?'

Cobb turns.

'The Mayor's going to hear about this! I know the Mayor personally, Pete Wilson, and when I tell him – '

'Ma'am, we – '

But there is no pacifying this outraged citizen of San Diego, and it's hardly the time to start explaining that, as flashers often have a history of more serious offenses than indecent exposure, the department considers chasing and catching them rather important.

14

Jaunty, jokey, never giving the impression of doing a damn thing, Sergeant Juarez stops off for his mid-shift meal at a barrio diner, outside of which two units belonging to his squad are already parked.

Lieutenant Rae Chassam: We were out on a little average stabbing the other night, a bar fight. Well, the average policeman out there would go in and say, 'Okay, what happened? What's your name? Who did it? What did you see?' They're going to tell you nothing happened, and they didn't see anything. Anyway, Eduardo walks in, and it's, 'Hey, everybody all right? *Qué pasa*, how're you doin'?' And he just talked for ten or fifteen minutes, never once mentioned the stabbing. 'Before I go though,' he says, 'didn't something happen in here?' So somebody says, 'Yeah, I think some guy stabbed somebody – I saw some blood on his shirt.' 'You know who it was that got stabbed?' 'Yeah, it was Marcel, y'know.' 'Oh, okay – who else was in here?' They tell him, and Eduardo walks out. I'm thinking, 'Jesus, he's not asking what went on!' But he stood outside on the sidewalk for a while, and the next thing you knew, a guy came out of the bar and said, 'Hey, Eduardo . . .' – and he starts telling him who was fighting, who

75

was doing the stabbing, everything. Ed said, 'Okay, okay,' and he never wrote anything down. He just stood there like he was just talking to him. The next day, they put the guy in jail for the stabbing. Eduardo is very, very good at his job. The guy is really cool.

There is a new waitress on duty, and Sergeant Juarez tells her she has the most beautiful eyes he's ever seen. It's almost a habit with him, on and off duty, making waitresses loath to hand him the menu in case he stops talking, flattering, saying so many wonderful things. Sometimes, when he's attracted to one, he may try for a date, but not before he's quietly checked out her arms for needlemarks.

Sergeant Juarez settles for tacos and a large Coke.

'Tacos – *con todo*?'

'Yes, with plenty of chili.' Although fluently bilingual, Sergeant Juarez does not wear the special name tag signifying as much, which is about double the regular size in order to accommodate the crossed flags of Mexico and the United States. He is very proud of his heritage, but fears the Mexican flag may make him appear partisan.

'Hey, Sarge,' says one of his officers, pushing aside the remains of a meal, 'I was talking to Julio – you know Little Julio? – and he wanted to know about the car-hop.'

Sergeant Juarez promises he'll catch up with Little Julio to explain the arrangements, and for a time the conversation stays centered on the event. There is a danger, it's agreed, that the car-hop could bring an outburst of violence between gangs, but nothing would ever get done to further community relations if a few risks weren't taken.

Then, hardly have they begun to discuss a course in body language, scheduled for the following week, when the three radios on the table top give warning of a fight that's broken out at a halfway house for delinquents. Having finished their meal, the two officers ten-eight themselves back into service and leave to give cover.

There is a strong *esprit de corps* in the Heights squad, engendered by more than the shared dangers out there in the barrio, where violence seems always on the simmer and outside help isn't often at hand.

Squad member: Our sergeant's very aware of the culture and all that, and he wants to surround himself with men that will stick to his idea of enforcement. If it has to be hard enforcement, they can do it, but that isn't something you do all the time, every minute of the day.

Not that this is always easy to achieve. In common with many police supervisors today, Sergeant Juarez's chief problem is the youth and inexperience of most of his officers.

In my squad, I have four with experience: one with three years, one with five, one with ten, and one, eleven. Then I have nine new officers – eight with less than a year on. The John Wayne approach, ones who are gung-ho, that bothers me. Now I'm a sergeant, I can do something about that, but it's kind of limited.

Starsky and Hutch may have jokes made about them in the San Diego PD, but no name associated with entertainment is mentioned more often than that of John Wayne.

Kim Benton, burglary investigator: Then I turned John Wayne. Oh, *God*, what a mess! Going through what we call your John Wayne syndrome is when your job is everything, you protect little kids, you've got your six-gun, and your badge becomes THAT BIG. You can tell a John Wayne by the way they stand, by the swagger. I watch them walk across the patio and it's hysterical – although the poor citizen has had it.

You get very blunt, everything's black or white, there's no gray: 'Hey, either you did it or you didn't – yes or no? The rest, I don't want to hear about.' There's no way of talking their way out of a traffic ticket if you stop a car. 'I don't want to hear any argument, just sign the ticket.' And if they don't want to? Just pull them out through the window! A *ghastly* period.

We get a lot of divorces at that time, because you're so hard to live with. Can you imagine, going home and saying, 'Why's there no damn food on the table? I don't want to hear your lip!' They recommend you to get counseling from the department psychologist at that time, because of the stress on you and the job and your family.

I don't think it stays that long, unless you're a complete psycho – we've had a couple of those! But everyone goes through it, and in fact they warn you at the academy, warn you to watch out for it. Maybe it takes a year, then you wise up, get a little bit more seasoned.

Alone, Sergeant Juarez eats quickly, and then returns to the streets again, after telling the waitress at Salazar's that he's pleased to see his recruiting poster on display near the check-out. The poster, a very striking design in black and white, shows a San Diego PD badge rocketing out of a Star Wars galaxy over the words *MAY YOU BE WITH THE FORCE*.

He loves it.

15

Communications has a job for Five-thirty-two William.

'At three-one-seven Pritchard Street, a possible two-eleven. Apparently he was the victim of a two-eleven last night. The suspect has just called to meet him downtown and, for a hundred and fifty dollars, he would return his papers.'

Officer Frank Cobb, immaculate once again in a fresh uniform, makes for the robbery victim's address, leaving the problems of Balboa Park behind him.

Being with the force isn't how he once pictured himself making a living.

> I had intended to be a career officer in the army. I was a captain. I volunteered for Vietnam three times, but I was in Korea by some fluke. Then all of a sudden, the Vietnam War was over, I didn't have any college and stuff, and they just dumped me. I came back to San Diego because it's where I grew up. For two and a half years, I swept floors at night and went to school in the day. Then I went down to buy some fishing gear in National City, and the clerk said to me, totally off the wall, 'Sir, are you a cop?' I said, 'Why?' And he said, 'You walk like a cop, talk like a cop.' 'No,' I said, 'I'm a janitor.' He said, 'You oughta be a cop. San Diego is hiring right now – why not go along and sign on?' I was gettin' tired of pushing brooms, and so, three weeks later, I was a cop.

The apartment house at 317 Pritchard Street turns out to be a discreetly fortified stronghold in a fairly select area. Cobb finds the right button to press at the entrance, and from the speaker comes a frightened voice demanding, 'Who's there?' Incongruous, on a sunny afternoon with water sprinklers making rainbows, it's like a fragment of some radio play.

Mr Larry Conrad, the two-eleven victim, lives on the top floor in Apartment 3F. He opens up to the sound of a waltz being played on a television show. He is a willowy, sensitive-looking man with red hair and eyeglasses. The sleeves of his mauve shirt are rolled only halfway up his forearms, and a gold nugget hangs on a chain around his neck, nestling in gray hairs.

'Come right on in,' he says, bolting the door again behind Cobb. 'God, I'm so shaky.'

The room is sumptuous, the carpet thick, the air sweetened by several vases of flowers. There is a bar in one corner, opposite the large television set, and above it hangs a signed photograph of a world-famous man.

Cobb sits on the edge of the well-padded chair offered to him, and invites Conrad to start at the beginning, since the message from Communications had been none too clear.

'I'm gay,' announces Conrad, perching on a bar stool, 'so let's get that out of the way.'

Cobb doesn't bat an eyelid. Some shifts simply decide on a theme for the day – and they stick to it.

And then, to the strains of truly gay Vienna, Conrad begins his story. Last night, he tells Cobb, he had been downtown in a dirty book store, just browsing round, when he'd met a young man named Gerard and had struck up a conversation with him. Gerard had invited him back to his hotel room, and there they had decided to have sex together. He had allowed Gerard to tie him naked to the bed, and while trussed up, he had seen the young man steal his driver's license, credit cards and personal papers from his clothes. Gerard had also helped himself to a gold ring and a wrist watch, worth about six hundred dollars between them. Later, he had refused to return the property.

But now Gerard has called him, Conrad goes on, right here at the apartment, and wants a meeting downtown at which he'll restore his 'papers' upon payment of one hundred and fifty dollars. Alarmed by this turn of events, and even more alarmed by the thought of Gerard following up his phone call by coming round, Conrad explains that he feels it's high time he told the police all about it.

'There's no fool like an old fool,' he says, smiling lopsidedly.

Not that he has quite told the police all about it, there are still some rather blurred areas in his story – what occurred, for example, between the alleged theft and Conrad's release? But once Cobb is satisfied he has the main elements of the complaint, he tells him that the matter will be passed on to the detectives for investigation. In the meantime, Conrad would be well advised to take care over who he admits to the building, and to inform the police if he receives any further phone calls from Gerard.

'Don't worry,' says Conrad, with a shudder. 'I'm not letting *anybody* in.'

Back at his threshold, whiskey sour in hand, he thanks Cobb very warmly for his prompt assistance and understanding attitude. It was nothing, says Cobb, who would describe his response as simply 'professional', a word in constant use in the department. Then, cutting off the waft of romantic music, still playing in the background, Conrad closes his door on the outside world and bolts it.

> *Probationary officer:* I remember one time at the academy they said, 'We're all prejudiced. I'm prejudiced, you're prejudiced, and it isn't just racial. You could be prejudiced by what sex somebody is, how tall they are, what kind of food they eat, how they eat; you could be prejudiced about fat people, thin people – all that. I'm not here to say you mustn't be prejudiced, because that would be stupid. But what I can tell you – that being prejudiced in the way you do your job as a police officer isn't professional, and that's how you've got to be in this department, professional.

Cobb doesn't resume patrol right away, but sits in his unit and writes out his report first. For all his apparent fear and trepidation, there had been something about Larry Conrad like a row of dots at the end of a sentence.

16

Sergeant Juarez is still out touching bases, as he calls it, when dusk comes to the barrio.

Traveling down a long slope, he notices his favorite Lomas girl, a plump teenager with a scarred cheek, minding her small brother on the steps of a stucco house standing almost on the sidewalk. Half a block farther on, he turns on to the parking lot of a fast-food joint, and parks behind a camper that has been abandoned there. He drinks the last of his Perrier. The Lomas girl, her small brother propped on her hip, appears at his car window.

'What you been up to, Eduardo?' she says.

'Hey, I'm sorry I couldn't stop the other night.'

'That's okay.'

Sergeant Juarez offers his ring finger to the small brother to fiddle with. 'Any problems in the neighborhood?' he asks.

'Nothing, nothing.'

'It's quiet?'

'Nobody hangs around any more.'

'They do hang round – Golden Park.'

'Right here, too. A bunch of hypes.'

'Where?' he says, his attention on the small brother, who is enjoying trying to get the ring off.

'In the back of the house.'

'Tell me, this house?' Sergeant Juarez glances up briefly at the adjoining property. 'Which apartment?'

'Right here at the back,' she says.

'Okay, I know it. How do you know they're selling?'

'Because everyone comes up and asks me where they stay,' says the girl, and she mimics: ' "I want a balloon for Perico." '

Sergeant Juarez laughs. 'Where's he keep it in the house, do you know?'

'I don't know where he keeps it. I just know he's got it in his house.'

'There's sure a lot of it goin' round,' says Sergeant Juarez, his attention again on the game with the ring.

The Lomas girl hitches her small brother up to a more comfortable position on her hip, and remarks, 'You know Carlos is locked up?'

'For what?'

'For stealing the truck.'

'But I saw Raul the other day.'

She giggles. 'Raul's dad blamed everything on Carlos.'

'But Carlos did steal it.'

'Yeah, but – '

'Can I tell him you told me that?'

'*Hey?*' she says, horrified.

The small brother grins at Sergeant Juarez's gleeful laugh. 'No, I'm only kidding,' he assures her.

'Then Raul's dad told the probation officer – '

'What he says doesn't really matter, because they have to prove it in court,' Sergeant Juarez cuts in, and then nods at the apartment house. 'My concern is, don't get involved with these people, because I don't want you to get hurt. When people come round asking, just ignore them. Have you seen any guns?'

'No, all they do is come.'

'Come, how?'

'Some car comes.'

'Is it stolen?'

'I don't know.'

'Don't cut your hair again.'

She smiles ruefully and tugs at a ragged fringe. 'I'm not going to cut my hair again.'

'Listen, let me come back tomorrow.'

'You're coming for sure?' she says, like someone often lonely.

'Yeah, about four or five.'

'Bye . . .' says his favorite Lomas girl.

'Bye!' says Sergeant Juarez, turning his ignition key.

Time and again, that's all there is to it. Just a few minutes' idle gossip, a warmth of feeling, and he has something worth passing on to his squad. On this occasion, information of interest to his two narcotics specialists. On others, this same girl has helped to solve several killings.

17

It's a beautiful night, up on Hillcrest, and the only people causing problems in Balboa Park right now are the roller-skaters. If it weren't for the radio, which is carrying an increasing number of calls from downtown and the Heights, Officer Frank Cobb would have every right to think all was well with the world. As it is, most of what he hears tends to sound fairly remote.

> We get the Chicano youth gangs, writing their names on the walls and shootin' each other up and stuff; but they're killing themselves off, not bothering the rest of us.

'Five-thirty-two William . . .'

Cobb acknowledges.

'A four-fifteen disturbance in the emergency room at Centre City Hospital on Elm.'

Unit 532 takes off, lights flashing, siren yelping at every intersection, with Cobb intent behind the wheel. Like a kitchen, an emergency room can become a deadly arsenal of improvised weaponry, and like police officers, emergency room staff have to deal with some pretty violent people. Every high-speed ride involves a considerable element of risk, but sometimes seems really worth it.

Braking to a sliding halt in the hospital yard, Cobb grabs his baton from its door holster and hurries over to a side entrance. The silence from within is ominous. Cobb pushes his way through two sets of doors and stops.

There, at his feet in the emergency room, is sprawled the slack-lipped, watery-eyed old Mexican who goes round trying to slip a hand into the pants of sleeping girls at the Plaza. Only this time he is the one asleep, and snoring loudly.

Cobb looks up.

'You got here quick!' says a very young doctor, smiling.

'Is he a patient or a walk-in or what?' asks Cobb, unamused.

'He came into the lobby, took a kick at me and missed,' says the doctor. 'He fell down and stated he just wanted to die there.'

Cobb nods.

'He'd been drinking,' the doctor adds.

Anybody could diagnose as much with a single sniff, just as they could also tell he was incontinent.

'Señor!' says Cobb, crouching to shake his shoulder. 'Are you comfortable? You look it!'

'Sorry I had to dump him on you,' says the doctor.

Cobb straightens up and unsnaps one of the fast-loader pouches on his gunbelt. 'One reason I refuse to work downtown is because of people like this,' he says. 'You see, this came out as a disturbance. I think we'll put an ammonia capsule under his nose.' He takes a glass ampule from the pouch and breaks the top off.

The effect of the ammonia fumes is dramatic. The drunk's eyes fly open and his chin jerks up off the rubber tiling like he's just had the Last Trump sounded in his ear.

'You awake, huh?' says Cobb, taking hold of him. 'Stand up, please, señor – c'mon, stand up!'

He manages to keep his fresh uniform from coming to any harm, but the same can't be said of the back seat of his unit on the way down to the detox. And although the night air has grown cool, the car's front windows are kept wide open.

The hour and the drop in temperature have brought the usual huddle of homeless people to the detox entrance. They want in, a roof over their heads and mattresses to lie on. And, as they can see through the glass front, there are plenty of mattresses as yet unoccupied. But only agency referrals are admitted after seven o'clock, which means they'd have to be drunk enough to be arrested first, and none of them has the money.

As Cobb escorts his protesting prisoner between them, they beg to be allowed in with him. One gray-haired old man, lying on his side holding a wooden crutch, says he has a fractured hip, and that the cold in the small hours will be agony.

The same old man calls out, as Cobb is leaving, 'Sir, you've got a gun. Why don't you just shoot me?'

18

Alert, self-assured, stifling a yawn, Officer Kay Pruitt continues to patrol her downtown beat, just cruising and watching. She has made friends among the community of storekeepers and others who work in the area, and likes it when they wave and say, 'Hi, officer!' Off-duty, however, she doesn't admit to being a police officer if she can get away with saying 'Oh, I just work for the city.'

The hookers are out in force now, and the sidewalks below Broadway teem with people in search of a good time. Pruitt parks at the Plaza under the big red letters spelling out Cabrillo, who named this land after a beautiful female warrior who led a nation of Amazons. Nearby sits a familiar figure on the Plaza, a slender young man who always has his sketchbook with him. Not that he seems to come there to make studies of anyone; his pictures are mostly religious, and his Christs suggest a series of self-portraits. Another familiar figure is missing, much to everyone's relief.

Fellow officer: His name is Jones, very crazy and very violent. He used to carry sharpened wires, knives, clubs – I took a board away from him once with a couple of razor blades stuck in it. When one of the other officers on the squad came up to him, Jones swung a bar at him and missed, and the officer split his head open with a nightstick. He was quiet for a while after that, then he pulled a knife on somebody on the squad one night and got taken down. He's now in the state mental ward, but he'll probably be out in a couple of months. The longest they put them in there seems about six months.

There's hustle and there's bustle on the Plaza tonight, and a group of possible illegal aliens is giving Pruitt sideways glances, but essentially everything is quiet. So she starts rolling again.

Round the block, north up Second Avenue past the Plaza, and then into B Street, behind the U.S. Grant Hotel. 'Walk on the sidewalk!' Pruitt booms at a slight figure, shuffling along in the street, her head bowed and her face hidden by a tangle of long hair. 'Walk on the sidewalk!'

The trash can girl ignores the command.

Pruitt frowns and pulls over, getting out to confront her. 'Did you hear me tell you to get on the sidewalk?'

'Yeah, I heard you,' mutters the trash can girl, who would also attract admiring glances if it weren't for her grime.

'Then how come you didn't do it?' demands Pruitt.

'Because I was walking here.'

There is a pause, and then Pruitt says, 'Get up on the sidewalk. It's dangerous to walk in the street – and illegal.'

With a shrug, the trash can girl obeys her this time, but Pruitt waits to see she doesn't step back into the gutter farther down, before returning to her unit.

She must have stolen some new clothes – she's got different ones from the ones she usually has. I don't ever want to touch her. She's maybe twenty-four or twenty-five, and she eats out of garbage cans, sleeps in the bathrooms under the Plaza. I can't even picture living like that; it must be awful. And she's got just about every disease you can think of. I really don't want to touch her.

The radio blurts: 'Five-thirty-two William?'

And Pruitt hears Frank Cobb make his acknowledgment en route back to his Hillcrest beat from the detox.

Communications has a message. There is a two-eleven

victim downtown, on the corner of Fifth and Broadway, who has just seen the suspect who robbed him. The victim's name is Mr Larry Conrad.

19

As it happens, Cobb is no distance at all from the corner in question, and within a minute or so, Conrad is there in his headlights, flagging him down.

'I've seen him,' he says, as Cobb gets out.

'Where, sir?'

'He was at the hotel.'

'Yeah, but where?'

'In the lobby.'

'Okay.'

'I wonder if he suspects what I'm doing now . . .'

Cobb is momentarily distracted by the strange behavior of a man near to them. 'Oh, he probably does,' he tells Conrad, 'but crooks are notoriously stupid.'

'Gerard acts like he's stupid,' agrees Conrad, running a hand over his hair. 'He knows that the cops are involved.'

Cobb shrugs. 'He probably took whatever money he got from you and sniffed it up his nose.'

Then he tells Conrad to get into the unit and they'll go round to the hotel, but first he has to transmit a message. 'Five-thirty-two William,' he says. 'North-west corner of Fifth and Broadway, there's a white male with a beard and a white tank top, blue shorts, crawling round on his hands and knees. Could you get a unit to investigate?'

The hotel is only three blocks away, Cobb has a cover unit meet him there, and then enters the lobby. Gerard is talking animatedly in a phone booth, with his back turned, when Conrad, jittery with excitement, points him out.

'Open up, we're police officers!' says Cobb, and as the man turns in surprise, he adds, 'You're under arrest.'

That's it. No struggle, no protests. The prisoner is handcuffed, pat-searched, and put straight into the back of Cobb's unit, where he sits peering out, apparently dumbfounded.

Cobb goes over to Conrad to double-check a couple of things before he takes this any further. 'How did he get the wrist watch and the other stuff?'

'He had my wrists tied.'

'Did he make any threats toward you?'

'No, he didn't do anything in any way threatening,' says Conrad, and he's trembling.

Back in his unit, after thanking the downtown officer for providing cover, Cobb picks up his clipboard and prepares to question the prisoner. He is small, unshaven and scrawny, dressed in a creased shirt and stained black pants, and his breath is like nail-varnish remover, suggesting that he doesn't eat too often.

'Well, sir,' says Cobb, ready with his pen, 'what is your name?'

'My name is Gerard.'

'Your last name?'

'Viper.'

'Viper?'

'V-I-P-E-R,' he spells out.

'Oh, like the snake,' says Cobb, not batting an eyelid.

Other particulars follow.

The light in the unit isn't too good, and so Cobb asks: 'What's your hair? Black or brown?'

'I have brown hair and brown eyes,' Viper confides softly, making it sound almost an enticement.

He has no address, other than the hotel, and neither has he any occupation.

'That red-headed gentleman who is standing over there,' says Cobb, pointing with his pen, 'claims you robbed him last night. I'd like to read you your rights, and then try to talk to you about it, see what your side of the story is.'

Viper nods, hears his rights read out, and then says, 'I'm willing to talk with you, sir.'

So Cobb repeats Conrad's allegations.

'No, that's not the truth at all,' says Viper, looking hurt. 'I didn't have him tied up. When I met him last night, he said, "Well, I'm gay", and that he'd like to get together with me, so I brought him to my room here. He said he'd give me some money, but I didn't take anything from him.'

'So you don't have the ring and the watch?'

'No, sir.'

'Would you mind if I went up to your room and searched to see if the ring and the watch are still there?'

'I don't mind at all.'

Cobb gets out of the unit, tells Conrad to wait around the corner, and asks Communications for someone to accompany him on the search of the hotel room. Kay Pruitt draws up in under a minute, and Cobb quickly outlines the situation.

Then, with Viper handcuffed between them, they enter the hotel, which was once patronized by Gary Gilmore, the murderer executed by firing squad in Utah. *No guests after 9 o'clock* warns a notice on one wall. There is a wire rack for empty bottles. On the left, the lounge has been roped off, denying the use of its few sticks of furniture, and on the right, the reception counter is barricaded by a high iron grille. Safe behind these bars, the hotel clerk, a moody-looking man in a black tee-shirt, is taking wax from his ear with a kitchen match and spreading it on a corner of an open copy of *Penthouse*.

The prisoner's room is on the second floor, so it is much easier to take the stairs than to attempt to ride in an elevator that looks like a shipping crate and has no buttons, just a lever sticking out of a battered control box. Stepping carefully, to avoid discarded bottles and the odd slippery puddle, Pruitt leads the way up, and then out into a hall with lime green walls, where a midget in a red bathrobe rushes up in great excitement.

'What's goin' on? What you doin'?' he squeaks.

'Left,' says Viper.

The midget follows them, skipping to keep pace, and collides with another wire bottle rack. A black couple, both down to their undergarments and arguing outside a room, dart back inside it and slam the door. The hall is filled with noise: drunken sounds, happy sounds, wild weeping, radios tuned to a clash of different stations. Nobody is playing a Viennese waltz, though.

'My room,' says Viper.

Conrad must have stood out in it like an orchid on a meat block. Bare boards, bare walls, an iron-frame bed covered by gray sheets with long rips in them. Torn drapes at the window, no mirror above the cracked handbasin, a razor without a blade and a paper bag half-filled with soiled clothing. Disturbingly, for so small a space, the room has two other doors, each nailed shut. Even a thorough search takes hardly two minutes.

Down around the corner on F Street, where Conrad has been standing, nervously fingering his gold nugget on its chain, Cobb tells him that the search has been fruitless; the gold ring and the wrist watch, worth at least $600, simply aren't there.

'I'm going to charge him with grand theft,' Cobb adds, 'rather than robbery, because he didn't use any violence.'

Conrad nods, expresses his thanks once again, and walks away, chin up, stepping out briskly, trying to ignore the smiles of some watching hookers. He never did really explain what had brought him downtown again.

Then, just as Cobb is about to swing Unit 532 out into the traffic on Second Avenue, Conrad reappears for a last lingering look at the prisoner. Viper stares back at him through the car window, expressionless and unblinking.

It is a curiously private moment, which Cobb notices yet pays little heed.

> Conrad probably felt used and stuff, wanted his revenge, but the case isn't prosecutable. I mean, when it comes down to him getting up on the stand and testifying to what sort of sex acts were going on between them, do you really think he'd do that? Before a jury of twelve men and women? No way! So, in effect, I've sentenced this guy to three days in jail – street justice. Because, seventy-two hours from now, the detectives will drop the charges, since Conrad won't want to bare his entire life before the world, and the guy will go free.

And besides, Cobb's shift is almost over.

20

One by one, the units of Second Watch return to the back lot at the station. For the first time in eight hours or more, there is suddenly no need to look round warily before stepping out. The moment also holds a decided if fleeting sense of achievement; being still in one piece is something nobody ever gets to take wholly for granted.

Then comes what is often a difficult period of readjustment, and Kay Pruitt speaks for most of her fellow officers when she acknowledges the adrenalin 'fix' that is so much part of patrol work's attraction. 'The excitement's a kicker, a high in a way, but after a shift you've got to come down again, and that makes it a little bit harder to do at times.'

Second Watch begins to disperse. Pruitt heads for the shower. Frank Cobb climbs on his bicycle to make for his home in the suburbs; the long ride helps to keep him fit, and isn't always without incident.

> I was just puffing along on my bike, and there was this Chicano standing at a stop sign. He went, 'Hey you, honky – what you doin' in my part of town?' And he started toward me. I said, 'That's far enough.' But he came on, so I drew on him and just went, 'Stop.' *Zzzzwit!* He was gone! I don't fool around in situations like that.

Cobb is passed on West Market by his supervisor, Sergeant Dave Shepherd, who has with him his latest acquisition, a .22 magnum derringer no bigger than the butt of the huge handgun he uses for patrol, a .357 magnum on a .44 magnum frame. Off-duty officers are under no obligation to be armed in San Diego, contrary to established practice in most police departments, but Sergeant Shepherd lives his life in a state of constant readiness, being not only a gun buff but a part-time fireman and an EMT (emergency medical treatment) expert as well. He has a number of bleepers on his belt, and uses a radio scanner in his car to monitor police, fire and ambulance messages while he's driving. He switches the scanner on.

Looking ready to party, Sergeant Juarez crosses the street behind them in his jeans and bright beach shirt, heading for his sports car in the parking lot, cracking jokes with a couple of members of his squad. They separate and the two officers go into the 153 Club, which takes its name from the form that has to accompany every crime report.

The no-frills bar has a no-frills blonde serving behind it, with tattoos on her arms. The notice on the wall above her head reads:

ROBBER/BURGLAR
BE WARNED
THIS IS A POLICE
STAKE-OUT

There is nobody else in the place. One of the officers orders two beers, the other makes a selection on the juke box. The blonde tells them about the trouble she's having with her car, and about how she nearly didn't get to work that day from National City. They nod, don't talk a lot, seem interested only in getting that first beer down.

'I like it,' says one.

'What?'

'That.' And he lifts his beer toward another sign up on the wall behind the bar.

Doing a good job
is like wetting
yourself in
a dark suit –
you get a warm feeling
but nobody notices

Back out on the parking lot, breathing easier now that Sergeant Juarez has driven off round the block behind the station to Seaport Village, the city's latest tourist attraction, a senior member of his squad works on the trunk lock of a colleague's car. The trunk opens and he places in it a six-pack of beer that he took during the shift from a couple of under-age drinkers. He has been putting six-packs in this trunk for a couple of weeks now, and his colleague, who knows how strict the department is about 'freebies', is beginning to show signs of acute anxiety.

'My God, but you've got intelligent eyes,' Sergeant Juarez is saying to a very goodlooking cocktail waitress at a sophisticated nightspot in Seaport Village. 'Are you at school? What do you study?'

And the cocktail waitress, obviously flattered, lingers to tell him about the classes she's been *thinking* of taking next semester, while he covertly checks her inner arms for needle marks.

21

Life was rather different when Officer Dan L. Jackson, the area commander's aide, joined the department eight years ago.

Back of the station was a big empty lot and we used to call it Sea Wall. After Second Watch, we'd build bonfires and stay out there until four or five in the morning, drinking beer and shooting the beer cans. This was like five nights a week, real heavy choir practice.

I guess I drank a lot just to forget stuff. Various times I went home and I was so upset I literally cried a lot, just to get it out. I told my wife there was a great demand on me. Shit, I'd been in battle and I'd seen a lot of things, people blown up and guts trampled all over the place, but to see in *a society*, where everything is supposed to be laid out clean and proper, kids being beat up and whipped and – that was hard to take.

It's the waste. Whores walking the streets, people preying on the runaways, people getting murdered, and the *reasons* they're getting murdered. Like some guy'd kill a gal because she wouldn't make the dinner, and we'd say, kind of joke about it, 'Well, at least that wasn't a senseless homicide.'

This Sea Wall stuff almost drove me crazy, almost turned me into an alcoholic. But the sergeant I was working for at the time – y'know, the camaraderie – made the group real tight, and it was important to me to be accepted. I think that's why all the guys went to Sea Wall; they didn't want to be left out of anything. We had a lot more problems back then, a lot of ride-overs from the sixties. There wasn't much love for us at all.

22

The bad, bad sixties. 'Terrible times for law enforcement officers in California,' a veteran of those days remembers. 'Violent times, a lot of political issues, human issues, the Vietnam War, the draft, the mass demonstrations when the officers were getting rocked and bottled. Really, a very traumatic experience, and it impacted me personally. I had a daughter going to elementary school, and I had to warn her not to tell her classmates – or even her teacher – what her father did, because she'd have been subjected to abuse, verbal and physical.'

Yet recruits still came forward, and among them was Norm Stamper, a veterinary assistant who 'stumbled into the job' in 1966, when he accompanied a friend to the civil service examination, killing time before they were to have a beer and corned beef sandwich together. 'My friend was one of those people who'd wanted to be a police officer since he was about three years old. I passed and he failed.'

Now thirty-six, bearded, with the dress and demeanor of a pipesmoking faculty member, Norm Stamper would not strike many people as a veteran police officer – perhaps it's the way he speaks, which would certainly puzzle many street cops.

But what he actually has to say, as formal and intellectualized as it may appear, strikes at the very nub of the problems that beset policing in many departments, and gives some idea of how and why San Diego decided to make a number of radical changes.

> In my academy days, I had the distinct impression I was entering a very noble calling, an honorable profession, and that police officers were here to do those textbook things: to prevent crime, to detect and apprehend offenders, to stop people hurting other people, and to provide an extremely important community service. I learned that a police officer was knowledgeable about and sensitive to problems, and adopted that kind of problem-solving orientation.
>
> But once I got out of the academy, I soon came to realize that my peers didn't see it that way, and that in this city in 1966 a 'good police officer' was one who was extremely busy writing traffic citations, making field interrogations, keeping his car free of Jack-in-a-Box trash and sunflower seeds, smiling when his sergeant walked by, and making sure his reports were filled in properly – in other words, responding to the internal bureaucratic requirements.
>
> Nobody at that time was expecting Norm Stamper to be knowledgeable about his beat, to really know its people and their problems, the crime trends, the patterns – that wasn't part of police work. In too many cases, good police work was being done by accident.

But young Stamper had still to come to this view. Paramount at the time was his need to 'belong', to prove his worth among his fellow officers, and this wrought changes in his personality that would have been almost unimaginable a year earlier.

> There were some very understandable reasons for this. Police work – which is conspicuous and has all the visible trappings of authority – is enormously attractive to any person who has held unexciting jobs in the past. Because of my youth, my probationary status, my impressionability – if that's the word! – I experienced a very profound adjustment period.
>
> For example, I think I'd always avoided the kind of racial

93

prejudice so common in this and other countries, and yet, within two years, I was using the same racial and ethnic slurs my peers were using. It was not just acceptable to do this, it was *expected* of you.

And anybody who did not perform in that fashion, who was not out collecting numbers, who was not engaging in war stories about blacks and Chicanos, who was not adopting the 'we-they' attitude to the community – well, there was something wrong with that officer.

I'd never had such awesome authority in my life, and for two years there, I was right in among them as one of the swaggering, boasting unprofessional cops. I'm not at all proud of it, but I'm glad I had the experience of going through that kind of psychological change, and later I got to really think through what I'd done and how I'd done it.

I was given credit – or blame! – for the introduction of community-oriented policing to San Diego, through an experiment conducted in 1974, and then I resigned in 1977.

By the time of his resignation, Norm Stamper had made a meteoric rise to the rank of Captain in less then ten years, and was in charge of one hundred and thirty patrol officers.

The work was very rich, diverse and satisfying, but it was all taking place within a paramilitary bureaucratic structure I had become increasingly tired of. I felt stymied and stifled; I wanted more autonomy, more freedom and much more officially sanctioned discretion. After I told Chief Kolender I was leaving, he asked me to first talk to the City Manager. The irony was that I came right back on a contract to provide in-house assistance, and then, in 1979, I became a city employee again as Special Adviser to the Chief. I don't know of any other police department where a civilian is intimately involved in organizational values and can advocate changes in programs, policies and procedures.

Norm Stamper may indeed be a civilian now, but one of his strengths is that, unlike so many who seek to bring about reforms in policing, he has himself been a police officer. This makes him impossible to dismiss as simply 'just some intellectual, some bleeding heart fulla crap ideas that'll never work,' as one patrol officer puts it. Moreover, a great deal of his thinking is based not just on hearsay and on statistics, but on his own memories of those first two years he spent out on the street.

Over-reactions, physical abuse, excesses on the part of young officers, are often the direct result of fear. My contention – and the contention of many others – is that the better informed one is about the community, the fewer monsters there are out there.

COP can de-mythify a lot of community and social problems that police officers are expected to do something about. I may be twenty-one years old, but if I'm committed to a course of action where I'm constantly developing information that is useful to me, the less impulsive I'll be. I think COP means that it now takes maybe only two years to be comfortable with the role of police officer, instead of four or five.

In fact I take the view that the younger and more inexperienced one is in law enforcement, the greater is the need for a system that supports the COP approach. Because what it says is, 'You're a new cop in the city, you're struggling to make it in this new world, to find out what it's all about, and here is the way you do it.' And, as most people want to please the boss, then that's probably the kind of work the boss is going to get!

Sure, the attitude may be, 'I'm in this for my own self-interest, and I don't give a damn about the community', but even in those cases, I've seen police officers being responsive to the community. Maybe the attitudinal change is five-ten years, a generation or two away, but the *behavioral* change – hard as it may be to accomplish – is something the organization does have control over.

Sea Wall has gone, obliterated by the instant antiquity of Seaport Village, where Sergeant Juarez has just made a start on a frosty glass of margarita, and only a couple of weeks ago, eight San Diego police officers who discharged firearms at an impromptu choir practice were suspended.

Part III

Wing of bat, hair of trigger

1

The yelp of Second Watch sirens being tested on the back lot disturbs the afternoon calm in Lieutenant Pat Evans's nearby office, where, as head of in-service training, much of his work is concerned with forming behavioral attitudes.

Pat Evans is in his forties, a robust, clean-cut graduate with a broad amiable face, a relaxed manner, and 24 years as a police officer behind him, including a spell as SWAT commander in San Diego. Unlike most officers involved in COP, he has personal previous experience of being part of a 'people's police', albeit on a somewhat unstructured basis.

> I worked for my hometown police department in Clearwater, Florida, which probably had about thirty-five people on it. It was a very unsophisticated, backward department in terms of human rights, training and procedures, but it was a community style of policing that the community wanted.
>
> They had a lot of foot patrols, which many departments had gotten away from years before. The duties involved going into Joe's Cafe at four o'clock in the morning and turning on the stove, the air conditioning, ready for Joe when he came in at five-thirty. Then you'd double back at six for your free breakfast! Very unprofessional, but that's the way it worked and everyone loved it. I loved it too – we didn't know any better.

Then came a career move from smalltown policeman to big-city cop in Phoenix, Arizona. Pat Evans found the switch from 'a wet region to desert-style country quite a shock', especially as the patrol cars in Phoenix were not air-conditioned at the time, and a temperature of 118°F 'was no big thing'. This turned out to be, however, the least of the adjustments he had to make.

> I had to learn a lot about people in Phoenix. In Florida, ninety-nine percent of my work had been with white people, half a percent black, and the rest, Spanish-American people from Tampa. In Phoenix, probably half your contacts were with another culture.
>
> It was not a tight, homogenous community. You had like nine major Indian tribes, most of whom didn't get along. You had a large population of Mexican and of black people – they didn't get along with each other, nor with the Indians. The place was divided into some very, very poor racial groups; a pretty broad middle class; and a very, very moneyed class. The police were

caught between two extremes. Those at the bottom didn't like you, saw you as the oppressor, and those at the top, the wealthy, didn't like you either.

That change was really significant for me. In Phoenix, you enforced the law until you found out the guy was a high-ranking Republican – or until he flashed a card, signed by one of the chiefs, which said: 'Mr So-and-so is not to be issued with any traffic citations. If you have any questions, see me.' Shit, he goes sixty-mile-an-hour in a forty-mile-an-hour zone, and all he does is flash his little card! And if he got his car towed out of a red zone, the officer'd probably end up driving it back for him and legally parking it for him.

Okay, so you write the ticket. They'd probably not say anything to you upfront, but it'd be voided – a study in futility. Or if you made it a crusade, then you'd be labelled a guy who didn't want to go along with the plan.

I really began to see for the first time in my life the dynamics of power politics and all that stuff. I didn't care for it at all because I'd been led, as a former Marine, to have feelings that one standard fits all. I understand that department has changed a lot, but then, looking back to Clearwater, it may not have been professional, but at least it was honest.

And so Pat Evans, having broadened his experience considerably by also working in accident investigation and as a detective handling a number of homicides, decided to move to San Diego, where he had once been based as a Marine.

In San Diego, I wrote tickets to anyone – doctors, lawyers, politicians. I'm not saying a judge somewhere hasn't used his own discretion over a citation or something like that, but nobody has ever put that pressure on *me* – that was refreshing.

It began to clean up its act after World War Two, and it's a damned clean department. I was *shocked*, as a new officer, to see them arrest a policeman and put him in jail. You think, 'How disgracing for the department – it's revolting to think a police officer would do that.' Then it dawned on me that, in the long run, it might be an advantage to us for the public to know that we did all the investigating, that we prosecuted one of our own without waiting for the FBI to find the bad apple, or for a grand jury. That's healthy. Healthy for the young men and women on this department to look at that and think, 'If ever I'm tempted, there I go . . .'

Boy, it was tight when I came here in 1965! We had very military expectations of conduct and procedures, protocol – lots of 'sirs' and ranks and stuff. As a beat officer, you were expected to make an entry in a journal every twenty minutes of your shift or you were in trouble.

Then, in the middle of the seventies, the 'open door' policy began: 'If you have a problem, come in and see me . . .' And another healthy thing happened: we began to wean ourselves away from the idea that if I'm a lieutenant, I'm obviously smarter than you because you're just an officer. Now the idea-sharing thing is promulgated throughout, and some of the most significant developments have been from ideas that *did not* come from the top.

I used to sit down and think, 'Why is it like this? Why don't we have things a little more static in San Diego? Why does everything change so fast?' Well, it's just the nature of the animal. California has a moving life-style; somebody's here for two years, then they move on someplace else – it's a rare thing to be a native Californian. How do you deal with a million-plus aliens coming across the border from Mexico?

So, there's a lot of movement, a lot of different cultures, shifting values, and if you don't shift and adjust as a police officer, then you're out of tune. Take the Cambodians who've settled here; one of the first things we learned about them is that they don't like to be touched. Shake hands, and it's, 'Hey, only immediate members of my family do that.' So when you say, 'You're under arrest, put out your hands,' you don't raise up their hands for them. If we didn't adjust to their culture, we could probably lock up every one of them on some technicality, but you can't do that!

And so, if I think we're light years ahead of a lot of other departments, that's not because we're so wonderful, but primarily because we've had the problems thrust upon us. I enjoy the job. If I wasn't a police officer, I'd probably have been a career Marine. I think you'll find there's some Pony Express rider in many police officers! Adventurous types. Not too many scholarly people come on; there's a degree of the unsavory and the distasteful.

2

Officer Luke Jones, his Second Watch colleagues say, is most definitely a scholarly type, notwithstanding his wrestler's build – height six-three, two-twenty pounds – and the penchant he shows for 'cop humor'. It was Jones who answered the pay phone at the Plaza the other afternoon, pretended he was a hustler, and arranged to meet the john outside the U.S. Grant Hotel.

Cruising downtown, watching the afternoon crowds, listening for a call on the radio, he turns into Fifth Avenue below E Street. Three hookers on a corner, clinging together as they cackle over some wisecrack or other, momentarily attract his attention, making him give a slight smile. He is working on a mystery novel, set on a college campus, that has the tentative title of *Dunsinane Whore*.

> The main character is very similar to me: he's a large-framed, very masculine patrol officer who speaks with a lisp – obviously I do, too – but very, very quiet, very unassuming, albeit intelligent, and I make him give a commentary on police work. Able to infiltrate where the wily detective would be rejected, and through his knowledge of *Macbeth*, he solves the homicide – but he gets no credit for it.

Luke Jones, twenty-five, who says he is 'part English, part Creole and part Red Indian' in origin, and has straight black hair and a strongly blocked face, comes of a family that has never had any connection with law enforcement. His father was a pastor, and so is his brother, while another brother is in accountancy.

> I went from high school to college: natural philosophy, Pope, Dryden, Swift, Chaucer – I concentrated more than anything on Shakespeare, and got a BA and an MA. I was interested in teaching but, as a university teacher, you have a tendency to live the ivory-tower existence, and everything you know, you know through books. I'm not the Eugene O'Neill type that's going to put on my tennis shoes and sweat shirt and travel around the country on a train, and so this is my way of getting some experience while I'm younger. My ambition is to be a full-time writer.

Unit 521 is reflected briefly in the window of The Dirt Store, which primly warns hard-porn enthusiasts: *No shirt, no shoes, no service*. The radio chatters on. A cab, illegally parked, hurriedly leaves the curb. Two men in a doorway break off their conversation until the unit has passed by. The sun is still high, the colors bright, the streets filled with life and bustle. But, through the eyes of Luke Jones, after three years with the department, no blasted heath could offer a vision more desolate.

> We respond to a radio call: 'Female down, Fifth and Market.' It turns out to be not a female at all, but a transvestite. We roll him over, there's a wallet beneath him, and we rush him to hospital. He tells us what happened.
> The transvestite had picked up a john, trawling for a whore

downtown, and they'd gone to a parking lot. While the transvestite's performing an act of oral copulation, he reaches inside the john's pants, which are down around the ankles, and pulls out the john's wallet. He is now a grand theft suspect. He gets up and starts to get out of the car.

Then the victim of the grand theft, who doesn't realize he's had his wallet stolen, pulls out a gun and says, 'Give me all your money!' The transvestite says, 'That looks like a capgun to me,' and starts to walk away.

'I heard a pop,' he tells us, 'and there was a pain in my arm – a pop, a pain in my leg. There was another pop and I felt a pain in my chest, and then I ran like hell, because I knew I was dyin'. I ran until I fell down.'

So now the victim in a grand theft is a suspect in an armed robbery attempt, and for an assault with intent to commit murder. We had his wallet and his identification, so we go knock on his door and we arrest him.

One week you arrest a guy, next week he's a victim; victim-suspect, victim-suspect, almost all the time. It's real rare for an average citizen, for a businessman, to be a victim – to my mind, that's more of a tragedy. So when people say, 'What's it like, working downtown?' – that's the story I tell them. That's what it's like.

Passing the fleabag hotel where Larry Conrad and Gerard Viper parted company, Unit 521 takes the next right and stops beneath the CABRILLO sign on the Plaza. Luke Jones gets out, slips his baton into the ring on his gunbelt, and begins a foot patrol.

Investigating? Being a detective? If I've got to be sitting at a desk, I'd rather be grading papers.

3

Being a detective in San Diego has altered quite considerably since Sergeant Will Braun joined the department some three decades ago, when he was twenty-four and fresh out of the Navy. 'In those days,' he recalls, 'all the investigators wore felt hats, regardless of the assignment.' And, in many other respects, they conformed to the popular idea of a detective: out until all hours, barhopping, living the life of a glamorous elite.

Not any longer. With some exceptions, and allowing for the

occasional weekend duty, detectives in San Diego now work from 7:30 a.m. until 4 p.m., Monday through Friday.

This gives them time, it is argued, to organize themselves and to catch up on paperwork before telephones begin to ring. Then again, from the standpoint of contacting witnesses, complainants and suspects, it is much easier to get hold of people while they're at work, rather than in the evening, when they could be anywhere. Or, should the people concerned be nocturnal and perhaps elusive by nature, then the chances are high they'll be found in bed in the morning. Either way, although these hours militate against some of the most jealously guarded 'detective traditions' (in which sentiment and alcohol play no small part), they have been found to be the most productive.

> We used to have night detectives, but a lot of times they'd just kind of spin their wheels – they wouldn't do a lot, and a night detective would just transfer the case to someone working days. Now our patrol officers are trained to lift fingerprints, conduct neighborhood checks when making their preliminary investigations, and do a lot of what was once considered detective work.

And as for drinking on duty, that's out. Should a detective feel it imperative to drink with someone during his shift, then he has to get written permission beforehand, or if the occasion presents itself without warning, then he has to submit a full report afterwards. Moreover, any drinks have to be paid for; no police officer in San Diego is allowed to accept anything for nothing, not even a cup of coffee.

> When police officers from departments back east see how this department works, most of them don't believe it. Like they go out and they see our officers pay for the drinks – it's strange to them. Because, back where they come from, they have places where you drink free and you eat free, like there were here, thirty-forty years ago. Then the department started being run by younger administrators who weren't just content to settle in; they were ambitious, aggressive, looking for some recognition, and the word went out that some things were acceptable. It isn't unusual for officers to transfer here from the east and not last. I think this town has been clean for so long that, the first time a cop tries to shake somebody down, they'd be reported *that* quick!

Sergeant Braun, now nearing his retirement and working as administrative aide to Chief Kolender, has something of

Spencer Tracy about him, plus high blood-pressure and a cynicism he attributes to twenty-odd years as a detective, working everything from burglary to vice. Unlike many detectives, he has never been divorced, but is still happily married, after thirty-five years, to his childhood sweetheart from Minnesota. And, unlike many detectives, who regard homicide as the most satisfying form of investigation, he has other ideas.

> In my opinion, the worst crooks are the robbers. These are the people who arm themselves, conspire, go out and commit a crime, planning on hurting or killing somebody if they're interfered with. Murders are a spontaneous situation most of the time – husband and wife, boyfriend and girlfriend – but a robber is cold, calculating; he prepares himself. It made me feel good when we could go out and catch them.

And in going out to catch them, Sergeant Braun has often been in extremely dangerous situations, facing desperate men of the sort so familiar from police shows on television. But, as his personal experience would suggest, the popular notion of a detective has never quite matched the reality.

> I was involved in investigations for twenty-two years, and I've been in a lot of raids, a lot of arrests, and I've probably pulled my weapon about four or five times in all that period of time. I've never been shot at, never been seriously injured – just bruised and things like that – and I've never shot anyone. I think most people can be talked out of just about anything.

4

'Patrol is definitely the most exciting part of the job,' in the view of Luke Jones, the aspirant novelist. 'Not that it's always exciting, but what interests me is the fact that every second has the *potential* of being exciting . . .'

Whereas, by inference, the 'wily detective' has little to do with spontaneous situations. Instead, he operates in a fairly predictable world, which allows him to be cold, calculating, and to conspire with his colleagues while preparing to make an arrest, say, under the most favorable circumstances.

Noticeably, however, Luke Jones is not carrying a magnum

on his gunbelt, the weapon that so often signifies an awareness of that potential for sudden excitement.

> When I got this job, I'd been in school, getting federally-insured loans, and I had to spend several hundred dollars to outfit myself, buy the uniform, so I wasn't about to spend a couple more hundred dollars on a gun when they were going to issue me with one. It shoots as straight as the others.

Crossing the Plaza on foot, dauntingly large-framed and muscular when seen in the midst of so many frail with old age, with undernourishment, with drug abuse, alcoholism, Luke Jones encounters the slack-lipped, watery-eyed old Mexican, presumably on the look-out for sleeping girls among the low life. Sometimes, when drunk, the man imitates a matador, and down at the detox they've nicknamed him El Toro.

El Toro has a switch in his hand, which he flourishes as though it lends him a certain officious dignity. Jones takes it from him and begins breaking it in pieces. 'You don't need a stick,' he says, turning away.

'Hey, that my stick!' says El Toro, shuffling after him, demanding to know why this action has been taken.

Luke Jones ignores his protests, and carries on breaking the stick in his huge hands, repeatedly making an ever-thickening bundle of the pieces, but snapping it with ease. He could break a human arm without trying.

> It's really strange, because I've had a very liberal education, and I came on with very liberal attitudes, but I've found they *just don't work*. You've got to take a very firm stance against these people, because once they've fronted you off, you've lost your effectiveness – you might as well pack up. And I'm more likely to make a racial slur – let's face it, ninety percent of the criminals I deal with down here are black males. But, under the surface, I still have the same feelings about socio-economic tensions, and my racial ideas haven't changed, not at that level.

Then El Toro falls back, wary of Jones now he is approaching a gaunt, gray-haired man who lies sleeping on the grass. Jones draws his baton and strikes the worn soles of the sleeper's shoes.

'Hey, wake up!' he demands.

The old man winces, but it takes another blow from the baton before his rheumy eyes open wide in alarm and he jerks his head off the ground. 'What's goin' on – ?' he gasps, pathetic with fright.

'C'mon, get up,' says Jones, his voice cold. 'You're drunk.'

Inevitably, there are protests, and the old man finds he is bleeding from a cut hand, but Jones maintains a relentless, detached manner. He places a wristlock on him and leads him over to the unit. People all around the Plaza are staring across at Jones, and some are frowning, but he ignores them as totally as if they didn't exist. He gets behind the wheel of his unit and heads for the detox.

The traffic down to Market is fairly heavy. The old man on the back seat croons softly over his injured hand; it's a soothing sound his mother might once have used to ease a hurt in a small boy. Luke Jones gives his attention to the progress of a small blue car about fifty yards in front.

> A lot of things I've encountered have resulted in a loss of certain types of sensitivity – I was also very passive once, always very, very nonassertive. I've never become super-aggressive, but the job has altered the way I relate to people. I'm a little more outspoken and a little less tolerant, and this had something to do with my break-up. I was engaged.

The small blue car suddenly swings left out of the middle lane, wanders wide on the corner, and straightens up only just in time to avoid hitting a parked truck. Unit 521, flashing a red light, and with one quick wail of its siren, follows the car round and brings it to a halt.

Luke Jones gets out and approaches the driver's door. Patrol officers making a 'stop' in San Diego do not do so with guns drawn, as is policy in other cities, for fear of needlessly alienating the public. They show great caution, however, as this is possibly the most potentially lethal situation they find themselves in, on a day-to-day basis.

What a picture the couple on the front seat make – the sort which Norman Rockwell, had he ever shown any malice in his illustrations, would have contrived to show how a police officer, by just doing his job, can contribute to the demise of a promising relationship.

Instantly.

Although the man behind the wheel, flushed and happy, hasn't realized that yet, and is still making motel eyes at his companion. 'Sure, we've been drinking,' he admits. 'Isn't that right, honey? Great little party, over at the office!' She ignores him, stares grimly ahead, and does up the two top buttons of a blouse which, a moment ago, was showing cleavage.

'Honey?' he says, touching an arm that's jerked away.

Very tactfully, Luke Jones remarks, 'Well, sir, if your wife will stay in the car, I'd like you to step out here and – '

'Oh, she isn't my wife,' the driver whispers loudly and most apologetically, as though hating to correct a police officer.

'God!' she says. 'Oh, Jee-*zuss* . . .'

Forgetting his injured hand, the old man in the back of Unit 521 perks up and watches the scene with interest. It isn't often that the middle-class, as it were, becomes part of the downtown action. A scrawny man steps out of the small blue car, and produces a driver's license for inspection. He has a shaven head, aviator's glasses, and a big deep-sea diver's watch on his thin wrist. Another unit draws up, and after a word with Luke Jones, the second officer moves the car to a parking space. Moments later, handcuffed and smiling sheepishly, the driver is sitting there on the back seat beside him.

'I mean I'm fucked up, I'm drunk,' says the old man, with a sympathetic nod of welcome. 'But what has he got you for?'

'He got me for doing intoxication, I guess.'

'Shee-it,' says the old man, impressed.

And side by side, ragged jacket brushing shoulders with blue silk shirt, they begin a murmured, comradely conversation, touching on the vagaries of fate. It is cut short, however, when the second officer removes the old man, having agreed to take him down to detox, and they barely have time to wish each other luck.

Then Luke Jones returns to the unit, tells Webb that he is going to be taken down to Central to have his sobriety tested, and warns him that a refusal to cooperate will automatically result in his driver's license being suspended for six months.

'Which test would you like to take?' asks Jones.

'Whichever is . . .' says Webb, distracted by his erstwhile lady companion.

Tight-lipped, hugging her purse to her, and ignoring him completely, she is having to set off on foot through an area of

winos and grinning low-life that obviously frightens the hell
out of her.

'Blood test, breath test – urine test?' persists Jones.

Webb, still distracted, says, 'The breast test.'

5

The Intoxilizer machine down at the station has to be operated
by an officer with the required twelve hours' training. Luke
Jones and his deuce – SDPD slang for a drunk driver – have to
wait while Sergeant Jean Cummings is summoned from
Community Relations.

Sergeant Cummings is tall, elegantly slender, in her
mid-thirties, and wears her very long fair hair in a tight roll.
'I'm a feminine person,' she says, 'and I always have been, it's
part of my makeup. But when I put my uniform on, I'm a
police officer – and I expect people to know it.'

There can be little doubt that this is the first impression of
her anyone gains, thanks not only to the uniform but to the
brisk authority she exudes. One gets the feeling that she
surveys the world from well within herself, and that it would
be rash to raise an eyebrow when she says, with unboastful
simplicity, 'I'm very good at my job.' Sergeant Cummings has,
after all, plenty of proof she can point to.

Four years ago, she became the first woman ever to rise to
the rank of sergeant in the San Diego Police Department. In
fact, the whole idea of policewomen – as opposed to females
hired to work as detectives only – is relatively new in the
city.

There were only eight women when I started in 1965, and they
didn't hire another woman until 1969. My father's in police work,
and he encouraged me. I was just twenty-two.

At that time, the women were required to have quite a bit more
in the way of qualifications than the male officers, who needed
only a high school education. We had to have either two years of
college, or two years' working experience in a public job – I had
both.

We had the same training at the academy, but we didn't work
patrol – we worked as detectives in Juvenile, Sex Crimes, and
Forgery. It took a long time for us to learn as much as a uniformed

109

male officer could learn in a year – knowing when something was wrong, spotting someone with a guilty feeling.

Then in 1972 seven additional women were hired, and there was a slight change in policy. Two female officers were assigned to Traffic Division to work school patrol, and others were placed at the border checkpoint to keep an eye on juveniles. There was a special uniform we had to pay for, designed by a Los Angeles couturier. The dress was relatively short and there were no pockets, and so for a while we carried a policewoman's purse (which served also as a holster). The Chief we had at the time wouldn't allow us to wear gunbelts, because they didn't look feminine. Depending on where we were working, we had to wear either one-inch or three-inch heels. They finally let us wear a small two-inch gun on a gunbelt when we were directing traffic.

What had been missed, however, was that in trying to preserve the 'feminine look' of these officers, their modesty had been placed at risk whenever they bent over, in their short skirts, to search a vehicle. Once an alert captain had pointed this out – figuratively, one must assume, in such gallant company – dresses were shortened to tunics, and slacks were introduced. (Today, of course, everyone wears the same uniform and it's equally flattering; in some departments inappropriate clothing is used, so female officers allege, to pursue a subtle form of discrimination.)

But any truly significant change had to wait until the following year, and Jean Cummings was to play a major role in it.

In '73 they transferred two of us to Patrol for eight weeks of field training as a test case. We were told that they didn't expect it to work, and that they were going to show it wouldn't. But we both succeeded.

So they took the rest of the women – except those hired before me – and arbitrarily transferred them to work Patrol. Most of them quit. It was a ploy on the part of that particular police chief to show women didn't want to be patrol officers.

But towards the end of '73, they started hiring women specifically for patrol, and there were fifteen women out of fifty recruits in my class at the academy the next year.

Chief Kolender is very supportive. We had the first woman Homicide detective in California, and even a woman in our SWAT team for a while. Also, percentage-wise, we have possibly the highest number of women in any law enforcement agency in the nation. We've about one hundred and forty of them in uniform – out of one thousand three hundred, whereas the LAPD has only one hundred and sixty out of seven thousand.

And so, from a shaky start, San Diego has set the pace for employing female officers, much to Sergeant Cummings' satisfaction.

> I have never considered this just as a male's job. It is a profession that can be taken up by anybody who likes making decisions, working with people, and helping people. Even if we end up wrestling them to the ground or whatever, putting them in jail, we're still helping them out of that particular situation.

At the mere mention of 'wrestling', many male officers would want to point out that women are physically incapable of fully meeting the requirements of the work. Sergeant Cummings is unimpressed by this argument.

> I've worked patrol for seven years, and I don't recall being injured, other than for a few bruises. Women get into less physical confrontations than men do – we aren't necessarily offended if we don't get the last word, and in many cases, having a woman present will calm the situation down.

All of which has naturally made it more difficult for male officers, and gung-ho recruits in particular, to sustain the idea of a police officer as Macho Man, and this may explain a reaction that Sergeant Cummings has found surprising.

> I thought that when women began proving themselves in greater numbers, the young male officers – having grown up in the seventies, with women's liberation and more liberal attitudes – would accept us more. That isn't true. From what I've observed, they appear to feel threatened, and some of the discriminatory attitudes are coming back. But the older ones have accepted us: we've proved ourselves, and that's all they want.

A number of 'older ones' might want to question that last assertion, while also voicing disquiet about the fact that almost half the current list of prospective sergeants is made up of women. It does seem true, however, that some male officers aren't only reconciled to having women working with them, but that they are prepared to be positively indulgent about it.

> If a woman officer's hair is longer than the top of the shoulder, it has to be worn up. But male supervisors will not enforce that, especially in detectives. I'll go to a sergeant and say, 'So-and-so's hair is too long', and he'll say, 'I like it that way.' 'Like it or not,' I tell him, 'it's unsafe and it's unprofessional!' Because if I walk up

to somebody like that, they'll see an attractive woman maybe, but not a professional who is there to handle their problem.

Neither has she that handy hank of hair available for somebody to grab and use to smash her head against a wall – a point apparently overlooked by many other departments.

Sergeant Cummings hopes discriminatory problems will eventually disappear, but is ready to concede that, human nature being what it is, female officers will always have a tougher time in certain situations. A policewoman attending a family fight in the barrio, for instance, can make matters worse because Mexican machismo – which probably sparked off the fight in the first place – won't allow men to take orders from females without loss of face.

But the ironies can run deeper than that:

> Where women suspects are concerned, the woman officer is at a disadvantage. They'll try to get round a male officer, with tears or whatever, but they can't use that with a woman officer, so most of them just get downright nasty and no holds barred. Also, when you're dealing with a lady of the streets – or with a barmaid – and she's the victim, she may find it difficult to talk to a woman. That's because she's so used to working with men she's uncomfortable around another woman, particularly a woman with a professional job – and she may feel we're looking down our noses at her.

6

Second Watch is gathering momentum, but back in Burglary, the day is almost over, and Officer Kim Benton is trying to clear her desk before four o'clock, like the other detectives around her.

'How would you like to be a real cupcake,' she asks, handing a name to a passing colleague, 'and take that down to Records and run it through for me?' Then she turns back to sorting through a batch of mug-shots, selecting five 'look-alikes' for a photo line-up identification.

Although overcrowded by gray metal desks, the long room, with its wall-to-wall carpet and butter-yellow walls, is quiet enough for the soft Muzak to be the dominant sound.

A long-stemmed rose stands in a narrow white vase on Kim Benton's desktop. For a more robust 'mood elevator', as she calls it, she need only look up at a very large sepia-toned photograph on the wall, which shows a group of Burglary detectives in Wild West costume outside a saloon. She's the long-legged dance-hall girl; the others are sporting Stetsons and six-guns.

Right now, however, she is dressed in a smart dark jacket, white blouse and light slacks, and has her own six-gun, hidden away in a shoulder holster. Kim Benton is thirty, stands five-six, weighs a lithe one-twenty, and has her fair hair up in a style that accentuates her strong, fine featured face. Yet a hint of the Wild West persists – perhaps, taking into account her size, self-assurance, and tough, wry sense of humor, one is reminded of Annie Oakley. She certainly talks just as straight, and seems to regard many of her sister officers as a posse of Calamity Janes.

They just aren't pulling their weight, in her opinion, and are allowing fear to make them shirk their duty, while basking in the 'glamor' of the job and in the relatively high rate of pay for women. 'I hate most policewomen on the force,' she says, then laughs. 'Hate is maybe a very strong word! I *intensely dislike* a lot of the women – if they're afraid, then get out!'

Quality, not quantity, is what concerns her. She joined six years ago, and was in the second academy to include regular policewomen: 'We had to do the same things the guys did, physical requirements and that sort of thing, and now they've slipped back a little bit.' Furthermore, she says, that whereas female officers of her generation were content to prove themselves, now they are apt to go and complain if criticized for their shortcomings.

There's definitely a need for female officers, but we're women involved in a man's world – it always will be, by the nature of the job. I love the chivalry, I love it! The guys are really protective of us and that's fine.

You have to use a lot of guile because you haven't any size. I've promised people anything in the world to get them into the back of a police car – I couldn't care less what I say! And if they're taller than you, they think they're superior, so you use things like standing on the curb to give you the extra four inches to look them in the eye. I've stood on orange crates, car bumpers – wherever I could, just to get up to their level!

But when it comes to arresting a violent female, Kim Benton believes a policewoman is at a definite advantage.

113

A man knows he can knock a woman out with one punch, so he usually tries to restrain them – and she usually tears them up, with the clawing and the biting and all this. I prefer being a woman, because I'll walk right up and punch them, see?

The telephone rings. It's her husband, to say he has been delayed at the DA's office, and won't be able to come by the station as arranged to pick her up. This sort of thing happens quite often in their lives: Roger Benton is a detective himself, working narcotics. But they don't have any family to worry about – 'I won't have any children,' says Kim Benton, 'I'm not like that' – so the effect of these disruptions isn't too catastrophic.

And clearly, she enjoys being a detective too much to ever want to give it up.

It's nothing like working patrol. I come in, get the cases assigned to me, and I just tell my sergeant where I'll be going and when I'll be back. I have anywhere from three to six cases a day on my desk, and I shift that in my day. The most I've had was eight – although, when I worked Juvenile, I averaged twenty.

Placing her final selection of mug-shots on her desk, Kim Benton glances at the time, notes it is nearly four, and then looks back at the line-up of black faces, each with braids and a mustache. They should do fine, when an eye-witness in the case comes by in the morning.

People thought I'd be the last person to be a cop. I was wild as a teenager – used to throw bottles at cops and then sail over six-foot fences!

I went to college and did sociology. To support myself, I was a waitress and then I was a meter maid. I had a police radio and I was able to see what the job was like. It's not so much the variety of the calls, as the variety of personalities you run into.

When I was in Vice, I arrested one of my sociology professors. *That* was an experience. I said, 'Oh, my God . . .' and he said, 'What can I say?'

7

There is a restlessness about the Plaza this late afternoon, and it has nothing to do with El Toro having just been arrested and taken down to the station on Market.

Groping isn't his only weakness. He also tends to start fights with whatever comes to hand, and a few minutes ago, not having his stick any longer, he'd started using his belt, lashing out left and right – apparently indifferent that a pair of unsupported pants don't help a man when he's trying to escape.

Neither has the restlessness anything to do with the bus lines growing longer as shoppers head for home, nor with the activities of their attendant purse-snatchers.

Scattered about are several groups of youths, possibly members of less celebrated street gangs. United, they would constitute quite a mob, but Luke Jones and his colleagues can do nothing at this stage, other than keep an eye on things.

A crippled American Indian, with silver medallions around the crown of his black hat, approaches Unit 521 and asks Luke Jones for the address of the Indian Center. It's a request he frequently makes, and it isn't easy to guess why he keeps repeating it, unless it simply reassures him to have a cordial exchange with a police officer.

The tedium of making the same reply encourages Luke Jones to set Unit 521 in motion as the cripple backs away with his thanks, and he turns right down Third Avenue. There, just round the corner, another downtown unit is standing empty. By its number, Jones recognizes the car assigned to Dave Swithin.

Even here, out of sight of the Plaza, that sense of restlessness still seems tangible, held in limbo by a gut feeling.

8

Officer Dave Swithin is out, walking his beat.

> I walk a lot downtown, so I've got to know a lot of the bouncers, some of the dancers in topless bars, the little coffee-shop waitresses and waiters, people who work in the shops down here, the hookers. I like to get to know the people, and to know there are people down here who might help if you get into some trouble on the street.

He notices Luke Jones leaving his unit a block away to talk to a black man in a green tank top who has arms as thick as most

115

people's legs. Every field interrogation – or interview, as senior officers prefer to call it – is meant to be recorded on an FI pad, and the information, however meagre, finds its way into SHERLOC, the department's own intelligence-gathering computer. Without needing to approach any closer, the reason for Jones's interest having been aroused seems fairly obvious.

> We stop a guy: he's very muscular, big arms – he's usually spent time in a state prison, pumping iron. They come back like a *rock*. Why not? They don't do anything else, so they work out in the gym, get as strong as hell, get so they can run real fast, learn the martial arts. I think the martial arts is a bit over-rated, because you've got to be awful damn good to know what you're doing. Most of the guys you meet, who say they're into the martial arts, I find you can take them out.

Swithin is not a particularly big man himself, being on the spare side at one hundred and seventy pounds spread evenly over a five-eleven frame. The most noticeable thing about this sandy-haired former naval officer, who hails from Connecticut, is his sensitive yet unflappable air.

> Being a cop is the last thing I thought about, then I got some information about the department and I liked the idea of getting out, being my own boss. It's changed me. I used to put up with a lot of things – like poor service in a restaurant – but now I won't, so I guess maybe I'm more assertive. But I've also seen so much that, in some ways, I'm more compassionate – things that've made me *sick*. Talking to a rape victim and those questions you've got to ask; to a six-year-old boy sexually molested by two twelve-year-olds; a child neglect case – seeing a cute little girl smile, and she has no teeth because they're all rotting out . . .

Swithin has two children, by his first marriage, and is in the process of securing his second divorce. Most of the people he associates with are not police officers, but service friends. 'I read a lot – I've always done that; pretty much anything. I go to movies, I go to plays.'

He pauses to look into a bar. Only a couple of the customers are watching the topless dancer, a pale, unshapely girl who jiggles in the greeny glow like a larva on a fish hook. The thudding beat seems to have stunned everyone else, and over against the wall rack of pool cues, a bouncer gives him a bored shrug.

Generally, the owners and the bouncers take care of any hassle, because they don't want us coming down on them. Most bar fights I've been in, it's just the two people involved and everyone else just keeps out of the way, so it's not difficult to break up. If it looks bad, you hold off and call up some other units; you let the people beat the living daylights out of each other, and then, when they're tired, you go in and pick up the pieces.

Back out on the sidewalk, Swithin turns and retraces his steps to his unit. Suddenly, he's running.

9

Fifty or so people are fighting on the Plaza, in a possibly gang-related clash, and onlookers are fleeing, standing stunned, finding it all so unreal. As the police move in, however, most of the combatants break and run too, leaving only a few still at each other's throats.

Luke Jones, with a ticket to Sunday's performance of *Two Gentlemen of Verona* in a breastpocket, plunges in and grabs a youth hellbent on pulverizing another, who is already sinking to the ground. And as he handcuffs his prisoner, he orders two others to stop where they are. But they start to walk away, and then one of them – tall, skinny, long-haired and looking like a scarecrow with a bloodied mouth – breaks into a sprint, followed by his companion.

A chase begins. There's confusion. Luke Jones gets his prisoner into Unit 521, and returns to the fray, but just as suddenly as it began, everything seems to have quietened down. People have started to laugh nervously. Then, through the crowd of onlookers, come the pair who had tried to escape; they've been arrested about a block away. The scarecrow man is fighting every inch of the way; handcuffed and with his arms pinioned, he keeps kicking out and spitting blood into the face of the arresting officer, making noises like an animal. There is certainly not much that is recognizably human about him at this moment.

Into the back of a unit he goes, and the car door is slammed shut. Time for the police officers to engage in nervous laughter, as their own reaction to the conflict sets in. But it isn't over, not for the scarecrow man.

Turning berserk, ranting and screaming, he hurls himself on his back on the rear seat of the unit and starts trying to kick out a window. The door is jerked open, and he's manhandled out. Luke Jones lifts him easily, as though he were no more than straw and rags, and forces him down over the hood of the unit, smearing blood over the paintwork. Other officers set about hog-tying the prisoner, by placing another pair of cuffs around his ankles, and then drawing the two sets of cuffs together, linking them with a plastic strap, so that he ends up arched backwards, his feet and hands almost touching. The scarecrow man resists violently, twisting in a frenzy of unnatural strength, but Luke Jones has his sticklike arms held so tight that his efforts are of no avail. Finally, trussed up, still spitting, screaming, hurting only himself now when he heaves about, he is tossed back on to the rear seat of the unit, face down.

A parcel for the patio, and later, the county jail.

Luke Jones returns to Unit 521, checks on his own prisoner, finds him behaving himself, and sets off down to the station. For a scholarly type, he might seem remarkably unaffected by his recent, almost casual exertions.

I've always been involved in very divergent things. For example, when I was wrestling in college – I wrestled for the AAU, one weight below heavy-weight, and was active in all sports, baseball, football, boxing – the rest of the wrestling team kind of looked upon me as an enigma, because I was much more erudite than they. I was continually helping them with their report writing, and whenever they had a paper to do, I'd help them. But, by the same token, they seemed unwilling to allow me to really get involved with them – I was resented, in a way, for my interest in the theater, in dance and stuff like that. Of course, wrestling's a very macho-oriented area, like police work is.

I get over here, and they had a tendency to feel the same way about me. They wondered, 'What's this guy really like?' I'm also a minister's son, so they automatically assumed I probably didn't want to do the things they wanted to do, which wasn't necessarily true. But I've developed more personal friends than I ever had before, when I used to be regarded suspiciously because of my other interests. You don't openly think about it, but every cop realizes that when you go out of that lot, you may never come back – or your best friend may never come back. It helps to build a strong sense of camaraderie.

Somewhere out here in Central Division, right at this

moment, there's a very upset man with eighty-one rounds of ammunition in his pocket, and another six rounds in the twenty-two revolver stuck in his waistband.

10

The scarecrow man is delivered to the county jail where, if his attitude doesn't change pretty soon, he'll be put in the 'rubber room', a padded cell. The charges against him are fighting in public, resisting arrest, and battery – spitting blood in the face of the arresting officer, which constituted 'unconsented-to touching'. The steel door slides shut behind him.

Outside, it's a perfect evening. A slight breeze, at least an hour's daylight still, and Officer Dave Swithin is thinking about taking another stroll down a street on his beat. He exchanges a wave with a female accident investigator, as she passes by the other way.

> With male officers, you get real good ones, real bad ones, and then there's your average cop. But the women, for some reason, seem to be just either really good or terrible.

The accident investigator from Traffic is another policewoman who prefers to keep her bullet-proof vest in the trunk of her unit. Dave Swithin, who has experienced about ten incidents involving firearms during his two years' service, is somewhat ambivalent about body armor.

> A friend of mine in my academy was shot through the neck. Another friend of mine took a rifle bullet in the shoulder. But I generally wear my vest. You'd probably get a few internal injuries, but that's better than have a bullet go through – although apparently, just the shock can take you out.
> I wish they'd do more to people carrying guns, because I like going home at night. I don't like knowing that just about anyone I contact could be carrying one.

Anyway, he has his vest on tonight, as he picks out familiar faces on the sidewalks.

> I like working the street, but like most everybody else, probably after a while I'll get tired of it, feel I need a break. I've worked plainclothes a few times, and I enjoy it. It's scarier, but

it's nice to put on some ragged old clothes and not to shave for a couple of days. One night I spent four hours as a drunk in detox.

11

'*Detox?*' exclaims the dishevelled man, steadying himself against the back of a bus bench. His tone indicates that an outrageous suggestion has just been made to him, and he looks round in disbelief at the circle of smiling faces. 'Do I have to go with this crazy son of a bitch?'

'Detox,' says Luke Jones, lightly, 'is a *whole* lot more fun than jail.' And places his handcuffs on him.

'No, wait! I'm not what you think I am!'

But he is: a routine drunk.

Very routine, as he makes clear once he is in the unit. 'You know,' he says to Luke Jones, through the grille, 'I've been arrested about two hundred times. How do you like that shit?'

'What's your name?'

'Harold. My name is Harold.'

Unit 521 starts rolling, and the prisoner falls silent for about six blocks. He has the head of a Roman senator, the finely scarred hands of a sheet-metal worker, and the crumpled gray suit of someone two sizes bigger than him.

Harold leans forward and confides in a shy whisper: 'Besides, I love my sister, you see. Do you understand that?'

'Sure I do.'

'*I* don't understand it!' explodes Harold, indignantly.

The detox comes in sight, with its usual huddle of hopefuls around the door. They watch Luke Jones go in with his prisoner, reclaim his handcuffs and then leave again, looking preoccupied.

'Hey, officer, just listen a minute, will ya . . . ?'

But his broad back remains turned towards them as he strides over to his unit. It's all happened hundreds of times before. A man in a light shirt and light trousers stares at that back.

A few minutes later, seated in his parked unit several blocks away, Luke Jones is writing out a report when the radio warns of a white male, possibly armed with a concealed weapon, outside the doors of the detox. A lot starts to happen very quickly.

12

'A white male,' repeats the voice on the radio, 'possibly wearing light blue pants or light green pants, possibly a light blue shirt.'

Dave Swithin is the second officer to arrive at the scene, and sees the man, who is roughly his own height and weight, sitting on the detox steps, with a revolver lying beside him.

As I get out of my unit, he picks the gun up, so I draw my revolver and duck behind a car parked on the lot. I tell him to drop it, but he won't drop it. Two other units roll up; they're about twenty-five feet from the guy, and I'm about fifteen. A reserve officer comes up and gets behind a car. The guy keeps waving the gun around.

He keeps cocking it and uncocking it, and then he cocks it and waves it around some more. He waves it in our direction a few times, but he never actually aims it. He doesn't take a good grip of it, kind of like a limp wrist. A couple of times, the way he's waving the gun around, he is almost pointing it at his own head, and I think he's going to shoot himself. I begin to get the feeling that one of his main problems is that he's crazy and he *wants* us to kill him.

So orders are put out to keep the street blocked off, and to keep all civilians out of the area – then, if we do have to shoot, nobody will be in the line of fire.

Well, after a while, he fires a shot in the air.

Luke Jones hears the shot but can see nothing, because he's outside the immediate area, helping to keep it sealed off. The radio is frustratingly short of the sort of information which builds up a picture of what's happening outside the detox.

'Four-fifty-six William, where do you want me to stop?'

'Okay, I want you west. Five-thirteen William, block off Ten and J.'

'Five-fourteen William . . .'

'Five-fourteen William, just cruise around. As far as I know, all entrances to the area are closed.'

'Hutton . . .'

'Hutton? Where are you from?'

'El Cajon.'

121

Help is coming from all points of the compass. Dave Swithin, crouched only yards from the man with the gun, has his clear field of fire.

He starts fooling around with the bullets in his pocket. He gets up and starts walking down the street away from us, so we follow him. As I'm moving from behind a telephone pole into a doorway, he spins round and catches me wide open. I almost shoot him. But his gun's pointing at the ground, or I'd shoot him without thinking.

Out on the periphery, things start to sound really bad, especially when a hoarse voice warns on the radio: 'He has reloaded his gun!'

And an angry supervisor almost shouts into his microphone: 'Forty-one-eleven, get the hell out the street! You are under fire! Get off the street!'

Then the man with the gun stops, and Dave Swithin, still following him, freezes.

He lets the gun dangle by its trigger guard, with his hands about shoulder high, and he starts walking back at me. I keep telling him to stop, to drop the gun, but he won't. When he gets close enough, *the hell with it.* I grab his gun, throw it behind me, and tackle him. Another officer comes in too.

Over the radio, Luke Jones hears: 'Five-fourteen William – he's in custody! The suspect is in custody.'

Not only that, but Dave Swithin is all right, apart from a wrenched shoulder and having dirtied up his uniform.

I almost shot him three different times. It was just it was never really . . . I don't know, maybe I just didn't like the idea of killin' somebody unless I absolutely had to. I came close.

13

'It's not like shooting a rabbit,' remarks Officer Dan L. Jackson, the Sea Wall choirboy, in his lazy Texan drawl. 'Although there are guys around who probably feel that way, and maybe it's good. Officers that've been involved in six or seven shootings, and have killed as many people, who do their job well, and are able to live with it. But a lot of people might not want to invite them over for dinner either.'

Dan L. Jackson has been fired at on two occasions during his eight years with the department, and last time, he shot a man himself.

I'm not going to tell you it's not exciting – you train all your life for a set of events like what happened to me. There was no mention of a vehicle put out, no description of a car, but by using good police sense, I found the guys and I *knew* they were the guys.

We had a robbery up in Hillcrest. They broadcast it as a couple of minutes old; two black males, both armed, and they'd cut out on foot. I was ten-twelve blocks away, so I just took what I thought might be their escape route. I saw two black guys in this white Continental. Part of the description was that one of them was in corn rollers, the other had a medium Afro, and one had a blue jacket.

I went to stop them. I started calling for cover, and I didn't get any until I was way down Market Street. We wound up in a high-speed pursuit, chased them all over south-east San Diego, and they finally went into a dead-end street.

They bailed out with their guns and started running at me. I hit the emergency brakes on my car, and figured I was going to get my lunch – that it was all over right then. I jumped out with my shotgun and I knelt down, leveling at the driver. But my car, still being in 'drive', lurched forward, hit me in the back, the shotgun went off, and I was knocked to the ground. I thought I'd been shot – in fact, I got up and I was lookin' for the holes!

In the shoot-out that followed, Jackson set off in pursuit of one of the suspects, firing twice to no effect.

The third time, he was runnin' and about forty yards away. I remember going through in my mind the department instructions on when I could shoot and when I couldn't, and I read 'em all in just that flash – I fired and he went down.

I took a lot of heat around here from guys because I didn't kill him. He was a well-known crook from when he was a teenager and I'd first come on. They said I could have saved the state and the courts and probably everybody else a lot of money, because when he gets out, he'll be doing the same thing all over again. They wanted to send me back to shotgun training and everything, until finally I got the range master to come and tell them that, from the distance the guy was away, I was lucky I hit him.

Guys can say what they want to, but it's easier, I can live with myself. If you kill somebody, no matter how big a crook or screamin' asshole he is, it's still somebody's kid and somebody must care for him, someplace.

'I've been in this job three years,' says Norm Stamper, Special Adviser to the Chief, 'and in the first year I had probably about five hundred counseling sessions with employees, many coming back two or three times. Much of it was the type of counseling for which I'm not trained, so I'd make referrals, but I'd listen first. That's what many people were looking for, just to talk to somebody who wasn't going to affect their career-advancement possibilities.

'They'd walk through the door and say, "My sergeant's just changed my days off, I'm going to school, and it's screwing up my life." Blah, blah, blah. And after five minutes of that, they're into the real subject: "My wife and I are getting a divorce and it's breaking me up" – or, "I'm *scared* out there . . .'''

All of which confirmed his belief that he'd been right to include a psychological services program in his original COP outline, drawn up in 1974, and a few months ago, the department finally hired its own psychologist, thirty-two-year-old Dr Michael Mantell.

Dr Mantell's duties are to provide a free and completely confidential counseling service for officers and their families, psychological screening of recruits, expert advice for managers, and educational and training programs, with an emphasis on how to cope with stress.

There is also, for those who undergo a particularly traumatic experience, such as at an accident or shooting, a psychotherapy program.

Back at about the time Dan L. Jackson joined the department, Norm Stamper actually killed a man.

Maybe two or three times a year it'll come to my mind, and I'll sit and reflect and I'll tear-up about it. I think that's normal and healthy. It was a very tragic, unfortunate thing, but to me the salvation was it had to happen.

It was in '72: we were trying to track down a twenty-three-year-old man who was threatening to kill his three-year-old son. He had him with him. And his wife told us horror story after horror story of what he had done in the past, including stringing her father up in a closet with baling wire and leaving him there for two days.

When we found the man, he ran around a gas station, jumped in his car, took the kid and said, 'Get outa here! – or I'll kill him.' He had a thirty-two revolver.

It was not one of those split-second things when you don't get a chance to think. It's true what they say: seconds took minutes. It was amazing how an event that lasted such a short space of time was so pregnant with thought and considerations of what to do and what not to do. I shot him in the back of the head from about twelve inches.

I relive it from time to time. I remember reaching in and pulling the child out of his dead father's arms. There was blood all over the child, and he was screaming and crying. But he'd not been hit – I'd made sure of that.

14

Luke Jones, his broad back to the Cabrillo, leans against Unit 521 and watches the passing show on the Plaza. Darkness has long since come to San Diego.

What you don't see is more dangerous than what you do see. One of the witnesses said that as I walked out of the detox, that guy shifted the gun in his waistband.

There's a white male of about thirty-five, sweat-stained and looking as though he has just crawled out of a trash can, taking careful steps in a very straight line across the lawn toward the fountain. He halts, his path blocked by a large, self-absorbed couple united in a heaving embrace like a pair of elephant seals on a deserted shore.

'Detox,' sighs Luke Jones, starting forward to make the arrest.

'Hey, Luke!' calls out Sergeant Juarez, who has dropped by with a ride-along. 'The car-hop's Saturday – you didn't forget?'

But Luke Jones has to hurry before the drunk literally puts his foot in it, provoking the sort of reaction with which disgruntled elephant seals enliven call-of-the-wild documentaries.

And a minute or so later, he is on his way down to the detox again, probably for the last time this shift. Suddenly there's an urgent call for back-up from an officer in Hillcrest. Unit 521 does a one-eighty, burns rubber, goes banshee wailing up the slope, running red lights, racing the imagination.

Armed robbery? Wife hacked up by husband? Shoot out? Could be pretty well anything . . .

It's a seventy-year-old, respectably-dressed white-haired

old guy, standing beside a Volkswagen bus and waving his arms about, working himself up into a frenzy. 'Persecuted!' he shouts in guttural German accents. 'Down through the ages! There is no escape! You know what happened, my momma, my poppa, in *Auschwitz*! Holocaust! What I do? I come to America – America for the free! What happens? Show me your driver's license! Let me see your Jew's name, Jew! And I will persecute you! Is *this* why I come America?'

'He didn't stop at the stop sign,' explains the officer at the scene, highly agitated. 'Won't show me his license – you can't get near him. Hey, listen, sir, all I want – '

'I know what you want, Mr Policeman! *Mister Gestapo!* For how many years now I'm driving and not one ticket? I go!'

And he starts to climb back into his Volkswagen, but pauses in a glare of headlights as three other units arrive screeching to a stop, and the officers jump out.

'All for *me*?' he says, smiles nervously, and gives up his idea of making a run for it. He signs the ticket.

J. F. Kennedy, the Holocaust – it's striking how often history has a way of getting mixed up in a street cop's everyday experience.

Luke Jones goes back to his unit, swings it round and heads for the detox again.

Back-up depends on tone of voice. That officer was angry when he put out the call – I thought he was in trouble. In a way, that was true: one officer sure can physically subdue a seventy-year-old man, but he may have to hurt him. With two or three officers, there isn't that problem.

The drunk on the back seat mumbles.

Out there, away to the right, so dark and vast it doesn't bear much thinking about, the Pacific. Here on the left, coming up in a moment or two, the floodlit bridge across into Balboa Park and its fourteen hundred acres.

Still the drunk mumbles, his words indistinct yet lilting, as the park drifts by, fragrant with eucalyptus. Canyons, mesas, lawns and formal flowerbeds, natural forest, a dance of fountains. Massive baroque silhouettes, Spanish cupolas, Moorish geometric decorations. Museums, galleries, theaters, restaurants, the zoo, a planetarium. Cabrillo Bridge, the House of Charm, the Hall of Champions.

'What you doin' back there?' demands Luke Jones, glancing up into his rear-view mirror.

Silence.

Then the drunk's speech clears. 'So twice five miles of fertile ground . . .'

And Luke Jones says, 'With walls and towers were girdled round . . .'

Together, they recite:

> 'And here were gardens with sinuous rills,
> 'Where blossomed many an incense-bearing tree,
> 'And here were forests Ancient as the hills
> 'Enfolding – '

The drunk breaks off to exclaim, 'Hey, man, I never knew dumb cops knew nothin' about poetry!'

'And I never knew,' says Luke Jones, 'dirty old downtown drunks knew anything about poetry.'

'You're right!'

They laugh out loud together. And then, riding down the long slope of San Diego, not in any hurry, they begin again at the beginning.

> 'In Xanadu did Kubla Khan a stately pleasure
>   dome decree:
> 'Where Alph, the sacred river, ran
> 'Through caverns measureless to man,
> 'Down to a sunless sea . . .'

Part IV

Ghosts and Billy Johnson

1

There was the usual batch of burglaries in San Diego yesterday. One will have repercussions on the department undreamed of by anyone glancing casually down the list. Another will have an indirect bearing on the tragic aftermath of tomorrow's Mexican car-hop.

But, in the meantime, it's Friday – and for some, just another day in the working week.

> I wake up in the morning time to the sound of music. I get out of bed dancin', and I dance my way into the shower, and I sing and dance and make jokes with my lady, and I laugh and have a good time and kiss the kids goodbye, and I'm off and runnin'.

Officer Billy McGuire is on his way down to the station on West Market. Rangy, lean-faced, proud of being still thirty-two inches around the waist at thirty-seven, he has been with the department for close on twelve years, making him one of its veteran black officers.

> I've worked Narcotics, Training, Burglary, Auto Theft, School Task Force, and in the Personnel Division – came in from the Navy, a machinist's mate. Prior to the Navy, I worked as a skilled machine operator for the Baldwin Piano Company. I made piano strings and I learned everything except how to play a piano. Worked for myself since I was eleven years old; I come from a family of very poor sharecroppers in Southern Mississippi. By the time I was seven, my grandmother made me this little tiny cotton sack, and I worked right beside her in the cotton fields, and she said, 'Pick, baby – pick!'

2

Officer Dan L. Jackson is also on his way in, steering his car with a bandaged hand. He gashed it on duty up at Hillcrest, and the injury has placed him on light duty as area commander's aide to Captain Walker.

Which is why Dan L. Jackson, a confirmed street cop, has on his three-piece suit, as egg-shell blue as the early morning sky above, and is carrying a snubnosed handgun for a change.

Standing a hefty six-two, and exuding an air of casual competence, he was born thirty years ago in Japan. When roughly his small daughter's age, his ambitions were already fixed.

> I had a great-great-great-something or other uncle who was a district attorney in Dallas when it was a rip-roarin' town, and he was pretty famous in his way – I'm kind of named after him. I wanted to be a policeman since I was about five or six years old; be a policeman and play the drums.

He went on to become a drummer in his high school orchestra and marching band, and in rock-and-roll groups. For a while, however, he wasn't too sure he'd get to twirl a night-stick.

> I was about sixteen and we were at a fair – you know, where you paid a buck and they read your palm. This gipsy told me I probably wouldn't make it to twenty-one, because my life-line was so short. I joined the Navy. On my twenty-first birthday, I was sittin' in Da Nang harbor, right in the middle of the war, and had cause to be very cautious.

3

With his earlier starting time, Officer Joe Cronin is already parking his car at the station.

When he went off to war, he gave the matter his customary cool appraisal, decided that all Uncle Sam required of him was a body, and saw no reason to hazard good clothing and foot-wear which he'd probably not see again for a long, long time, if ever. 'I left home,' he recalls, 'in shower shoes, shorts, and a tee-shirt – they thought I was just going out for the day.'

And when Joe Cronin returned from war, there wasn't a great deal he wanted to say about it. Mainly this: 'When they said casualties were moderate, "moderate" was really heavy.'

Then the Vietnam veteran changed uniforms.

> When I came in the department in '69, there were seventeen black officers – today, we're talking of fifty-six, including the guys in the academy.
>
> I've seen guys come on, and they've been called 'Uncle Tom' by their peers and they've quit. I've been called every derogatory name in the book, but I don't let it get to me. You see, my mother and my family told me, 'Hey, no one out there is going to help

you!' – and I don't like to be dependent on anyone, on welfare or anything, so what people say don't hurt me.

I lost my cool just once. This guy was calling me racial names and I got down to his level – I should never have done that. He spit on me, so I got out my first-aid kit, and I took some tape and I wrapped it round his mouth, around his whole head! He looked like a mummy. When he came in the station, the Chief of Police at that time said, 'He's really pissed you off, hasn't he?'

Now Joe Cronin is back out of uniform again.

At thirty-seven, he stands five-eleven, weighs a solid one-ninety-two, has an Afro hairstyle, a mustache, glasses, and a gold ring. When he left home this morning – he lives with his Italian wife and their two children at La Mesa, about twelve miles from the station – he was wearing a stylish vest with a caramel suit, and took with him some business cards that describe him as an investigator.

Joe Cronin works Burglary.

4

Dan L. Jackson has some cards in his pocket too. They also give two telephone numbers, one for use in emergencies only. But instead of being conventionally white and emblazoned with a facsimile of a San Diego PD badge, he has chosen to make his own cards rather special: they are buff-colored, have a textured surface, and his badge is only a small part of the head-and-shoulders portrait of himself.

It shows an officer with a broad, genial face, glasses, a mustache, and long fair hair almost covering his ears; it hints at Scandinavian forebears on at least one side of the family; it confirms his pride in wearing uniform.

They say the best job in the department is the beat officer. The only fault I can find in it is the shift work, because you wind up going to court mostly on your days off, and that's hard on you and your family, planning things. In New York, you go from silver badge to gold as a detective – here, everybody has gold and you just lose money. A lot of them don't get overtime. And guys who make agent – the two-stripers in Patrol – lose those stripes if they're chosen for detectives, which means about five percent off their pay, plus they have to put out all this money for suits and stuff. Some of the specialized assignments, they're really neat, but there are some that are just the paperwork jungle. In patrol you're doing a multitude of things; the guy in Burglary is dealing with burglaries, the Sex Crimes guy with sex crimes and doesn't see other things. But you need that kind of people for their expertise and they do a lot of the leg work for you. Other people may think there's status in being a detective, but Patrol are the front-line guys: they either screw it up or make it right.

5

And that's something that bothers Lieutenant Rae Chassam, patrol commander of Second Watch, Central Division, who is also on his way down to the station.

> The big thing to me is the preliminary investigation – if we don't get the information, the chances are that person isn't going to be caught. In my opinion, that's one of our failings. Our patrol officers should become more and more involved in that, but they're not all doing it.

Normally, Lieutenant Chassam wouldn't be traveling into the city from his home in El Cajon at this hour, since Second Watch doesn't begin until the afternoon. But he and Sergeant Juarez have last-minute arrangements for tomorrow's car-hop to see to, such as making sure the bleachers are transported down from Balboa Park. They are old friends; he tutored him for sergeant.

> When I came on the department, I formed my own prejudices, although I was not nearly as prejudiced as a lot of blacks you ran across who hated white people, *period*. But at my age now, forty-seven, I'n not going to waste time on something like that; there are too many nice people in the world to worry about what color they are, or where they come from.

He may be approaching fifty, and his Afro hairstyle could seem very gray against his deep suntan, but Lieutenant Chassam leaves many of his young subordinates looking like crotchety old men, especially the John Waynes among them. Enthusiastic, warm, with a quick, keen mind and a great capacity for having fun, he doesn't mind admitting, 'Oh God, I love Disneyland! I'm hooked! I'm an addict!'

And he still goes there given any excuse – despite what happened back in 1958 while he was in the Navy.

I needed a pyrotechnic operator's license for the State of California. To get it, I worked at Disneyland for two months. Every night we would shoot off fireworks as a grand finale, and Tinkerbell would fly down from the Matterhorn with a big spotlight on her. Tinkerbell, in reality, was a retired aerialist and must have been, I guess, about sixty-five years old. They had a big cable, strung from the top of the Matterhorn, which went all the way across where the fireworks were – you couldn't see it – and down to this big telephone pole, wrapped with a mattress, where a fella called the 'catcher' would save her from hurting herself.

One night, after I'd been there a couple of weeks, we were setting off the fireworks that came before the grand finale. *Boom!* – and everyone would go, 'Ooooh-aaaah . . .' *Boom, boom!* – 'Ooooh-aaah, oooh-aaaah . . .' Then *BOOM!* – one of the damn things exploded at about hip level, blew my pants off. It was a hell of an explosion: burnt me and the guy I was with, cut all communications, and set off the grand finale. Tinkerbell saw the grand finale and jumped off the Matterhorn – but the catcher, knowing it wasn't time for it, had gone to get a Coke. And so, she came right across Disneyland in the dark, no spotlight, nobody to catch her, hit the pole and . . . The truth of the matter is, I almost killed Tinkerbell.

So Lieutenant Chassam hardly needs reminding that, even with the most innocent of pleasures – like tomorrow's car-hop – things can still go horrifyingly wrong.

6

Pick, baby, pick!

Billy McGuire gives the impression of having lived his life to the beat of that exhortation ever since. 'I've got no big degrees on my walls,' he says, 'but I'm sort of self-educated and a radical.' He numbers among his acquaintances Rap Brown and Stokely Carmichael, founders of the Black Power movement.

He is also one of three officers chosen for the department's recruiting team, which places an emphasis on hiring black Americans, Chicanos and female officers. The team's first duty, however, is to attract the right sort of candidates for the COP approach, and to insure they have some idea of what they're letting themselves in for.

One thing we're faced by is the television image of the police officer. Guys who come in and they think, 'Hey, the world's going

135

to change, bells are going to ring, and lights are goin' to flash!' The only perception they have of law enforcement is Koquack and Colimbo and The Three Little Girls That Chuck Owns, and within thirty minutes they can investigate a murder, collect all the evidence, and get a conviction in court – whereas, in that amount of time, we sometimes don't even make it to the scene.

Billy McGuire's liveliness and candor are part of what he calls 'impacting people', and that's something he really believes in. Any prospective black officer with questions to ask is likely to find the answers coming back at him like an Arthur Ashe volley, without compromise.

Let's face it, police work is a very different atmosphere for a black person, an environmental change. Number One, you're being introduced to laws that affect you negatively. And, Number Two, police work centers round white middle- and upper-middle-class values, right? It's a job that has been dominated by white male Americans, and this *whole country* is designed for right-handed, five-foot-eight to six-foot-two, two-hundred pound white male Americans – not left-handed, because Marines WILL NOT SEE Joe Blow firing from the left shoulder!

So, in police work, it's not easy to get recognition as a black, whereas I've seen white officers, who go huntin' and fishin' and campin' with the boss . . . Well, the guy does anything other than write a ticket, and they're saying, 'Hey, *look* what a good job he did!' I've worked for a lot of good supervisors, but I've also worked for guys who, no matter what I did, it was never as great as, say, what my white counterpart did, who'd come to me for advice.

It used to *sicken* me, the way I'd have to come into the station and hand my reports to some two-year guy, a rook, acting in the sergeant's absence, and there I was, with eight years on (then), a competent police officer. For a long time, we never had blacks in acting-sergeant positions – that came about just within the last four or five years.

We're not looking for something to be handed out. We can get what we want out of the system here, if the system is willing to give us what we deserve. I'm president of the Minority Officers' Association, and I'm somewhat between optimistic and pessimistic right now, though things are going great for me personally.

So what's it like being a black police officer out on the streets of San Diego, especially when confronting whites? Is being black automatically a disadvantage?

When I was working the beach, I did things – by way of handling situations – I would not think of doing in my own community. For instance, I'd drive up to where all the big macho bikers hang out, and I didn't feel threatened. I'd get out of my car and if some guy gave me some guff, I'd tell him what was going to happen to him if he didn't comply. Nobody thought of jumping me – it was a mysterious type thing. 'God,' they're thinking, 'here's this guy and he's black and maybe he wants to get revenge for the way his rights have been handled in this society, so we'd better not offend him!'

The chief problems of a black officer seem to occur, according to McGuire, within the police community itself.

There have been many times when I've been hurt by my relationships with white officers – you have dreams and expectations shattered. I've ridden with guys and developed such camaraderie that we've even had social evenings together: 'Hey, bring along the family and we'll go to Crystal's, have dinner together tonight!' But as soon as we've transferred to different divisions, it's dissolved. That's a very shattering thing, because to me it shows that that was just a working relationship.

There can be hurt, too, even in the best of such relationships, those which don't fade away, and are strong enough to allow fun to be poked at racial bigotry.

To call a black person 'boy' is like calling him a nigger, right? But Craig – the big tolerant white guy he was – and me never called each other anything except 'boy'. In the locker room, he'd say, 'Mornin', boy!' – and I'd say, 'You're going to hate to go to line-up, boy, and tell the sergeant a boy just kicked your ass!' One time I made an arrest in a very sensitive black area, and I called for a back-up unit. Craig gets there and says, in the regular old customary manner, 'What you got, boy?' Well I understood him, but God, did I get rousted! The crowd went, 'Wooo, he's a fuckin' Uncle Tom! If that pig'd called me boy and I'd had a gun, I'd have shot the motherfucker!'

Should this anecdote cause a black candidate some confusion, and lead him to ask Billy McGuire just exactly where he stands on racial issues as a self-confessed 'radical', then this is the reply he's likely to get.

I've gone into divisions that have been previously all white, and in many cases it wasn't me they discriminated against – it was against somebody in the group that didn't fit in. Y'know, the sort of guy who walks in and says 'Good morning!' and buys you a cup of coffee, but no matter how hard you try, you can't get to like the son of a bitch. We're talking about individuals, and people are just naturally prejudiced. I've felt that way about a lot of white

137

officers, and a lot of black officers too – I just don't identify with the same things as they do. But you'll never hear me use terminology like 'spics' and 'chinks' and 'honkies' – nor will I allow my three kids to. Once you start that, it's reinforcement of stereotypes. People give radicals a bad name, but you'll find the most militant black people are usually the least anti-white – look how many of them have white wives, not that I do.

This reference to 'fitting in' may well lead a black candidate to ask Billy McGuire to what extent he's had to compromise – or develop a 'hole in his soul' – in order to carry out what he considers his 'community commitment' by being a police officer.

In the late sixties, when I came on, and through to the mid-seventies, a black person coming into law enforcement was considered to be an Uncle Tom. I even had one of my own relatives say he could not respect me, because I'd been hired to kill my own people. Through peer pressure, because of department expectations, I've done things I've not always wanted to do at the time, but I've never done anything so grossly wrong to an individual that I've had to regret it. In almost twelve years, I've never shot anybody, I've never Maced anybody, I've never hit anybody with my night-stick, I've never used a choke-hold on anybody – and I've worked every area of this city, including two years undercover, Narcotics. Sure, I've drawn my gun many times, and I've had more than one opportunity when I'd have been justified in killing a person, but I'm not a killer. Most police officers are not killers – the television stuff leads you to believe that.

Which brings the conversation virtually a full circle, but for one last, almost inevitable question: Just how did Billy McGuire himself become a police officer?

I was here in the Navy, and one night some friends and I were going to the bowling alley, all piled into Tommy's raggy old car. These two officers stopped us. Tommy said, 'Oh hell, here come the damn cops, man . . .' He was also born and raised in the Deep South, and when a carload of blacks got stopped there, I mean it was *The End*. But I got talking with the two officers, and they were really friendly. This was not something I was accustomed to, and I got the impression, well, maybe all San Diego cops were that nice – I hoped so. That's why I wanted to become part of it.

To this day, I've never known why those two officers stopped us.

7

Somewhere in there seems to be a cautionary tale for those who paint too bleak a picture of police officers during the 'bad, bad sixties'. Lieutenant Chassam would want to add to it.

> We tend to identify the old breed of officer with being hard and harsh all the time – that's not really true. There were a lot of guys with the ability to talk to people, to manipulate them that way; they just didn't recognize it.

He would also want to set the record straight on where, in his view, the San Diego PD stands at the moment.

> We're in a state of change. Obviously, you're always going to have those traditionalists who say, 'We don't wanna change' – and a lot of ranking officers feel that way.
>
> I say we're going to change in another ten or twenty years. It's going to take time, but it's the only way we're going to survive.
>
> My God, there's almost a million people here, and we've got just over a thousand police officers. *There is no way in hell we're going to control those people unless they're on our side.*

That's what the average street cop likes about Lieutenant Chassam: he spells things out in terms a person can understand, and doesn't go in for a lot of multi-syllabic philosophizing. In fact, it's difficult to recall whether he ever mentions COP by name, although he's clearly 100 percent behind it – and behind the man he considers its prime mover.

> Old-time police chiefs – some big cities still have them – were very autocratic: they ruled with an iron hand, there was no management and no direction. You either did the things they said, or you were out. Then, around the sixties, we started seeing some changes. Chiefs of police were no longer coming from the outside, and they were managers instead of the paramilitary thing.
>
> Chief Kolender's a perfect example. He manages, he isn't autocratic in the true sense of the word – he has a participatory approach. Now that we're starting to get some real good management, the next logical step is to let that filter down to the rank and file.
>
> In order to do that, we're having to be more thoughtful, more scientific, more *social*, if you will. We're having to realize that our job is not strictly fighting crooks – in fact, we spend less than a third of our time on it. The rest is spent helping old ladies; taking drunks to detox; writing traffic citations, which aren't strictly

criminal. We're having to realize that we're a social organization, and have been since we came into existence.

So instead of just going out and knockin' heads and throwin' people in jail, we're sitting down and talking to them. We're asking, 'What are your needs?' – 'What are our needs?' – 'Why do *you* do those things?' – 'Why do *we* do those things?' I think it's valuable.

And that's what is so exciting about this car-jumping thing we've organized. These are kids that, five years ago, police officers wouldn't talk to. 'Hey, they're the pukes, we don't want to mess with them, run 'em out of town' – and all that. But these aren't really kids, and ten years from now, they're going to be leaders in their communities, so it behooves us to have them with us, not against.

There's a cheery beep-beep on a horn, and Sergeant Juarez's sports car follows Lieutenant Chassam's Buick into the parking lot, across from the station.

8

No shotgun to book out, no handie-talkie to collect either; no weight of penal codes, no heavy gunbelt, no armored vest . . .

A detective travels light. It's one of the first things that strikes anyone just out of Patrol.

Crossing the patio, Investigator Joe Cronin carries on through the main gate and takes one of the sedans parked in front of the station. Unmarked cars are called 'pastels' in the San Diego PD – not that many of them have pastel bodywork in common. But they do all have distinctive fat tires and a give-away radio aerial, which means they are 'unmarked' only in the eyes of the virtuously ignorant.

Even so, when Joe Cronin swings his pastel out into West Market, the feeling is very different to that when a unit leaves the station. It's as though one is suddenly going about without bull's eyes painted on the doors.

He switches on the car radio.

' – four-fifteen, Greyhound bus depot. Three white males, one possibly armed with a weapon. Are there any units in the . . .'

It could be happening a world away, instead of a few blocks north; it simply doesn't concern him.

So he turns over in his mind the three cases he has left after about four hours at his desk this morning. Patrol's preliminary investigations into two of them are disappointing, but the third one sounds more promising – even if the beat officer was unable to find and 'lift' any fingerprints.

9

'About twenty-five percent of the latents we receive are good,' says Officer Drew Hubbard, 'no matter if they come from the lab or experienced detectives or rookies.'

Drew Hubbard has been part of the two-man Latent Prints team for the last five of his twenty-five years with the department. 'Our function is to receive, grade, store, compare and testify. We don't file known prints by classification; we keep them in the person's jacket at Records. It has its drawbacks.'

They're called 'latent prints', rather than 'fingerprints', because not all such incriminating marks are made by hands. 'There was the guy who made the mistake of washing himself up, took his shoes off, and there they were on the floor – sole prints. We find latents on wood, plastic, an awful lot on paper.'

Some are sent off to the FBI and other agencies for comparison, the rest Drew Hubbard and his partner handle themselves. 'There's no required number of points of comparison,' he says. 'We're more or less required to find eight, but we like ten. If it's not of good quality, we want more – and below seven, I've never gone.'

Occasionally, the work can be very gratifying, as in the Case of the Impossible Fingerprint, which threatened for a time to cast doubt on Drew Hubbard's expertise.

Two guys were found outside a bar that'd been broken into, and one of them had a coin box from a cigarette machine. I dusted the box and found the other guy's right thumb print. 'But it couldn't have been me,' he said, and he showed the detectives his right thumb, which was wrapped up in an old bandage and had a cut in it. 'Oh yes,' his mother said, 'my son cut his thumb – I forget, seven or eight days ago – and I bandaged it.' The detectives didn't know what to say to me: 'Sure it wasn't his *left* thumb?' 'Right thumb,' I said. Then someone finally had an idea and came up with a case three months old. The same bar'd been broken into, only they'd left the coin box behind that time! He pleaded guilty.

But, when considering the amount of work that flows in every day, it must be difficult at times to keep one's spirits up. 'We identify about thirty latents a month,' says Drew Hubbard.

10

Joe Cronin makes his first burglary call, only to find the householder has had to go to the doctor for tranquilizers. So he tries the neighbors, hoping to pick up some unconsidered snippet of useful information. Another blank, even though everyone he interviews would like to help.

Which only confirms his personal summation of working Burglary: 'About sixty percent of the time, nobody saw anything – so you're out chasin' ghosts!'

Back goes his slim briefcase into the pastel, and he sets off for a Mexican fast-food stand that had its cash register taken last night.

There's another general statement he could make about his work: 'You get less hassle as a black officer in Detectives, because people think you know it all.'

So much for the public's reaction. Once again, though, the reaction of one's fellow officers can be a different matter.

People resented my transfer to Detectives. There was a grievance letter about it, written by some white (patrol) officers with two or three years on the department – and I've got over ten. And in order for a black officer to be transferred, he has to prove himself twice as much as a white officer.

It shouldn't be that way. We've met with Chief Kolender and told him we'd like to see some changes – we don't expect them overnight. He's understanding. He knows we're not (in the Minority Officers' Association) trying to over-run the department, the belief of most white officers. We're trying to make conditions better for all of us, and we've had a lot of success. The administration now contacts us first when making decisions. This is the first time they've had blacks recruiting blacks, and we want a qualified black.

There are eight or nine black detectives; none in Robbery, Auto

Theft, Forgery, Intelligence, Sex Crimes or Fencing. I was the first black in Intelligence and the last one.

Clearly some sort of paradox is involved. If, as so many white officers say, much of their work concerns black criminals, then how is this helping the cause of detection? Rapport, an essential element in interrogation, would surely be more easily established in many instances were the interrogator black himself. Furthermore, it isn't clear how Robbery, for instance, arranges surveillance in black neighborhoods, unless it's always on the basis of seconding nonspecialist personnel from Patrol.

When I was a trainee, I did a lot of undercover work: dope assignment, Vice, SCAT – Special Crime Attack Team. We teamed up in pairs where they had a lot of robberies and burglaries, did stake-outs, and in three months we'd a total of ninety-eight felony arrests.

In fact, it's Joe Cronin's contention that, when it comes to detective work, the black officer has the greater versatility.

11

A burglary report has just been assigned to Hillcrest beat officer Jimmy Fellows. It's half an hour old, but his morning on First Watch has been hectic – a fact not altogether appreciated by the couple of impatient young Texans who made the call. They're also taken aback to see a black officer step out of the unit, and make some crack about it between themselves.

In his experience, their reaction is unusual.

I strongly believe that few people ever notice the color I am. The only thing they see is this car, this uniform, and this badge. It doesn't give me any trouble at all.

Then the Texans get a closer look at Jimmy Fellows. He is thirty-one, has a long mustache, and stands a compact five-ten. He has the quiet self-assurance of a man who doesn't wear body armor. He's polite.

Next moment, they're talking.

'Hell, like we just got here.'

'We're on vacation, right? Rented this place and – '

'Car was in the driveway. We – '

'We were taking stuff inside, y'know? Then these – '

'Two guys came by. Took both our cases and – '

'I mean, all our goddamn clothes, right? And we're on – '

'They were in some kind of liftback.'

'It was orange.'

'No, yellow. Anyway, we – '

Jimmy Fellows interrupts: 'These guys, sir? What did they look like? Can you – ?'

'Two guys – white guys, I guess,' says one.

'Maybe Mexican,' says the other.

When further questioning fails to elicit a better description of the suspects and their vehicle, Jimmy Fellows passes on what he has to Communications, and then says he'll take a look round the neighborhood, as there's a chance that the yellow/orange liftback isn't far away.

Plainly skeptical, the two Texans watch him drive off, and mutter some unkind things about San Diego.

Jimmy Fellows is somewhat ambivalent about it himself, having transferred here from a police department in New Jersey just over two years ago, bringing his wife and young son with him: 'It was the weather – I didn't even know the place existed.' But it hasn't been easy to set up home again. Houses cost twice as much as he's accustomed to, and he can't raise enough for a down payment. What has 'totally shocked' him is that the city doesn't pay medical insurance for dependents, which means that although his salary is greater than before, he has less money in his pocket each month. He and his wife also miss their families, and he feels that Californians are far too self-absorbed. 'You'll notice how each individual house round here has a fence around it. You put up a fence and say "Nothing matters to me outside it – I don't care if you live next door, I just don't care." Back east, very very seldom do you see a fence; neighbors walk over backyards, kids run in between.' Another problem is that his wife is now much more anxious about him. 'She thinks I was safer back there, because I always had a partner, plus cover all the time. Here she watches the TV and hears officers complaining about their cover being ten minutes away. But you're not up against such a hostile environment. The people aren't the same, and you get more respect. It's a whole different world.'

Twice, Jimmy Fellows pauses in his search for the suspects' vehicle but each time the vehicle he's glimpsed turns out, on closer inspection, not to be a liftback. He continues to cruise the neighborhood. It's a pretty part of town; lots of greenery, trim houses, fresh paintwork, wide streets and clean side-walks. Back east, as he says, was very different.

> I worked in an area with a lot of unemployment, there were a lot more fights, and people didn't think anything of shooting at a cop. It was nothing for a guy to come in with a bullet hole in his back window. I had a beat with six tenements on it, each of sixteen stories. You always walked round lookin' up – the garbage cans, the bricks! We walked in pairs, and the maximum time it took your cover was three minutes. I liked it for the simple reason you talked to people. Out here, you don't talk to people unless they flag you down, and it's not just talk, it's because of some violation. I'd be happy to work back there again, with a few changes in administration as far as corruption goes.

Passing an alley running through the middle of a block, Jimmy Fellows catches a flash of yellow. He backs up and takes a good look: yes, a yellow liftback, parked behind a small two-story house. He sets off to fetch the two Texans, waiting only four blocks away.

> San Diego's as clean as they say it is? Fairy tales! I'm a realist: there's nobody in the world that honest. It isn't human. But it's a *lot* cleaner than back east. Very seldom do you get offered a bribe. I think I've had it twice since I've been out here, both times it was people from back east. And the worst position in the world is knowing another cop's taking a bribe and you're there, and you know why he's gone into a particular store. You sell your soul. I've never taken anybody's money, I've never rolled a drunk – I've seen it done. I've seen them drop off the Christmas envelope. To me, this was wrong. You sit around and talk to cops here about it, and they say 'Hey, why didn't you turn him in?' And you say, 'Well, your life would be worth – (snaps fingers) – that much! You don't *do* things like that, you know.'

The Texans follow him back to the mouth of the alley in their own vehicle. One of them gets out and comes over looking delighted.

'Hey, that's the one!'

'It wasn't orange?'

'No, that's the car – do we go right on down there or what?'

Jimmy Fellows shakes his head and calls for a cover unit. Quite a few of his perspectives differ from those of his colleagues who have always worked in San Diego.

> When I first started back east, there were really bad vibes between black officers and white officers. I've seen it where blacks were on one side of the room, whites on the other side – I've seen them fightin'. Then they instituted salt-and-pepper teams, and I've seen it where a black officer is drivin', and he wouldn't respond to cover a white officer. I've seen it vice versa. And when you got off work, I went one way and the white officer went the other way – we did nothing together at all. They were just starting to mingle when I left, and then I came out here and heard about racism and all that other stuff. But compared to where I had been, this is a *dream*.

As his cover unit appears, Jimmy Fellows drives into the alley, followed by the Texans. They stop short of the yellow liftback, and one of the Texans goes forward on foot to take a proper look at it. He comes back with the news that their cases are still in the back of the vehicle, in full view of anyone passing by. Jimmy Fellows shares none of his jubilant amazement.

> The smart crooks don't get caught, they get away with it every time. The dumb crooks, *they're* the ones we deal with.

With an officer from a third unit covering the front of the house, Jimmy Fellows and his cover partner go to the rear door, knock on it, and a woman allows them inside. It's all very undramatic. After a while, Jimmy Fellows comes out again, and describes two jackets he has found in the kitchen of the house.

The Texans, suddenly realizing their jackets are missing too, now look close to giving him a big hug apiece. Then he adds that he has seen some marijuana on the kitchen table, and the people of the house have withdrawn their permission for the search. He'll have to call for a warrant, as there is a likelihood of other drugs being found.

> I hate narcotics. I had a cousin who died of an overdose. I feel sorry for the people that are on it, and I hate the people that sell them – they're really living off somebody's hardship.

The Texans settle back to enjoy the show. Within a very short space of time, more and more police vehicles arrive, including one carrying a narcotics team, and the air is loud with the sound of handie-talkies and car radios. Then a handcuffed suspect is led out to the yellow liftback, and questioned about the cases. His blue tee-shirt has KILLER printed across it, which invites – and receives – some very dry Texan comment.

Not long after that, Jimmy Fellows emerges again. As this is a job for Investigations now, he can return to the station, which suits him just fine: 'I wouldn't want to be a Burglary detective – that's just a secretary.' And besides, First Watch is at an end.

> I really enjoy this, but when it's over, I want to go home and be *my*self. When I first started, I wanted to live and eat being a cop, but now I don't spend my off-duty time around a lot of cops. Basically, I think most cops are dull people. That's why I go to school, to listen to people talk, to get away from the whole drama of being a cop – it's not my accounting degree, I don't *like* accounting. People say the cops did this, the cops did that, and you have to agree with them it was wrong. A guy says, 'I got arrested for drunk driving – you can't tell me that cop doesn't get drunk!' And he's right. In a way, being a cop makes you a hypocritical person. (Smiles) I write very few tickets and I lock up very few drunks.

But before getting into his unit, he pauses to collect a few details from the Texans for his report. They immediately begin thanking him for the great job he's done in recovering their property so promptly – now they can get back to enjoying a vacation which would otherwise have been ruined.

'Oh-oh, just a minute . . .' says Jimmy Fellows, realizing they have missed out on the Catch-22.

And he explains to them that their property has been impounded as evidence, and that they won't be able to have it back until after the trial, perhaps several months from now – maybe even a year.

Which is how he has to leave them, looking sick to the stomach and utterly at a loss to know what to do next. One of them does suggest just reaching into the liftback and stealing back their cases, but that's impossible of course, with so many son-of-a-bitch San Diego policemen around.

Then they vanish from his rear-view mirror.

> I still have those moments – y'know, the realization I'm a cop. I wonder what I'm doin' here! At the time I joined, I really hated cops.
>
> I grew up in Newark, and there a cop spoke once and you

jumped – if you didn't, he thumped on you. I got thumped once, and from that time on, it was just an anti-police attitude I had. Then, when I was about twenty-one, I was a mechanic and I got to hate working inside, to hate knowing what I was going to do the next day. I had a friend who was a cop, and he said, 'Why not come on?' I said, 'Oh, no!' – but I rode with him, and I really enjoyed being outside, really enjoyed the so-called 'helping people'. You had the opportunity to help the weak: they prey on somebody that's old, they prey on somebody that's young. And I hate to see a woman hurt.

That was when I decided you're not going to change something by sittin' around, hatin' 'em. The only way to change anything is to become one – and not to be what they are like. I liked it, but sometimes I wanted to quit. I still feel like that at times. It's not the most rewarding job.

12

Clack-clack . . . clack-clack. Shotguns are being loaded, sirens tested, and one by one, the units of Second Watch, Central, are leaving the back lot. Among the first to go, heading for the barrio, is a unit carrying Officer Doug Summers and a fresh-faced trainee with a collegiate haircut.

Trainees pose a problem in most police departments, particularly when it comes to introducing them to practical policing. Some simply drop them in at the deep end, and trust to their own instincts for survival. Others try to find an experienced officer to show them the ropes, but unless Patrol has status in the department concerned, this isn't always easy – experienced officers tend to become detectives, or go off into other specialist groups. And anyway, honest administrators would admit that mere length of service is no criterion of an officer's quality, so even that plan has drawbacks.

Doug Summers, a thirty-year-old former nightclub singer, first joined the police near Los Angeles a decade ago, after helping in the arrest of an armed robber one night.

You're under a high amount of peer pressure when you're a young policeman, so usually you'll pick an older officer and you'll try to emulate him. I had an idol like that. What did that officer talk about? 'Man, we *beat the hell* out of this guy – Did you see how I had to *strangle* that guy? – Boy, I *shot* that guy . . .'

I remember looking at the other officers going, 'Oh wow, that's

148

really somethin'!' And I remember saying to myself, 'How do I do these things, in order to be like him? I have to get involved in shootings, I have to get in fights . . . But how?' One thing led to another: you get out and you challenge people.

So how do you get away from that? What we do here in San Diego, is we have what we call FTOs – field training officers – and the goal of the FTO program is to give them good examples to set themselves by. You say to them, 'Hey, you're being a lot more trouble than the people we're dealing with! Let's see how you can avoid trouble, rather than get in it.' Or, 'Hey you've got to be a lot smarter and a *lot* more intelligent in order to talk somebody into custody, rather than fight them in, and so if you want to impress me, young officer, do good quality work and use good common sense.'

Doug Summers – unfairly perhaps, in the view of callow recruits – stands a good chance of impressing almost anyone he encounters. Six-two, broad-shouldered and two-twenty pounds, brown-haired and indisputably handsome, he sang with the Righteous Brothers when they first started out. He has also been a truck driver, salesman, factory chemist, Hertz employee, and met his wife – it's their eleventh wedding anniversary today – while a teenage usher at the Broadway Theater in Santa Ana.

Out of the eleven of us who worked there, two went into the FBI, Diane Keaton is now a famous actress, one is a professor at MIT, another is the elected leader of the Gay Liberation Lesbian Party in Arizona, and I went into law enforcement – it was a hell of a group.

I see a real lack nowadays of people who're dedicated. I tried to be the best at everything. I took body language, I took sign language, I did lip-reading – everything that would gain me that extra little bit. You should commit yourself, but most guys just drive around the eight hours and they go home.

You could talk to people, meet people, show them you want to be here and to serve them. If you don't get out, if you laugh at people, let them think you don't give a shit, it hurts us in the long run – too many people care only about themselves. One of the things young guys don't understand is you're *infiltrating crime*. If you get to be friends with people, and something happens on your beat, it's like they owe you because they know you, and they can't not talk to you, because you talked to them last time. Some young officers confuse being nice with being soft; it's not, it's being clever.

Two small brass badges, made up of the letters FTO, and attached to his collar, declare Doug Summers's membership of what is, in effect, an elite that ruthlessly guards its own reputation.

We took the FTO badge off somebody this weekend. We have meetings every two weeks. If you've got a problem with a trainee in a certain area, maybe the other FTOs have had it too, and you get feedback on how to deal with it. Or, for example, I had an excellent trainee for a while, and the next thing I know, I hear at the meeting he's a problem, he's stupid. I said, 'Hey, wait a minute! That's out of character.' We found out that it was not him, it was his trainer, and we said, 'Why don't you get your act together?' The thing I hate to see is a training officer that doesn't care, who wants that position for the money – you get two and a half percent on your pay.

13

Pay starts at $1110 a month for recruits undergoing the 16-week academy, for which they also receive college credit. Then comes two years' probation as a Police Officer I, with a salary range of $1304–1574. Police Officer II is worth $1489–1797; Police Agent (Patrol only) $1558–1884; and Police Sergeant, $1738–2099.

These figures reflect only basic earnings, however. Officers also receive overtime, about thirty-five dollars a month for being bilingual in Spanish and English, and there is an educational incentive scheme worth about fifty dollars a month. Certain degrees and other special qualifications are also sources of additional income, such as $105 a month for an advanced Peace Officer Standard Training certificate.

This means that when Doug Summers, for example, adds everything together, he receives roughly $26,000 a year – nearly $5000 more than the top rate for a Police Officer II.

'Pay ranks about fifth in the things a person wants out of a job,' says recruiter Billy McGuire. 'Right now, the California Highway Patrol is the highest paid agency in this area. We've a wider spread of ranks and more promotional opportunities, so we're looking for career-minded people. Out of the thirteen major agencies in California, our pay rates about third – a month ago, about tenth.'

14

As it happens, Joe Cronin's household has a double income from the department. 'My wife's a supervisor in Records; she takes fingerprints of suspects – that's where we met.' But money, to a man who says his reason for being a police officer is chiefly 'to assist in any sort of way with the problems of the black community', has never been a first priority.

His visit to the Mexican fast-food stand having proved another ghost hunt, he is now on his way, after a Chinese meal, to the remaining burglary address.

It comes up on the left, a modest-sized bungalow in a quiet, leafy street of modest-sized homes. The sidewalks are deserted. In the gutter, lies a torn handbill advertising the Mr Black San Diego contest for *Men who style, smile and profile*. A sun-bleached Stars and Stripes hangs motionless from a pole across the way. Some large dogs bark.

But they're also over the other side of the street, so Joe Cronin knocks at the green front door again. This time he gets a response, and is welcomed in by a shy black youth of about sixteen, who leads him down the hall into the back livingroom. All the drapes in the house seem drawn, and the light is dim, as though the occupants are in mourning.

A plaque on the wall reads:

> *Bless This House*
> *O Lord We Pray*
> *Make It Safe*
> *By Night And Day*

There is so often a plaque like that somewhere, ready to be the first thing that catches the eye, driving home a fleeting irony.

The shy teenager's mother is slumped on the couch, a Kleenex box beside her. She moves wearily to her feet, anxious to be polite, but too exhausted for more than half a smile. 'Don't let anybody say it can't happen to you,' she says to Joe Cronin. 'Because we've been living here since '53, and *nothing* like this has ever happened.'

He introduces himself, and they sit down.

'I mean,' she says, 'I've had clothes taken from the line, but not a break-in and stuff. It really devastated us.'

And he lets her talk on, doing nothing to indicate that he's heard it all many times before. Neither does he interrupt to point out that, everything considered, the family has escaped lightly, because some burglars, known as shitters, can make it seem impossible ever to live in the same house again.

What it boils down to is simple enough: while she and her son were out shopping yesterday, somebody broke in and stole a collection of coins, a rifle and a handgun.

'You left the house at nine-forty?'

'Right.'

'Got back at eleven-thirty?'

'Right.'

'And you didn't see anybody outside, hanging round?'

'Right – 'cept for a couple of young kids on the corner, the ones I told you about. Are you sure you don't want a coffee?'

Joe Cronin would rather see where the break-in actually occurred, and the son shows him a bedroom in which a wide chest of drawers stands with its top drawer forced open. He checks around, but can find nothing overlooked earlier. From the damage done to effect an entry through the window, however, it is obvious that the burglar was no bungling amateur, nor had he – she, or they – wasted time on anything other than the locked drawer, indicating a single predetermined objective: the theft of firearms, with the loss of a few foreign coins being purely incidental.

Returning to the livingroom, Joe Cronin asks, 'These kids on the corner, they live around here? They could have seen somebody?'

'Coulda done,' says the son. 'I never seen them before.'

'No? Can you describe them?'

'Young kids, one was pretty small.'

'What else?'

They were just two kids, dressed the way kids dress, in jeans and tee-shirts and sneakers and stuff. Although the shorter of the two, quietly persistent questioning reveals, had some colored beads braided into his hair above one ear.

Joe Cronin takes his leave. He has said nothing in his deep, slow, gentle voice directly to console them, but his evident

152

concern and professional manner have had a visibly cheering effect on the mother and son. Sometimes, it's all he can offer.

15

'I think the gun laws we have are fine,' says Officer Henry Marvin, the Robbery detective who deals with all impounded weapons and investigates any gun ownership violations. 'But if someone commits a crime with a gun, they should be punished, and unfortunately I find the penalties too frequently don't follow the violations. A slap on the hand and you're back on the streets. It's hard for people to respect a system that works that way.'

The most common threat to life and limb is the easily concealed, ubiquitous handgun. There are three criteria for ownership: you have to be over twenty-one; you can't be a convicted felon; you can't have spent any time committed to a mental institution. There is a fifteen-day waiting period between purchase and delivery, to allow your application to be checked, and if you want to carry the gun on your person, then a special permit must be obtained. Special permit holders are generally people like wholesale jewelers and bank workers, who can prove they move valuables about. So much, Officer Marvin's shrug implies, for the letter of the law.

> It's often violated to the point that a significant minority of people carry guns. Frequently, they have a good reason in my own mind and by law: they're afraid, they live in bad neighborhoods. Most don't even try them out to see how they work, or *if* they work – maybe thirty percent of the guns we handle are twenty-five caliber automatics, poor quality. They're quite often surprised they can't hit anything, and get powder burns. People who're into violent crime, go for the bigger guns, the kind that go through car doors and stuff, and for that you need at least a magnum. The rounds we use in our department will not go through a car door, and if the windshield's angled, they'll bounce right off.

16

Communications alerts FTO Doug Summers to a four-five-nine at Thirtieth and J. That's about six blocks away, giving him time to brief his new trainee on the first steps of a preliminary investigation. The extrovert ex-detective talks a blue streak as usual, popping pertinent asides into parentheses.

'When you respond to a burglary report, you go out with two things in mind. First, the report is a false report – I've been on three burglar reports in the last two days, all three of them were false reports. If it's a false report, the easiest thing to say is, "Oh, screw it, I'll take the report." A lot of guys will tell you that, but it's bullshit. Taking a negative stand, that's what takes balls.

'My technique is, I stand there, writing things down in my book (which shows it's official, and I'm receptive), and then I stop writing, put my book away. They'll key on you, know something's wrong. Then what you say is, "Hey, listen, you seem real nice people, but I've been a police officer (you lie, add five years) for fifteen years, and from what you're telling me – *Listen*, let me explain somethin' to ya, okay? I was in the same boat you are, and I've reported things to insurance companies (everyone hates insurance companies; they're the biggest rip-off, you never get your money back) and I'm not convinced this is a report of what happened."

'And you watch them, because this is the really crucial part. If they're telling the truth, they're going to stop you right there, ninety-nine times out of a hundred. They'll go, "What the hell are you talkin' about?" That's your key now, you back up and say, "Hey listen now, we're required by law to warn you about false reports!" and that gives you an "out", see?

'But if they don't do that, they're listening (and if people are listening to you, you can be sure they're not sure of what you know). Then you say, "Hey, listen, if I take this report, you know as well as I do what'll happen: they're going to investigate. *And*, you know as well as I do that, hey, this stuff isn't gone or a friend's took it away or whatever – it's just a tool to make up on the insurance." You go on that. It'll happen to you. You'll get a lot of them.'

The trainee hesitates, then nods, 'And the second thing?'

'The second is, ninety percent of the time, that burglar lives within one block of that house. And when you're talking to people, ninety-nine percent of the time your victim knows the suspect. If he doesn't know him by name and address, he has an idea who did it. Okay, lots of guys rush in and say, "Do you know who did this?" – and a lot of times, the victims will say, "No." That's what I call negative-type questioning; you're not going to get shit. Even witnesses will say, "Screw you, I know nothin'." Ninety-nine percent of the police department uses those phrases and it's stupid.

'What you have to do is say, "Listen, you know the area better than I do, I don't live here, and all I'm curious to know is if you think you know who did it. Just because you give me the name of somebody, I'm not going to tell him you told me – and we'll investigate it thoroughly." You relax the victim, then watch and see how soon he'll be saying, "Well, goddamnit, we've been having a lot of trouble with Billy Johnson down the street here. He's always out at night time, doing this and this and this . . ."

'And when you have that information, that gives you probable cause to go and talk to Billy Johnson.'

The unit arrives at the address given out by Communications. What seems like a whole family of agitated people are outside on the porch. A portly man, bearing a remarkable resemblance to the late Louis Armstrong, hurries out to the sidewalk.

'Hey, officer!'

'What's your problem, sir?' asks the trainee.

'Hell, it ain't just a *problem*! We all out back in the yard, see, 'cos Jimmy here's got a new dog, no mo' than six weeks old, a tiny little pup, y'know, and it's foolin' around, y'know, and this nigger come right in my home, come right in that door, and my lady's purse is, y'know, by the phone, and she had twenty-three dollars and – '

'Oh, okay. Now take it easy, sir – try to relax a little.'

'What I want to know, where the hell *were* you guys?'

17

'You'll always have your opportunist,' says the Burglary Division commander, Lieutenant Charles Gibbs, 'who sees that door or window open. Probably a large number of burglaries are by young people, living in that community, who will never break into somebody's home again. But a *lot* of burglaries are by those who actually make a living at it – especially residential burglary, which is quite profitable.'

Lieutenant Gibbs is a slow-talking six-footer, a gentle-seeming man who might once have been acted on the screen by James Stewart. He is forty-two, and has been a police officer for twenty years.

> You still have the same types of crimes, but the motives have changed and the number has increased. Part of it's to do with the city growing, and part's to do with this permissiveness. For example, most drug and narcotics-related offenses, quite serious in 1960, aren't considered as serious today – they've been downgraded by the courts and the legislature, and some are practically overlooked. I think that has contributed to the increase in crime. A lot of burglaries are committed by addicts feeding a habit, a lot of our violent crime is committed by people under the influence of drugs or narcotics, and a number of our murders are the result of robberies that're drug-related. Attitudes in the community can increase or decrease crime. A lot of crime isn't a police problem, it's a social problem, and cannot be handled by the police alone.

Joe Cronin passes his office door, and then a few seconds later, going the other way, Kim Benton walks by with a prisoner. Only a short while ago, he saw that prisoner sauntering in, hands in his pockets, a free man, but now he's heading for the county jail.

> It's not a situation such as is portrayed on television, where we're out there chasing crooks up and down the streets all the time! Many, many times, our detectives will identify a suspect and then, with Patrol having six hundred people, it's much easier and much better to give the uniformed officers the information so they can make the arrest.
>
> It's not unusual for detectives to call up suspects and make an appointment for them to come in. We tell them that if they won't come down, and tell their side of it, we're going to get a warrant

for their arrest. This is especially effective where you have crimes against the person, batteries and those kind of things. They come charging down, walk in and the arrest'll be made in the office.

Or, many times, if an individual knows they have been identified, and that a warrant will probably follow, they will contact an attorney, and he'll call us and say, 'Hey, we're going to bring him in.' The reason they do that – especially if you've got an old-time criminal – is they know they can come down, bail out, and be right back on the street, doing whatever they did before. All it's cost them is the bail money, and they've actually beat the system.

18

The trainee, looking a fraction smug, has managed to get himself a Billy Johnson to question, just a block down the street from the scene of the burglary, and has also made friends with the new puppy.

But Doug Summers is in no hurry to allow him to make a mess of the next stage of the investigation, and so tells him to sit tight in the unit until the further briefing is over.

The scenario begins with a sound effect, as Summers raps his knuckles on the dashboard.

'Knock, knock! "Will you step out here a minute? I want to talk to you. I'm Officer So-and-so, Billy, and I'm investigating a burglary down here. Before we get into a lot of bullshit, before I start reading you your rights, and doing those things you've watched a lot of times on TV, Billy, I've been a police officer five years and I've gone through all the phases. I've gone through the phase where I like to put people in jail, and – "

'He won't interrupt you, because he wants to know what you know about him. Okay?

'Then: "Billy, I want you to know I didn't just walk up to your house and knock on the door. I'm here because somebody told me something, okay? Somebody that *knows* what's going on."

'Now Billy's standing there, and what is going through his mind is: "Oh shit, somebody's seen me, somebody's snitched me off." Worry, worry, worry . . . But you've told him nothing; absolute zero information. This is all perfectly legal.

'Then you say to him, "Now I want you to picture yourself as a judge (*this is always very successful*), as a judge. You're a judge, Billy, okay? And I walk up with this guy, about your age, and I say, 'Your Honor, I saw this, I saw that, I investigated. I got witnesses who saw this person do this, do that,' and then those witnesses testify against him. I show it was all true. Then you – sorry, Judge! – then the other person gets up, and he says, 'I didn't do anything!'

' "Now, Billy, as a judge here in California, you know you are going to think two things because the person said that. You are going to think, number one, '*He's a liar.*' Right?

' "And, number two, Billy, you're going to think: '*He needs to be rehabilitated.*'

' "How do we rehabilitate people in California? Billy, you know as well as I do that the only way we rehabilitate people is we put them in jail – and you know damn well, Billy, that *nobody* gets rehabilitated in jail. You know it, and I know it. It's the last thing in the world I want to do to you, Billy, because you're going to learn more *there*, Billy, than you ever did *here*, and everything bad will come to you.

' "Billy, now put yourself in the judge's part again, and I go up and I say, 'Your Honor, not only has Billy been truthful and honest with me during the investigation, we recovered the property. What do we do with a guy like that?'

' "And you know as well as I do, Billy, the judge is going to think, 'What the hell put him in jail for? We'll give him a chance!' "

'Lots of them will say, "God, I'm on my probation!" – that should key you.'

The trainee asks, 'But what do I say?'

'You can say, "They'll put you on more formal probation," ' explains Doug Summers, shrugging.

'And what if he doesn't, if he isn't on probation?'

'If he makes any comment,' Doug Summers goes on, 'like "what if this" or "what if that", that's the sign you've *got him*. This is the crucial part of the investigation, because anything he says now will go toward his confession. If he admits it, you say, "Hey, I knew it was you!" – and you go on from there.'

'But what,' asks the trainee, 'if the guy doesn't?'

Unfazed, Doug Summers does some acting. 'If he's crossed his hands, his legs, or he wants something in between you and him, those are all defense mechanisms, and so you push it further. You say, "Hey, come on, you know why I'm here. I think you were involved in it." *Involved in it* – you never call a guy a thief, a burglar. Just say simply – '

'Yeah, what can I say?' asks the trainee.

' "Hey, if that's what you want! If we get a search warrant, Billy, and if we find something in the house, then everyone in the house is going to jail!" But you must use the word *if*.'

'How come?'

'Okay, you start saying, "I'm *going* to get a search warrant, I *can* arrest everybody in the house . . ." – but there you're using a double positive, which is illegal in interrogation.'

The trainee blinks.

'You see, if you use *if*,' explains Doug Summers, 'you can use that statement to *anyone* – it's a true statement!'

'But . . .'

'Listen,' says Doug Summers, 'when you get to court, they're going to ask you for your exact terminology, your exact words. They're going to ask, "Did you threaten him?" And you can say, "I said *if* I got a warrant. I could say that to you, counselor!" '

The trainee glances toward the house. A probable Billy Johnson has come to stand behind the screen door, looking out at him anxiously.

19

'I think we have lost one of the best training tools we had,' says Lieutenant Gibbs, Burglary Division commander, 'which was walking your beat, the contact with people, having time to look around, to really observe a lot of things.

'I suppose I walked about eighty percent of the time in my first year, working reliefs in cars when somebody went on vacation. I certainly feel if you put an individual out on the streets with no communications – we had absolutely none – it developed a certain amount of tact! With this system today, some guy with a big mouth can call for all the help in the world.'

Back when Lieutenant Gibbs joined the department 'temporarily' during a slump in the aircraft industry twenty years ago, there was an older officer who particularly impressed him.

> I worked the beat adjacent to him on the night watch. There was a period of loud parties, people would call in to complain, and when the policemen got there, they'd be attacked. I covered him on this loud-party call, and there was a lot of drinking and potential for all kinds of problems. Right away we got the blast you always get when you go in, but he says, 'Now, now, take it easy . . .'
> There was a cold buffet there – I'll never forget this – and they had all kinds of cold cuts and everything. The people are telling him, 'You've got to have a warrant!' – but he says, 'We'll talk about that later.' And he walked down this table and he built himself a sandwich like you've never seen before! Then he said, 'Let's talk about this thing . . .' So he ate his sandwich, and they talked about this thing, and everybody loved him. They said, 'Sure, we'll keep the noise down.' And as we were walking out, he said to me, 'Hey, didn't you get a sandwich?'

20

Crestfallen, the trainee watches as Doug Summers, who had to take over the interview half way, locks the burglary suspect into the back of the unit. Somehow things just didn't work out the way they should have done, back in the livingroom of that house there.

But Doug Summers has his man, and if anything, seems more exuberant than ever, as he comes up to where the trainee is waiting by the unit's right fender.

'What you've got to learn,' he says, 'is they hide behind a chair, behind a table or whatever. You remember where that table was? Where you were? If I sit and talk to you across a table, that's no good. If I talk sitting at the side of you, that's no good – you want direct eye contact. Okay?'

The trainee nods.

'You've got to remember that the closer you get to somebody, the higher the anxiety you induce. You get close, you're attacking – you back off, you're retreating. Like this . . .'

Doug Summers brings his face closer.

'Yeah, I think I – '

'If you want to take, you approach – if you want to give, you back off.'

Doug Summers backs off, and the trainee's shoulders drop slightly.

'So, if I thought he was guilty,' continues Doug Summers, 'I'd come in close and I'd say, "Hey, you know as well as I do you did it – now let's knock off the bullshit!" And then, when he says, "Well, er . . ." I'd back off and allow him to talk. Attack and retreat, attack and retreat.'

'Attack and retreat,' repeats the trainee, picking up the rhythm.

'You got it,' says Doug Summers.

21

Every trainee has to prove himself or herself within the twelve-week FTO program, it's make or break – although occasionally someone is allowed a little more time.

'He has what they call a "critical pass booklet",' explains a lieutenant in Patrol Administration, 'that has to be signed off by the FTO. Even just arresting a common drunk is included, and he must do that until his FTO can say, "Yes, he is competent to make drunk arrests." This is to get us off being sued by people saying we don't train our people properly. This is when we weed them and fire 'em, during that twelve-week period.'

Or at least, they try to get it right at this stage, because firing isn't so simple later on, as Captain Walker knows all too well.

I remember an officer walking his beat, and two other officers got in a heck of a battle with a guy. This other officer just stood across the street, watching – he didn't move to help. Our then Chief of Police, Sharpe, heard about this and fired him the next day.

Today, you can't do that. It's really complicated and very difficult to get rid of incompetents, even on probation. They have a right to an attorney, and you have to prepare packages as if you were going to trial.

I've just gone through that experience. Evaluations by three different sergeants indicated this officer did not have the support of his peer group, because he did not cover calls and tended to let others do the work. We also had an indication he was visiting a lady friend on duty, and he even complained to me when he was changed from one beat to another. But in the end, I terminated him. But it was a tough job to argue with him and his attorney, and that's why our (continuous) personality evaluations are so important: if you don't document every officer's progress, then you may not be able to get rid of someone not cut out for the job.

22

It's rising four o'clock over in Burglary Division, and Joe Cronin's day has almost ended. Not a bad day at all, everything considered.

Among other things, he has more than likely identified the burglar who stole the rifle and the handgun from the house opposite where the big dogs live: Gary B. Wilkinson, aka Zizz, black male, age thirteen – and confirmed by the gang file on the computer to have recently braided colored beads into his hair above his right ear.

Moreover, according to someone over in Juvenile Division Zizz has lately developed some real style, and can now be described as an 'ace burglar', quite capable of a good clean job far in advance of his years. He is very elusive, though, and Juvenile are already trying to catch up with him, helped by the Gang Detail and by Patrol, for several assorted offenses.

So Joe Cronin has added his name to the list of interested parties, and although the firearms will undoubtedly have passed out of Zizz's hands by now, there is still hope that, with the right sort of interrogation, the case will be cleared.

Leaving just a desktop to tidy, ready for a fresh start on Monday morning. It isn't nearly as large a desktop as Joe Cronin once had offered him during a gathering in the city, attended by Maynard Jackson.

We got into conversation. He asked me about my experience, and said 'Would you like to be Police Chief of Atlanta, Georgia?' I said, 'Are you serious?' 'Yes, I'm serious,' he said. At the time, he was going back to Georgia for police chief interviews. But I enjoy this department and I was still gaining experience – Homicide, that's my ultimate goal.

23

Things are also going well with the preparations for the Mexican car-hop tomorrow. Just after five, Sergeant Juarez comes enthusing into the Central Division command office and announces that the bleachers have been taken care of – two banks of them, as Lieutenant Chassam had ordered.

'Fine, Eduardo – fine! That's great.'

'You still coming, Captain?'

'Sure I am.'

And off goes Sergeant Juarez again, to touch bases in the barrio.

If Lieutenant Chassam has a personal goal (he isn't the sort of man who often shows the serious side of his nature), then it would be to become more closely involved in setting up new computer systems in the department.

It is already possible for any patrol officer to request an ACE (Area Crime Evaluation) report on his beat from the Crime Analysis unit. Such a report includes detailed information on: crime type, specific areas affected, date range, case number, time of day, method of operation, victim profile, suspect description, lists of suspects, vehicle description, and maps of crime locations. Quite often, it also contains surprises.

We've always thought the weekend was always the heavy time – wrong. On some beats, it's Wednesdays and Thursdays. And we've found out something else. Traditionally, December was the big month for burglaries, around Christmas time. That's not true, it's October – and it's been that way for years and years and years! That's the difference between gut feeling and facts, and we've done our work by the seat of our pants for too long around here.

24

The working day done, Billy McGuire is also on his way out of the station. Two nights a week he goes to school to teach Process and Issues in the Criminal Justice System, and another class entitled Introduction to Law Enforcement.

We might get into rape, for instance. We'll discuss the issues, the fact that more Caucasians commit the crime of rape, and yet more blacks are convicted for it. Social values.

Teaching is one of the things he likes best.

I was very, very successful as an FTO, and very successful as an academy adviser. Any new officer, he's just like a baby; he knows little more than what is influenced upon him. If the FTO is macho, the new officer is very macho. If the FTO carries a lot of gear on his belt, the recruit will turn up the next day with as many things on his belt as he can justify! They'll even duplicate your manner of speaking. But they have to develop a personal technique because we need those individual styles – we couldn't afford to have thirteen-hundred Billy McGuires runnin' around here!

I have certain animosities towards procedures in law enforcement, especially concerning the treatment of people. I'm very conscious of it, and sometimes I'm so sensitive about it that it bugs me, to be part of that type of thing. It's been very difficult for me to understand macho cops, and we get a lot of it. I'm very skeptical of them. Either he has some inferiority he doesn't want noticed, or he is a sadistic person who doesn't see himself in that guy he's kicking around – 'I've got a gun and a badge and I'm not like him.' But in many cases you'll find that these guys who're so bent on harassing people would be in the same position as that guy if they were not police officers.

Reaching his car, Billy McGuire tosses some recruiting material he's preparing on to the passenger seat, and slides in behind the wheel.

If a person was to watch me on a daily basis, he'd probably think I lead a dull life. He sees this guy who goes to work, comes home, gets out of his suit and tie, puts on his overalls, works on his old car, digs in the yard until dark, goes in, takes a shower, maybe has a snack, goes to bed, and then starts his routine all over again, wakes up to the sound of music. But on Fridays, I'm in the Administration baseball team, and I go and play my nasty little heart out.

Part V

Lust, lowriders, and the little ugly duckling

1

Saturday sizzles like frying bacon.

'Hey, when was this car-hop thing supposed to start?' asks a downtown beat officer, opening a can of 7-Up on the city parking lot right across the street from the Holiday Inn.

'Oh, a couple of hours back, I guess,' replies a barrio beat officer, taking off his sunglasses to polish them. 'But we're into Mexican Time here, amigo. So relax.'

Sunglasses aren't a bad idea on this parking lot, where several ranks of customized cars gleam, glisten and glitter, holding captive in their immaculate chromework a brilliance of tiny suns. Most of the cars started out as Buicks, Chevrolets and Oldsmobiles, but have since undergone modifications that place them in the $25,000–40,000 bracket.

These lowriders, as they're known, have disproportionately small wheels, and rest about a hand's breadth above the asphalt, allowing their substructure barely any clearance. A few are parked, however, with their front bumpers a good twenty inches in the air, while others are poised nosedown, their rear bumpers elevated.

'I've never took a close-up look at how they do that,' says the downtown officer, a recruit.

There's a loud clanging behind him. He turns round, just in time to see a squirt of sparks from under a lowrider that has entered the parking lot too quickly, scraping its underbelly on the sidewalk. Almost instantly, the lowrider rises high above its wheels, leaving room for the average house dog to pass beneath it unscathed. Then, as the lowrider comes to a stop, it sinks back down again, almost touching the ground.

'It's Little Julio,' says the barrio officer. 'Wanna take a look in his trunk?'

They go over.

Little Julio couldn't be more delighted. 'You don't know how it works?' he says, going round to the trunk of his lowrider. 'Here,' he says, opening the trunk lid, 'isn't that so beautiful?'

'It's a whole lotta batteries,' observes the downtown officer, sounding impressed.

'Eight. Eight batteries, sometimes nine. And there, you see the dump valves? Hydraulics.'

'Give him a hop, Julio,' suggests the barrio officer.

'Okay.' Little Julio has in his hand a long gray lead extending back into his car, and his thumb on a button. 'Now watch!' By squeezing the button, he causes the front of the lowrider to jump into the air and come down with a thump. 'Pretty neat, huh?'

'When did all this get started?'

'I don't know – twenty years ago? It was some guys from Los Angeles. You know the Citroëns? Some German teacher, phys. ed. teacher – I think he was the one that got it started, when Corvairs first came out. Everybody got a big kick out of them. A lot of guys try to steal them.'

'I bet. Must be a big investment.'

'I got three jobs,' says Little Julio, closing the trunk lid, which has an elaborate painting of a jungle scene on it.

'How much did that cost?'

'One hundred and eighty dollars. I'm saving for the hood.'

'No shit – a hundred and eighty!'

'The guy is a great artist. I got blue velvet floorboards.'

Not only velvet floorboards. The downtown officer examines the lowrider's velvet-all-over interior, which is so filled with shiny things and plush padding that it's not unlike being in a jewelry box on wheels. Then, his appetite whetted for the bizarre, he takes a look into the next lowrider in line. It has a dish-sized circle of chrome-plated chain, with its links welded together, for a steering wheel.

'That's neat,' remarks Little Julio. 'But I gotta better idea. It's with – '

'Uh-huh?'

'You will see,' says Little Julio, grinning.

'Hey, and something else,' says the barrio officer. 'Julio here can make his lowrider kind of bounce up and down off the street when he's ridin' along, y'know.'

'Sure,' says the downtown officer, with a curt nod. 'But it's illegal, right? How many citations you got, Julio?'

He isn't telling; he laughs though, and seems immensely flattered. They talk for a while, about the afternoon's contest, about gang activity in the barrio, and then, when an announcement is made over the organizers' loudspeaker system, off goes Little Julio, parting on first-name terms. Across the back of his sweat shirt is embroidered the name of his car club. Most clubs follow this practice, so it's possible to identify, as present today, enthusiasts from the Latin Low-riders, the Amigos, the Classics, Brown Image, Korner SD, City SD, the Oldies, and the all-female club, Lady's Pride.

Within seconds, Little Julio, bobbing along rapidly on his short, stubby legs, disappears into the crowd around the organizers, and the officer from the barrio says, 'A great little guy . . .'

'He could get a lowrider ticket just *walking*,' says the officer from downtown.

2

Usually, on a Saturday afternoon, Golden Hill Park can be pretty busy, and the Heights families who come here to picnic, to bask, to watch Baby Jorge crawl around on the green lawn, have a tough time getting any real peace. Even the teenage girls can be a pest, because when they're out cruising, two or three to a car, they seldom stay anywhere more than a few minutes. Back and forth, they move; doing maybe only one lap of the park's circular drive before taking themselves off some other part of the barrio for a while. The young men aren't as restless, but they often unload speakers almost the size of washing machines from their cars, and what with the deafening disco beat and all the drinking that goes on, their presence is no comfort either. What's worse, of course, is when rival gang members arrive to take up positions under the palms, and then pass the time glaring sideways at each other. One wrong word, uttered too loudly; one wrong look, glancing off somebody's lady; one wrong almost-anything, and it's knives, chains, even guns.

This particular Saturday afternoon, however, the car-hop has provided a counter-attraction, and Golden Hill Park is so quiet that there's almost some poignancy in the words SAD GIRL LOMAS – gang graffiti, sprayed blood-red on a tree near the entrance.

Through which, coasting almost silently, comes a unit

driven by Officer Carl Brunner, twenty-three, who has been in the department for fifteen months. His radio is turned down, making the female voices from Communications sound more matter-of-fact than ever. Still coasting, he begins to circle the park, and directs a dark stream of spittle out of his window.

'. . . a white male,' Communications is telling some beat officer in Hillcrest, 'says he feels like taking his life, but he'll wait for a unit.'

'Okay, I'll take it,' says the officer.

If Carl Brunner sees an unintentionally funny side to this exchange, he isn't showing it.

'He's in a brown suit and tie,' adds Communications.

'Ten-four.'

In fact, Carl Brunner possibly didn't hear any of that, having his attention fixed elsewhere. In the middle of the park, under some palms, are the restrooms, and a Mexican man with a faded backpack has just suddenly ducked back behind them, like someone caught unaware.

The unit rolls to a stop. Any moment now, a jet liner should pass very low overhead. San Diego has its airport on the edge of the bay, barely five minutes' ride from the center of downtown, and Golden Hill lies directly on a flight path. The noise can be tremendous at times, but most picnicking families, being so used to it, don't seem to regard this as one of the more serious threats to a peaceful afternoon.

Carl Brunner watches and waits. Out of the corner of his eye, he can see a Mexican father teaching his daughter to rollerskate. Then comes the thunder of a DC-9, climbing up over Logan Heights, and as the sound reaches a level when it's almost impossible to hear anything else, the unit door opens.

Sprinting, Carl Brunner reaches the nearest wall of the restrooms, and then begins to edge his way toward where he saw the Mexican backpacker duck back. Silence has only just returned to the park when, suddenly, he takes a look round the corner.

'*Dios!*' exclaims the Mexican, starting violently, being no more than a few inches away. 'How da fuck . . .'

Then he shields his eyes against the sun to take a better look at the police officer confronting him, being probably already aware of a decided sense of presence, very pronounced and predatory. Five-ten, built slim and hard, with long hair the

color of a cougar and tawny eyes to match, Carl Brunner puts a crackle into the air, which, when combined with his stance, invites the most obvious of immediate associations: gunfighter.

'Hey, now, jus' a minute!'

But the tawny eyes never blink. The tension builds, sharpens, becomes intolerable. One wrong word, one wrong move, the moment suggests, and there is going to be blood and bone all over the place.

3

'Say, are we gettin' some action?' the downtown beat officer asks, crushing his 7-Up can with a quick squeeze.

The car-hop crowd seem to be settling on the bleachers, leaving an area clear in the middle, and the organizers have started fiddling again with the loudspeaker system. Over on the left, a couple of lowriders are revving their engines, which also seems promising. Abruptly, disco music blares out, and the cleared space becomes a dance floor.

'See, that's Olga,' says the barrio beat officer, pointing out one of the dancers. 'The chick in the white pants and the top with the red stripes and patches? Queen of the Barrio.'

'Oh, okay. A five.'

'A *nine*, pal.'

'It's your beat,' sighs the downtown officer, and wanders off to find somewhere to discard the crushed can.

He skirts a group where Lieutenant Chassam and Sergeant Juarez, both in jeans and beach shirts, are in a happy huddle over some list with members of the Classics and the Korner SD.

He passes Kay Pruitt, who is also on duty and in uniform like himself.

'Hi!' says Kay Pruitt. 'How're you doin'?'

'Hi,' he grunts. 'Just great.'

There are gang members everywhere, including six who sometimes come down and hang around the Plaza, and whose faces he knows only slightly better than their names, ages, occupations and addresses, having FI'd them many a time. Their girls are here, too; probably 'carrying' – those knives, chains, and guns have got to come from somewhere when trouble breaks out. Right now, however, they all seem preoccupied, admiring the lowriders and listening to the music.

Which stops, giving way to another announcement, and the dancers have to make way for a lowrider that reverses into the arena between the bleachers and switches off. The downtown officer ditches his 7-Up can in a container beside one of the portable restrooms, and goes back to where the barrio officer is still waiting.

'Any time now, and you'll see that car start hopping,' says the barrio officer, with a jerk of his chin toward the lowrider being made ready.

'Oh, yeah?' says the downtown officer, with another of his sighs. 'I'd settle if I saw the damn thing just stood there on one leg.'

The signal is given for the first attempt to begin. A pair of officials crouch on either side of the nose of the car, ready with wooden rulers to measure how high the front wheels can bounce into the air. The lowrider's owner, lead in hand and standing back to watch how well his hydraulics perform, starts thumbing a button. The front bumper jerks up, drops. It heaves up, drops. Then a clumsy, thudding, battering rhythm develops, and soon the tires are leaving the ground, bouncing a little higher each time. Ten inches, fifteen, eighteen – the gap grows greater, and by now the motion is almost frenzied. At nineteen inches, the front end of the car can bounce no higher, and is allowed to come to rest again. There's a final burst of applause, then the clapping and the cheering dies away.

'Is that *it*?' asks the downtown officer.

'That's it,' says the officer from the barrio.

4

Carl Brunner takes another pinch of Copenhagen snuff, tucks it behind his lower lip, and replaces the tin on the dashboard of his unit. He turns up his radio. He twists his ignition key, and drives slowly out of Golden Hill Park, traveling straight down Twenty-fifth Street toward Tony's Liquor Store, a notorious trouble spot, there on the corner of Imperial at the foot of the slope.

> That guy who ducked down, who had the bag . . . He had a camera, a calculator and a radio in it. I knew damn well it was stolen, but there was nothing I could do about it. Then a friend of his came up and says, 'Hey, he's had that stuff for a long time.' But I got a good FI on him. He's a transient person, living in a car on Thirteenth and Broadway. He had a harmonica with him. I've never seen a male Mexican with a harmonica.

One more small fact for the department's computer system to store away, just as it's an addition to Carl Brunner's own zealously hoarded collection of minutiae.

> A lot of guys just drive around, and the things they see, they take care of. I try to work on a knowledge basis of the area. I try to learn everybody on my beat, I try to learn them by name. That way, when crimes come out, and a witness gives a suspect description, I can say, 'Oh, I remember that guy! He lives down at so-and-so.' And I'll go down and check it out. Misdemeanor arrests, you can make as many as you want; felony arrests, I've made three this week, which is good. I try to get things as they happen and *before* they happen.

Three felony arrests in a week is actually better than good; it would be fairly exceptional even if he weren't still in his probationary period. Before joining the department, Carl Brunner went to college, worked a year as an FBI fingerprint clerk, and then drove a truck. His accent is Wild West, his handgun is a jutting magnum; he and a fellow officer share a small ranch outside San Diego, where they keep and ride a number of horses. If this suggests a syndrome, then it would be one owing little to John Wayne but a lot to Clint Eastwood.

Leaving Twenty-fifth Street, Carl Brunner cruises, taking in everything around him. The building on the next corner announces *Apartments for Rent* – 'Everyone moves out, because that joint gets ripped off every day.' To judge by the abundance of similar signs in the neighborhood, it can't be easy deciding where to move to.

Then Carl Brunner spots three Mexican boys, ambling along the sidewalk. Their clothing is good, they're clean and tidy, and their faces, still child's faces, share a look of bemused innocence when his unit draws up beside them.

'Hey, where you going?'

The tallest boy shrugs.

Carl Brunner gets out, and they tense up as he confronts them, sensing that presence.

'You, what's your name?' he asks the tallest boy.

'Muerto.'

'That's right, they call you "Loco". Who're your buddies?'

The other two mumble.

Carl Brunner says nothing, just allows the tension to grow and sharpen. He stands very close to them.

'Your name?' he demands again, of the next tallest boy.

'Carl – Carlos Tapia.'

'Carl?' says Brunner, moving back out of his body space. 'Hey, that's my name too! How old are you, Carl?'

'Thirteen.'

'You're going to show me what's in your pockets?'

Without hesitation, the boy reaches into his pockets. Brunner has no right to search him himself, just as he'd no right to go through the Mexican's backpack up at Golden Hill Park – the man had emptied it out personally, almost the moment the steady stare relented.

'Hey,' says Muerto, 'you got no right!'

'He wants to show me.'

'You still got no – '

Back comes that crackling tension, and Carl Brunner says: 'Just shut your mouth, understand? You get in the back of my police car.'

'What've I done?' challenges Muerto, looking tough.

'You just get in there.'

Muerto can't hold the stare, and obeys.

'What's he got busted for?' asks the smallest boy in a very small voice.

'Hey, Carl,' says Brunner, relaxed again, 'let's see what you got. What's this?'

'Library cards.'

'You go to the library?'

'Yeah.'

'You got a knife?'

'*Knife?* No, no knife.'

'And you?'

The smallest boy has some gum, a Kleenex and a rubber band.

174

'What's your name?'

'Ruben Gonzales.'

'How old are you, Ruben?'

'Eleven.'

Muerto, out of earshot in the back of the unit, watches as Carl Brunner chats easily to the other two, who laugh a couple of times. Muerto's frown deepens.

'Okay, out,' says Carl Brunner, fetching Muerto from the unit, and pats his pockets. 'What's that?'

Muerto reluctantly produces a red felt-tipped marker.

'What do you use this for? To write on walls?'

'No!'

The felt tip is worn down by having been used on rough surfaces. Carl Brunner, scribbling in the air with it, says in a Mexican accent, 'Barrio – Sherman!'

'No!'

'If I see anything that's got red crayon on it, I'm going to come and get you. I know you now.'

Muerto, still acting tough, shrugs. It's unlikely, though, that he knows a police officer cannot make an arrest for a misdemeanor he hasn't witnessed.

'Is that all you've got to do,' Carl Brunner asks the other two, 'is to write on walls?'

'I don't write on – ' begins Muerto.

'You be quiet, you don't say *one goddamn word* – you understand me? These guys here don't think you're bad, they think you're an idiot. Next time, I'm going to kick your ass straight to Juvenile Hall. You're being a big asshole.'

Muerto's cheeks burn.

Carl Brunner looks the trio over, as they now stand divided on the sidewalk. There are two things he doesn't tell them. He says nothing about having earlier noticed some new red graffiti on a school wall about two blocks away. Neither does he disclose that he has known for some time that Muerto is, in a sense, a recruiter for junior members of the Sherman gang.

Moments later, the unit draws off.

I used to go round and do my thing, y'know, and it gave me a street knowledge. I never robbed or burglarized places, but I wasn't the nicest kid on the block. Those guys thought they were

175

pulling a fast one on me – bullshit. Around their friends, they try to act tough, because that gives them an image of being '*loco*' or a crazy person. But I grew up just the way they did.

5

Lowrider after lowrider has taken up position between the bleachers, hopped up and down, and has been driven off into the wings again. Most hops work out at between nine and fifteen inches, but twenty-two inches is now the height to beat.

Sergeant Juarez, apparently loving every minute of it, is everywhere. Not that he takes much notice of the car-hopping itself. He talks to club members, to gang members, to ordinary spectators, to tourists who have happened to stroll by this way, attracted initially by the forest of masts along the bayside.

In his view, the event is already a decided success.

Last week, Lieutenant Chassam and I, we rounded up all the leaders of the car clubs (for a buffet lunch at the station), and we told them there's too much violence going on in the community. Car clubs do not present a police problem, but when they have gatherings, gang members are attracted and they relate to them.

It's one way, in other words, of trying to affect gang behavior by example, and by bringing to bear peer pressure. Furthermore, by providing first-rate facilities for a car-hop, the police department is able to underscore its interest in community activities, and in particular, its alliance with the car clubs.

'Hi, Captain!' says Sergeant Juarez, pausing for a moment. 'Hi, Mrs Walker! Having a good time?'

Mrs Walker, a very friendly, attractive-looking woman, and her husband, who is also casually dressed, exchange a few pleasantries with him. The Walkers are plainly trying to take an interest in the competition, but like almost everyone else here who isn't a Mexican, its joys seem to have somewhat eluded them.

Captain Walker certainly gives the idea of the alliance his full support.

Rae Chassam has set up this Rumor Control and Information Group with the president of the lowrider car clubs. This means if there is an incident involving the police in the community, he can go to them and say, 'Hey, here are the facts – make sure it doesn't get blown up out of all proportion.' The group can also come back to us with information that might be a help. We have (in the Heights) perhaps the most sensitive area of the city, and a potential for a blow-up.

Possibly mindful of that potential, Captain Walker keeps pretty much on the move, looks slightly on edge, and sees to it that Mrs Walker is never hemmed in.

6

Carl Brunner calls for a cover unit, and speeds on his way to a four-fifteen disturbance in the predominantly black part of Logan Heights, passing some West Coast Crips in their black derbies and hairnets.

The Crips, of course, regard lowriders and car-hopping as something alien to their culture, and are out in their usual strength. Even so, it's something that the Gang Detail may like to know about.

The four-fifteen is at a well-known address, and Carl Brunner predicts broken glass from seven blocks away. He's right. A truck parked outside the house has its windshield smashed in, and a very irate black man of about thirty, in a green baseball cap, is standing beside it. He is encircled by excited children, all grinning from ear to ear.

Carl Brunner gets out of his unit as his cover arrives; it isn't broken glass that makes him cautious, but what it can lead to.

'What's the problem, sir?' he asks.

'It's my brother-in-law, goddamnit!'

'You mean Rex?'

'He broke down my momma's window, he broke down my daddy's window, he broke down my grandmother's window, he done broke down my brother's window, he even pulled a gun on my momma, he told my momma to suck his privates – *and all this* happened within a two-week period. But today it *really* happened when he broke down my daddy's truck right there, and he done told my momma to suck his privates – why don't you kids go play down the street?'

'Just when – '

'I'm *tired* of this dude, man! When you took him to jail, he got right back out of jail, and he come right back down this street and threatened my brother, and he – '

'But how do you know he did this?'

'I know he did it! I *know* he did it! He just called and told us on the telephone.'

Carl Brunner remains poker face, but his partner has to turn away to hide a smile. An airliner passes overhead.

'You ever seen him do it?' asks Carl Brunner.

'A neighbor – '

'First of all, it's vandalism – a misdemeanor – and I can't arrest him for it.'

The son nods. 'Okay, okay, the detective that called me back on the phone today, he said the same thing you said: "If we don't see nobody do it, then we can't do nothing about it." "Okay," I said, "cool – no problem there. But therefore he could come back and break out the windows again, and you're not going to do anything about it. Therefore," I said, "it's going to lead into something more badder, and someone's goin' to get hurt."'

'Sure, but – '

'Okay, but this morning my father *seen* Rex do it, and he called up you guys and they said the only way we can do it is to walk up and call his name and place him under arrest.'

'Citizen's arrest. You need that in a misdemeanor, then we can take him to jail.'

'Okay, that's what my father did, citizen's arrest, and they took him and took him to jail. Now five minutes later, he's back out the front of our house – '

'*There goes the nigger, down there!*' shouts out another member of the family from the porch.

A running figure is glimpsed leaving a hedge on the property and bolting through the next house along. Carl Brunner sprints after him, while his partner takes another route round into the alley at the back. They've been told the man has a gun.

A startled neighbor appears at her open front door, just as Carl Brunner reaches it. 'Can I go through here, ma'am?' he asks, barely pausing, but mindful of the department's rules of conduct. 'Thank you, ma'am!'

And by the time she has followed him through to her back door, the air is filled with an uproar of barking dogs, squawking chickens and cheering children. There's confusion, sudden sweat, and the scent of eucalyptus, but no sign of the fugitive.

Out in front of the house again, the son continues from almost exactly where he left off: 'They took him to jail and – '

'What can I say to you?' interrupts Carl Brunner. 'We can't keep him in jail – that's the jail's business. We do our job by taking him down there. We don't make the laws. If it was up to me, bud, I'd take him to jail for life.'

The son laughs, but the father says, 'I get up, man, at four-thirty in the mornin', and get off at three – I work nearly six months for that truck, and he busts it up in five minutes! I got no insurance. That *hurts*.'

'Yeah, I know it,' says Carl Brunner, sympathetically.

And the son echoes, 'That *hurts*. My brother works, my daddy works, my momma works, and *I* works and – '

'That Pinto down the street,' says Carl Brunner, suddenly, 'isn't that his car? Rex's car?'

'Yeah, that's his.'

A closer inspection of the car, which must have been left standing there when the man went off to jail this morning, shows that its windshield has been smashed in.

'Who did his car?' asks Carl Brunner.

'I don't know who did it,' says the son.

7

A unit with snuff-juice streaks on its driver's door is parked on the high ramp of Community Hospital, overlooking the barrio and, there in the distance, the bridge across the bay to Coronado.

Carl Brunner has gone in to use the telephone in the staff coffee-break room off the main emergency treatment area. With a couple of FI slips in his hand, and a note of some other information he's picked up this afternoon, he is on the line to the Gang Detail, waiting for someone to answer.

A pretty nurse smiles at him as she short-cuts through into Emergency. 'Hi,' she says, 'that's nice – you look happy!'

'I love my work,' says Carl Brunner, and smiles back as though he means it.

Then in comes FTO Doug Summers and his trainee. Heights officers are in and out of the room all the time. Not only does the hospital have probably more than its fair share of good-looking, golden-tanned nurses, but it provides a refuge in an area where police officers feel constantly exposed to danger, and admit a need to take a short break from it now and again. In this much, it serves as a police station: somewhere to write up a report, to use the phone, to settle differences in private, to take some refreshment – the coffee, milk, orange juice and doughnuts are free, and there are coin-slot machines for those wanting soft drinks or candy.

'You'll never know what they'll buy,' Doug Summers is saying to the trainee, 'it's absolutely *astonishing* what people will buy.'

'Uh-huh?'

The Gang Detail answers its phone, and Carl Brunner starts passing on the intelligence he's gathered. With half an ear, he listens to another of Doug Summers's parables, this one concerning two robbers who shotgunned to death a market boy.

'I had Pete and his brother for marijuana, and Homicide said they might just have something to do with that murder. I went back to the one, Pete, and I said, "Hey, Pete, they've got you by the ass – if you did it, and it was accidental, tell 'em!" "God, Doug," he said, "I had that shotgun in my fucking hands and the guy moved and the gun went off and blew his head off!" I was real calm, but inside I'm going, "Yaaa, you stupid bastard!" They'd recorded that confession; he implicates his brother, tells me where the shotgun is, and I take him down to the market, where it happened, and they video-taped the whole goddamn thing! Afterwards, Pete is standing there and he says, "You know, Doug," he says, "I think I better get an attorney."'

This gets a big laugh, the biggest coming, perhaps, from a fair-haired veteran who has just come in and poured himself an orange juice. He glances at the trainee, noting the newness of his uniform. 'I think the difference,' he says, motioning with his Dixie cup between himself and the trainee, 'is that after four or five years you realize, "Hey, I'm not going to change the world, I'm not going to right all the wrongs." The big thing then is the job, and after 16 years, I'm still havin' fun. It's not work.'

Doug Summers nods. 'The most fun about this job,' he says, 'is trying to outsmart the motherfuckers, and trying to con the cons. *That's* satisfaction.'

Hanging up the phone, Carl Brunner puts away his FI slips, and gets to his feet, giving his gunbelt a hitch. 'Right now, I'm still young on the job,' he says, 'but I consider myself – as far as all the cops I know – the third-best liar on the department and I'm proud of it. He's first –' Brunner points to Doug Summers, getting another big laugh. 'And you can tell if somebody's lying when you're a better liar than they are!'

A doctor comes in for a doughnut and coffee, and Carl Brunner leaves. He describes himself as 'just a little bitty guy', but this is not reflected in the trainee's expression as he watches him disappear through the emergency room.

'He does things senior cops don't,' remarks Doug Summers, draining his coffee. 'He makes search warrants. He was Code Five – on stakeout – and he saw a guy breaking into a car. He caught the guy, and instead of just getting him for breaking into that one car, he talked to the guy. The guy took him round all these burglaries he did – a hundred burglaries.'

Carl Brunner was his first trainee.

8

Disco music is playing at the car-hop again, and couples are dancing. 'I don't get this,' mutters the beat officer from downtown. 'Five minutes ago, I thought it was all over – the guy in the red convertible had won the damn thing.'

The barrio beat officer shrugs. 'Yeah, with the twenty-four? Could be there's some argument.'

'Those dudes will not be too happy if he don't win,' says the downtown officer, indicating a group of gang-member supporters of the red convertible. 'This could all turn to – '

'Hey, just relax, okay? The people are mellow, they're havin' fun. The guys organizing this don't want any hassle. Don't you think it's been pretty great? Kind of like a carnival?'

'I guess so.'

There's an announcement over the speaker system. The downtown officer frowns as he tries to make it out. On one hand, the red convertible appears to have been judged the winner; on the other hand, a tie-breaker will be held at nine o'clock sharp tomorrow morning, down at Chicano Park. But if this leaves him confused, it doesn't seem to bother anyone else, including the gang members he felt leery about a short while back. The crowd begins to break up, there's laughter and lots of lively talk, people calling out farewells to each other, places to meet during the evening.

'Now there's just the mess to clear up,' says the barrio officer. 'Korner's helping us.'

'I can believe nine o'clock,' says the downtown officer, drily. 'Add how many hours? What's the attraction? Is it sexual?'

'Hey, how'd you make that out?'

'All the humpin' up and down, amigo – all this heavy talk goin' on about twenty-four macho-type inches.'

The barrio officer laughs. 'You look at it that way,' he says, 'it's more like some asshole with a heart condition tryin' to do push-ups!'

'Yeah, until his goddamn wheel comes flyin' off! Did you see that guy?'

Then the grins fade from their faces.

There is a sudden swirl in the departing crowd, over by some small trees on the parking lot, followed by a sudden rush of people – some toward the swirl, others away from it, panic-stricken. A voice shrieks, 'Stab him!' The sun flashes from a knife blade, then flashes again as the knife plunges.

'Here we go,' sighs the downtown officer, drawing his baton. 'I reckon there's somebody car-hoppin' mad in there . . .'

'Shit, this is *terrible*,' says the barrio officer, running baton in hand beside him.

'I knew it!' says a third officer, catching them up.

Seeing knives flashing, Captain Walker hurries his wife toward their car, sees her safely to it, then returns, looking very grim. He has his gun and his badge if the uniformed officers need any assistance.

In seconds, however, they have won control, despite the cries of 'Stick the pigs!' all around them. Kay Pruitt has grabbed the stabbing victim and bundled him away into her unit, where he lies locked in the back, out of harm's way. It's a move that also helps to defuse the clash between Logan and San Ysidro, and gang members soon take to their heels, leaving only the chief culprits in custody.

Sergeant Juarez, his voice full of wonder, is the first with the news of what actually sparked off the blood-letting, and as the ambulances arrive for the injured, word soon passes round.

'It was some chick,' explains the officer from the barrio. 'Logan chick, that some asshole from San Ysidro had to get smart with, insulted her or somethin'. Y'know, like that.'

Pale and shaken, the downtown officer just nods. Perhaps he's reflecting on those cries of 'Stick the pigs!' – and wondering what it was that dissuaded the mob from taking action.

He is far from the only person looking sick, car club members included. And when Sergeant Juarez says, 'Hey, guys, we've got a big mess to clean up!' most can't help murmuring about another mess that won't be so easy to handle.

But it takes Kay Pruitt, turning to an Irish-Mexican FTO from the Heights, to put the general feeling in a nutshell. 'Your beat,' she says, not unsympathetically, 'is going to turn to shit tonight, pal.'

9

And as darkness comes to the barrio, Officer Jim Bradford, who is acting-sergeant over the weekend, keeps in very close contact with his squad, both by monitoring their radio calls and by staying constantly on the move.

'We're afraid of retaliation,' he tells his ride-along, a holidaying detective constable from Scotland Yard, who happened to call in at the station. 'You're usually going to have it.'

'More stabbings?'

'Years ago. Now they've also got guns and they're not afraid to shoot people.'

'You mean, just like that?'

'I don't know what it is – they've no remorse about taking another life.'

'Nasty.'

'Yeah, you picked quite a night,' says Jim Bradford, without enthusiasm. 'Last time this – '

He breaks off to listen to the radio. But it's only Communications directing Doug Summers to a four-fifteen in a bar nearby on Market, so he relaxes again.

'Couldn't the bother start in a bar?' asks the Scotland Yard man.

'Could be anywhere. Thing is, just blacks use that bar.'

10

Doug Summers, on his way to the disturbance, has already primed his trainee with this information.

'They can be kind of hard to handle,' says his trainee. 'Y'know, they're not the same as the black guys in college – well, what I mean is . . . street blacks, is that what you'd call 'em?'

'I don't care much for them,' admits Doug Summers, 'but I'm able to suppress those feelings and be fair in my working with them. Basically, I think all human beings are prejudiced.'

'But when they come back at you and say – '

'That's right, you may have them for a righteous violation – and they *know* you've got them for a righteous violation – but they immediately say, "You're hasslin' me jus' 'cos I'm black! *You don't like blacks!*" Right? What they're looking for is, for you to say, "No, no, man! I figure all you guys are equal!" And you put up a defense, you see?'

The trainee nods vigorously.

'Now, I think a good answer is to say, "That's right, I don't like blacks." They go – ' Doug Summers lets his jaw drop –

'because there's nothing to argue about. And then you say, "If you were white, brown, or black, I'd arrest you for what you just did – your color has nothing to do with it." '

The bar is a four-sided stucco one-story building, as complicated in its design as a house brick with a couple of holes in it, and it stands alone on a corner, with a flickering neon sign over a small side entrance. Baton in hand, and followed by two officers who have volunteered cover, Doug Summers and his trainee enter the bar, which is no brighter than the night, and packed with people. It's easy to pick out the couple who caused the barman to call for help: they're the two managing to be heard above the sound of the jukebox. Quickly and quietly, Doug Summers has the pair of them escorted outside on to the sidewalk, where he draws the woman aside.

'You had better talk to me first, ma'am,' he says, 'here where it's private, okay?'

She keeps right on shouting for a while, listing outrages and wrongs, then adopts a sullen calm when told Doug Summers will speak to her man.

'You sure moved fast,' remarks the trainee, as they go over to where the man is standing with one of the cover officers.

'When you get two black people talking,' says Doug Summers, 'and one starts calling the other one "nigger", that's when you're going to have some kind of real confrontation.'

Then he also draws the man aside, confidingly, 'Okay, we want to talk to you, sir – okay?'

'Yes, sure,' says the man, scratching the small of his back, under his pink tank top.

'We got called here because there was some trouble between you and your girl friend. We just want you to know we don't want to come back here. A second time, and you go to jail – understand?'

'Yeah, but honestly, I never done anything like she – '

'Okay, I'm giving you fair warning, okay? We don't want no fightin' here, okay?'

'No fightin' – you got my word, baby!' The man reaches out clumsily to clasp his hand. 'My word's good enough, my word's *my bond*. I promise.'

'What's your name?' asks Doug Summers, shaking hands.

185

'Marvin Buckles the Fourth.'

'Okay, Marvin, take it easy now, Marvin . . .'

Back in the unit, Doug Summers says, 'Remember, in the day time, it's different. You know how you walk into a show, and shit, you're stumbling down the aisle and laughin' and stuff? But a few minutes later, you can see like it's daylight? So before you go into any dark bar or any dark place, when you're coming from the light, you close your eyes and count to ten.'

11

Lieutenant Rae Chassam has evolved his own personal variation on that little ruse. If he ever needs to go into somewhere dark on a bright sunny day, he drives there with one eye closed. And then, as he crosses the threshold, he opens that eye and closes the other.

'I got hit one time with a pool cue, walking into a bar,' he recalls. 'The person inside has a real advantage if you just walk in blind – I never did see the guy who hit me!'

But he really isn't in the mood for telling stories, not after what happened at the car-hop this afternoon. 'I'm sick,' he says, '*sick* . . . ' And very angry.

His efforts to further the ideals of community-oriented policing have taken a hard knock. Hard knocks are part and parcel of being a police officer, but this one seems to him entirely different to any he might have received in the past as, say, the head of the then narcotics bureau.

> I've done a whole lot of things – Patrol, the jail, Traffic, Captain's aide, but I could never work in the Vice Squad. Everything I hold near and dear to my heart is unlawful over there.

The time: 7:30 p.m. Still nothing from the barrio.

12

It is about now that the department's six Vice Squad officers gather for a briefing by their sergeant, before going out for a

Saturday night on the town which is quite unlike any other in San Diego.

The man in overall command of them is Captain 'Duke' La Mott, a big broad-shouldered detective in his mid-fifties, who looks like he could walk through a brick wall without creasing his suit. Tough, but no poseur, he is coming to the end of his career with the department.

> Thirty years is enough for anybody. Okay, it's been my life, and I know I'll miss it – but then again, a guy misses a cigar too. I'm looking forward to retiring. I'm tired. Maybe I'm burned out after all of this. I begin to worry that the whole world is crumbling, that our morals are decaying, worry about where this country is going to end up. I don't when I'm with my friends, playing bridge – very few I associate with off-duty are policemen any more – and so, if I got a chance to look at it from the other side, I probably wouldn't feel so bad.
>
> But working down here, day in and day out, you really start to worry.

As a native San Diegan, Captain La Mott has witnessed changes in his society that extend back over more than five decades, let alone three as a police officer.

> I don't know what it is about San Diego, we've always had a cleaner city than most big cities – and we're the ninth largest in the whole of the United States. But now we're getting more big city problems.
>
> It was a lot nicer when we could force all that stuff to go to Tijuana, to Mexico! The people used to go down there at the weekend. We weren't old enough to drink, but we could drink down there. They had whores, they had dirty books, they had anything you wanted. You could watch some girls put on a show for you: blow the smoke out like they were smoking through their snatch – or a darkie fucks them, that kind of stuff. Y'know, it was Sin City! It wasn't nice for Tijuana, but it was nice for San Diego; we had an 'out' for that kind of shit.
>
> Now they come up here to look at our book stores. And our dirty book stores are damn dirty, there's no two ways about it.

He has seen changes, too, in the way the department has permitted its Vice Squad officers to operate.

> I worked Vice as a patrolman, and I know how it used to be. You'd come to work and, hell, in two or three hours, you've had three or four drinks. It was just routine. Drink all you want, get drunk, do whatever you wanted – unless you got in the grease, nobody

187

seemed to care. But that's a bad, bad thing; it leads to all kinds of trouble. Now that's taboo.

But Captain La Mott hasn't only witnessed such change, he has himself been party to much of it, since taking over the Vice Squad seven and a half years ago. No longer, for example, can any officer expect to remain on the squad for an indefinite period.

> At one time, the whole night Vice Squad was either divorced, separated, or on the brink of separation. This was before we had any structured method of rotating them out. Now we only keep our officers about eighteen months to two years, and we've been doing that for about five years, I guess. It's not the best hours for family life: they work from seven at night until three in the morning, with Sundays and Mondays – or Tuesdays and Wednesdays – as days off.

Family life has a high priority with Captain La Mott who has three children and six grandchildren, all living in the San Diego area. The rotation scheme is intended, however, to act as a safeguard in other ways as well.

> Corruption is one consideration. We haven't had any I'm aware of, but we don't want anyone getting too entrenched, anyone to where they've got special friends they're taking care of.
>
> Frustration is another consideration. There's so much of it over here. These guys work hard, they go out and break their ass to put people in jail, and next morning, the people are back on the street: the prostitutes are there, the pimps are there. And the public says, 'What are you doing this for? Why don't you go and put robbers in jail? There's no reward for doing this work that the guy can *feel*, and pretty soon he's pissed off. It rubs off on the family – or, when a citizen resists arrest a little bit, he wants to beat the shit out of him. That's why we want him out of here, before that happens.
>
> The vice unit is, in our opinion, a critical job. Any misconduct by an officer could create an atmosphere which could cost the Chief his job, and so he always has approval of anyone who comes here.

Between 10 and 15 percent of potential candidates eliminate themselves from the running. 'They say they don't want to work Vice,' says Captain La Mott. '*I* wouldn't like to work it – I don't drink so I don't go into bars!' But for most officers on their way up the Investigations ladder, it's a prestigious assignment to be jumped at, given the chance.

188

We're looking for guys who can work alone, self-starters; guys who are innovative, and report writers.

We look at their sick leave. You're allowed 13 sick days a year. If a guy's using over six or seven, then he's using more than the average, and we don't want someone who's puny.

Besides, I like big guys. We're with people every night who have been drinking and they get false courage, and you can't send somebody out who can't enforce the rules. Size sometimes seems to affect that. Our guys don't get involved in melees as often as you'd think.

That's something else we're concerned about: the ones who get heavy-handed – we don't tolerate it. It creates more problems than we can handle if a guy, every time he goes out, has to fight somebody, and then there's an investigation for the sergeant, which takes him away from other duties.

Many other factors are also considered, which Captain La Mott sums up as: 'It's just a feelin' you get talking to him – it takes a different breed of cat, in my opinion.'

Then when the time comes to take somebody into Vice, the lieutenant and I sit down and lay out for them our own peculiar ground rules, so there's no doubt in their minds about what they can and can't do.

Like with drinking. There is *no way* you're going to work here and go and drink in those bars, unless you've got a special investigation and you get permission from your supervisor first. Or, if you're out in the field and something develops, as soon as you get out of that bar, you call your boss and tell him what you did, and why you did it.

You also *cannot* associate with our clientele off duty – that's prostitutes and barmaids and nude models and card dealers, and that kind of stuff. If you want to have a relationship or an affair with someone like that, you come in and tell us. No ill feelings, I'm not going to prevent you going to Burglary or Juvenile or someplace else, but you can't work here. You're *gone*.

It happens. Guys who come over and don't like it, or don't fit in, we move them out too.

Not that there are a great many new recruits to the Vice Squad who walk into Captain La Mott's office and ask for a transfer, simply because they want out.

It's a fun job, as bad as it seems.

We had a guy running a private-club deal, where you could go in his house and there's some guy sitting behind a door with a knot hole and you stick your dick through and he sucked your dick – or there was some broad, who would fuck anybody that came in. It was a sort of free-love affair. But to join, you had to go and have your picture taken nude. We sent two of our guys out there, and then we raided the place and got those pictures. We had a little fun with that – there's damn few rewards, so we have to have fun to keep our heads on straight.

There's also more work to do, more to learn, more contacts, more informants to develop. You get to see how the city runs – who works for who, who runs for who, who reports to who – and it kinda gives you an idea of what makes the machinery go round. We've got to prise 'em loose over here.

13

The two Vice Squad officers, now approaching their pastel on the moonlit patio, both have six years' experience as policemen.

George Wilson, jingling the car keys, was a black member of the Gang Detail before being chosen to work Vice. He is thirty-two, stands six-two, weighs one-ninety-seven, and is dressed casually in a light-weight blue jacket, gray pants, and an open-neck yellow shirt.

His white partner, Ric Thomas, thirty-four, came to Vice from Burglary. He is a dark-haired, dapper figure, more formally dressed in a checked jacket, gray tie and black pants, with large silver buckles on his shiny black shoes. He is about forty pounds lighter than George Wilson, and five-eight tall. Not a big guy, but a former Seal – the U.S. Navy's equivalent to such elite fighting forces as Britain's SAS – and more than capable of being as quietly forceful as he needs to be.

A low-key manner is something else that both men have in common, and the fact they are each married.

Before leaving the patio, they give the pastel a thorough search, and throw away any trash they come across. From now on, anything they find in the car tonight will have been left there by a prisoner, and may be used as evidence.

Then, checking in with Communications on the Vice radio channel, they begin their patrol, light-hearted and cracking jokes a lot, like two friends who have simply decided to take a ride downtown and enjoy themselves.

They make their first stop hardly three blocks from the station.

14

The barrio still simmers.

Ever active, Carl Brunner does a circuit of Golden Hill Park, goes down to Tony's Liquor Store, and then out into the black neighborhood, passing the statue of a black Christ, with his arms uplifted, outside the Reformed Progressive Holiness Church on the corner of Thirty-second and Imperial. The hands have been stolen.

Nightfall inevitably increases the dangers faced by officers working the Heights – fourteen square miles, populated by one hundred thousand people – even if it's only that darkness makes it harder to spot when a dog is rabid. One of the additional dangers makes Carl Brunner angry.

> Some guys know places to hide. It really pisses me off, because they're going to get other officers hurt, y'know. For instance, I could be around the park, gettin' my ass kicked, and this guy's around the corner, sleepin', not listening to his radio. It's real bad.

But it's early yet for that sort of thing.

Carl Brunner cruises the streets, passing innumerable KEEP OUT signs on garden gates, and others warning of dangerous dogs. *Ebony* magazine, according to Billy McGuire, has described San Diego's black community as 'the safest in the nation, but the most heavily policed'. Then, approaching some large billboards near a freeway, the unit slows down.

Over on the left is the Cool Water Motel, much patronized by prostitutes and drug addicts, and also a focus of a great many burglaries. It is always worth checking to see if anybody is walking out of the patio, especially if they seem unusually laden down. Tonight, however, the only sign of life is a taxi drawing away with two white men in the back, presumably a couple of johns who some whores brought out here.

And so, with 57,348 miles on its clock, the unit drifts back to the barrio. Patrol cars average about sixty miles to a shift, although Carl Brunner's must do much more than that.

15

The Vice Squad pastel is stationary. George Wilson, at the wheel, and Ric Thomas, beside him, are watching some distant figures, seated on the grass of a downtown park.

'There were three,' says Ric Thomas.

'Oh, is that right?'

'The other guy probably went back to go to the bathroom or something. There's two of them there.'

'One's brushing his hair back now. He already took a drink.'

Then their concentration is broken by another car drawing up alongside, and the driver calling across: 'Are you police officers?'

'No,' says Ric Thomas.

'Who are you?'

'What do you want?'

'I was wondering why you were sitting there.'

'Oh?'

'I need an ambulance,' the driver says, jerking a thumb at the man alongside him. 'I think he's pregnant.'

'You're probably,' says Ric Thomas, 'going to need *two* ambulances if you don't leave.'

The Robbery car leaves, amid much laughter of the sort that comes from cops who play night-games.

And now the game seems to have truly begun.

'The first two under the tree over there, okay?' says George Wilson, starting up the pastel.

'Okay.'

The car roars forward, its headlights coming on, and drives straight up over the curb, heading fast for the seated men. It is upon them before they properly take in what is happening and they're still getting to their feet when the two officers jump out and confront them.

'Police officers,' says George Wilson, and the relief this brings to two startled faces is momentarily comic.

Ric Thomas uses that moment to pick up two bottles of white port and another bottle of blended Canadian whisky, which he places on the hood of the pastel.

Still stunned by the drama of a moment ago, the two men don't seem to quite take it in when they're told that they have committed an offense by drinking in public. Perhaps the charge lacks a proportional sense of enormity, making it difficult to relate one to the other.

'Look, squire, we're just up from our ship, see?' says the older of the two men. 'Fancied having a few, out here on the grass where it's quiet. Smashin' night, really, and them palm trees – not one for your bars, to be honest, even when I has the money.'

'You guys are sailors?'

'Aye, deckhands, me and young Tony here. But I mean, what've we done that's so wrong, then? We going to be locked up?'

'You get a ticket – thirty-five dollar fine.'

'Thirty-five bucks!' exclaims young Tony, not another Englishman but possibly a New Yorker.

His companion points to the bottles on the hood of the pastel and asks the officers, 'Could we have a drink and talk about this?'

Remaining friendly but firm, George Wilson and Ric Thomas turn down the invitation, and fill in citations for each of the men, explaining where the fines can be paid. For their part, the two offenders continue to express befuddled astonishment, not really protesting, but uncertain if this law is a *good* law. What they'd hoped would be an inexpensive evening is in ruins.

Then Ric Thomas takes the three bottles of drink and empties them into the lawn.

'Terrible, that,' sighs the older deckhand sadly, as he watches the liquor drain away. 'Terrible.'

It isn't until the last moment that he comes out with a line that no fiction writer would dare to put in a modern sailor's mouth.

'That's *fifty* lashes for you,' he says to young Tony. 'You wasn't looking!'

And as George Wilson and Ric Thomas drive away, they're still smiling at that. It can be a fun job, just like the man said.

16

While the barrio still holds its breath, FTO Doug Summers carries on teaching his trainee precautions that may some day save his life.

The trainee has just made a mess of what looked like a simple drunk arrest. The suspect had been slumped on a bench in a small park, with his eyes closed, and the trainee had walked straight up to him and shaken him roughly by the shoulder. In an instant, the man had been on his feet, swinging punches – believing, as he explained a moment or two later, that he was being either robbed or assaulted in his sleep. What was more, he was perfectly sober, just very tired and possibly suffering from flu.

The correct approach would have been to go behind the man, to shake him gently, and to say, 'Police officer – wake up.' Not only would this get the contact off to a better start, but it would be less hazardous.

And then, to drive home the degree of hazard involved in ignoring this advice, Doug Summers turns to the subject of PCP – or 'angel dust', as this former animal tranquilizer has become known.

'You can take PCP and be very mellow – as long as things around you are mellow,' he says as they drive out of the park, having already said all of this at the academy. 'But let a police officer come up to you, shake you or speak loudly to you, and that'll key you off and you'll become violent. PCP users have abnormal strength. I've seen myself a PCP user overturn a car with his hands.'

'Yeah?'

'I myself have taken into custody a fourteen-year-old kid – who was five-six and weighed a hundred and ten pounds – and it took *six* of us, all over six foot, five or six minutes to handcuff him. You can beat 'em, gas 'em with Mace, nothing works – they feel no pain. I've lost two of my teeth, I've been stabbed once – and I want you to realize these have all been small people on PCP.'

In Los Angeles, the police have steel nets that they can

194

throw over PCP users who are tearing the place apart. The San Diego PD hasn't any, and couldn't afford them.

> One of the things I stress at the academy is that you talk calmly to them, if you suspect someone is under the influence, and if possible, close off all outside stimulants – music, lights. If you can cover their heads, oddly enough they become very docile, so we carry a blanket in our supervisor cars. If you can encircle them, simply hug them, they feel secure – like a baby in a crib, same thing.

17

At 8:30 p.m., opposite the Opera House in Fourth Avenue, the two Vice Squad officers give out three more tickets to people drinking in public, and empty their bottles into the gutter. The same sad, wistful looks; the same firm but not hostile enforcement of the law.

Five minutes later, four more tickets.

Six, a block farther down.

It happens without warning. Just two men pausing, stepping out of the crowd on the sidewalk. Nobody here on Fourth questions them on the reasons why.

George Wilson and Ric Thomas drive, stop, walk, drive on again, round and round.

Then a brisk, hard-edged woman's voice starts giving directions on the radio. She has seen a black whore picked up by a white john who is driving a flashy customized Chevy pickup.

Ric Thomas takes up the microphone. 'Want any help, Julie?'

'Yeah, might as well.'

For a while, things have been pretty humdrum. Now both George Wilson and Ric Thomas seem back in that party mood, and the pastel pulls away from the curb.

Radio traffic is incessant, as the two teams of Vice officers follow the pickup out into the Heights. Without the measured tones and conventions of a Communications broadcast, it builds up an excitement of its own, like a sports commentary.

'They're still rolling!'

'Okay, we're right behind.'

'Two heads are still up.'

'Coming up on . . .'

George Wilson laughs, and says to his partner. 'They chase them south, and I chase them west – where did you say the sea was?'

'They've stopped!'

And dead ahead, on a residential street in the black community, the vice pastel stops, too, about a hundred yards short of the truck.

'Two heads still up,' reports Ric Thomas.

If one of the heads vanishes from sight, then the Vice officers will make an arrest for a contravention of Penal Code 647(B): engaging in an act of prostitution – the preferred charge. Should things not work out as planned, they may have to settle for a charge of solicitation.

George Wilson uses his handie-talkie to say: 'I'll walk across the street and – '

'If,' his partner interrupts him, 'you can get across without being seen under that light.'

'I fit in this neighborhood, okay?' says George Wilson, grinning as he slips out of the car and disappears into some heavy shadow.

'What was that?' queries Julie, having heard only part of the exchange on the radio.

'George says,' Ric relays back to her, 'that he fits in this neighborhood, so they won't have a chance.'

Out of the night, whispered loudly through the speakers, comes one word from George: 'Racist!'

Laughing, Ric Thomas settles back to watch.

George ambles along the sidewalk, passing the parked pickup, and keeps on going.

A car comes slowly up from behind, and its headlights reflect off the back window of the pickup's cab, making it impossible to see through.

Another vehicle, coming down the hill with its headlights on full, dazzles for a moment.

Then Julie warns: 'Truck's starting to move!'

And move it does, at considerable speed.

'Going northbound on Twentieth,' reports Julie. 'Anybody with us?'

'Yeah, we are,' says Ric Thomas. 'We're right behind.'

But first he has to pick up George Wilson, who says as he gets in: 'I walked by. He came, I saw, I conquered – no, I didn't!'

More laughter.

Way ahead, the truck stops at an intersection, and is obscured by another vehicle choosing that moment to leave the curb and join the flow of traffic.

'She's gone,' reports George Wilson.

'Okay,' says Julie, 'he dropped her off. I'm going to make the stop.'

'Where are you at now?'

'Ninth and – '

But the stop has gone wrong. Suddenly realizing that he has been followed, the driver of the truck accelerates away, turning it into a real chase.

Patrol is alerted.

The driving is hard, fast, and just as suddenly, all over.

'I've got him,' says a voice on the radio.

'Who's got him?'

'I have, Market and Ninth.'

'Ten-four.'

The flashy truck is slewed across the street, its path blocked by a patrol unit. The driver is already out, his hands up against the side of his cab. He is bare-chested, dressed in only a pair of shorts, rubber sandals and a large buff Stetson. A singles-bar mustache completes a handsome face – he must be about twenty-six – and complements an expensive piece of hair-styling. His physique is above male-model standards, and his hirsute chest is heaving.

'Hey, what's goin' on?' he asks. 'What's goin' *on*? Shit, ya had me half-scared to death there! I'd done nothin'!'

And while he continues protesting his total innocence to Officer Julie Hofmeyer, a striking blonde in blue, Ric Thomas takes a look into the cab of the truck.

It's all something of an anti-climax.

Until Ric Thomas emerges from the cab with a smile, bearing the evidence required: a white hand towel which, when opened out, reveals a lipstick smear and about two cubic centimeters of expectorated semen, mixed with saliva.

'Wasn't that fun?' he says to his partner, as they drive away, leaving Julie Hofmeyer to process and jail her very pale prisoner.

18

Prostitution, like gambling and other activities under the 'vice' umbrella, is sometimes known as 'victimless crime'.

'I have a hard time believing that,' says Captain La Mott. 'Even the prostitutes are victims. Even if they're not working for a pimp – and our experience here is that most have a pimp who beats the shit out of them – the prostitutes are dehumanizing themselves.'

And he has no doubt whatsoever that prostitution should be dealt with rigorously.

> I think it was in January of '77, San Francisco got a new mayor, a new DA, and a new chief of police. They indicated to the media they were not going to prosecute whores any more – it was in all the papers.
>
> Jesus Christ, it just brings all the scum out from under the rocks. It isn't just the hookers, it's the people that follow them around: their pimps, their boy friends, the lowlifes, the burglars, child molesters. I don't give a shit what they say, if you don't have these 'victimless crimes', you don't have the crime that goes with it.
>
> That year in San Francisco, the crime rate went up by about *twenty-five percent* – I got my statistics from the FBI crime index.
>
> And by the time that year was almost over, there were so many prostitutes on the streets, hitting on the husband – y'know, the tourist man-and-wife, going into hotels – that the hotel proprietors brought pressure to bear upon the administration, and they started enforcing prostitution laws again about January '78. By March, the crime rate was down eighteen percent, then continued down to almost its original level.
>
> So it was an experience. Because of that, we believe that enforcing victimless crimes – and especially prostitution – has a very dramatic effect on the overall crime rate.

And what plainly irritates Captain La Mott is that, had San Diego been left to its own devices, then in his opinion the city would have far fewer problems.

> Probably ten years ago, we didn't have girls on the streets that would come up and solicit you – that's kind of new in our town.

Then the State of California enacted some laws concerning prostitution that pre-empted all of our local ordinances – we had ordinances (for example) that prohibited a woman from massaging a man in a massage parlor. The massage parlors really sprang up then, and made a lot of money from prostitution.

I know for a fact a lot of hookers were working in the parlors for up to a ten-hour shift. But if their pimp didn't think they'd made enough by then, he'd make them work the street until they got it. And from that come all of our street prostitutes.

On top of which, the whole practical side of enforcement became far more difficult to carry out.

Before that, we'd had cat houses, whore houses, of course, and as soon as we found out, we'd bust them. But the massage parlor made it difficult, because of locked rooms and problems with getting evidence legally. We've eliminated most of 'em, but now they've gone to things like rap parlors, other places you wrestle with a nude lady, and even camera places – for fifteen bucks, you go in the back room and screw the girl or whatever. We busted a picture place here two weeks ago, and they didn't have a goddamn piece of film in the whole store! If you could get the kind of enforcement we used to generate, we'd get back to where we were.

All things considered, however, San Diego is hardly much of a 'sin city' as far as large naval and military bases go.

I would say two to five hundred hookers work the streets around here, but they come and they go. The Navy pays out twice a month, and you'll get hookers *flying* down here – same as the three-card guys, guys with the shell game. Then there's usually a little more going on, although Navy pay days aren't what they used to be. Is it a new kind of sailor, more mature, who doesn't go for that kind of bullshit? I don't know – although it could very easily be more permissiveness among society. Out in Mission Valley, you can't tell the free stuff from the prostitute – I don't know how a whore could make any money down there.

19

George Wilson and Ric Thomas are back on foot, checking out bars and pool rooms in the F Street area.

Despite their plain clothes, once they enter a bar, the tension goes up. A number of things make them distinctive, among which is the fact they're smart-looking, enormously self-assured, and obviously acting in unison. Moreover, they're stone cold sober.

> *Captain La Mott:* When we really want to do a number on someone, then we'll bring in a brand-new cop or someone from another area, dirty them up, and they'll do the job for us. But these guys, you can't keep them cool. They're out every night.

And besides, it's a lot less dangerous to be recognized as police officers.

George Wilson leads the way into a long, poorly lit room, dense with disco beat and tobacco smoke, at the rear end of which is a pool table. He and Ric Thomas pause at a booth, identify themselves, and question a young girl seated there, taking her details for a check with Communications; they suspect she is under age and possibly a runaway.

They move on down to the pool table, where a scrawny man of about twenty, with long unkempt hair and tattoos, is lining up on the eight-ball. His posture reveals a large sheath knife on his belt at the back, where it would normally be concealed by his denim jacket.

'We're police officers, we want to talk to you.'

'Fucking shit! What you hasslin' me for?'

It's one of those moments when things can happen very fast, then a tall, lanky, beaming black man comes jive-walking round to the near side of the table, announcing loudly, 'Never fear, *Brother John* is here!' And he laughs, wild and high.

This distraction throws the pool-player, who lets go of his cue and of his anger, submitting sullenly to questioning. But when George Wilson and Ric Thomas walk out again, they are careful not to turn their backs on him completely.

The sidewalk radio check on the young girl yields nothing, and so the two Vice Officers decide to check out a few dirty book stores.

20

Up at Community Hospital, from where traffic on the Coronado bridge now looks like a string of cars flying in a gentle arc through the balmy night, FTO Doug Summers is having an orange juice, while his trainee writes a report on a simple case of battery.

Notwithstanding the young man's academic qualifications, the report has him chewing the end of his ball-point pen a lot, and there is about him an almost touching naivete.

> We see a lot more now of younger officers who still live at home. About half of my shift is under twenty-four, and around eighty percent of them are like that. Some do it for financial reasons; others because they're very attached to their parents, and haven't learned to grow up yet.

This particular trainee has in fact just moved out to live with his fiancee, and they intend getting married just as soon as he's through his probationary period. But whether that marriage will actually come to pass – or last very long – is a moot point, in Doug Summers's opinion. Part of what he has in mind is what could be dubbed the Ugly Duckling Syndrome.

> You'll find that eighty percent – or maybe higher – of all officers have remarried at least once. I have friends twenty-nine years old that've been married three times.
>
> I did some counseling at one time, and I did some research on this. It's really simple.
>
> Go back to when that young officer was just a young man in high school and college. I remember I had pretty much to do the chasing. If I wanted a date, I had to ask her. If you wanted to pursue an affair, you had to do it through the wining and dining and the flowers, type of thing. It's an inborn thing that a male has to do.
>
> Now what do you suppose happens when you become a police officer and, all of a sudden, that role is taken away from you? You no longer have to chase women, now *you're* the one who's chased! Chased continually.
>
> Not just by the groupies – and believe me, there are groupies – and not so much even chased. You stop a car, and the female says, 'God, I like you. How would you like to come over for a drink and spend the night?' Some are that upfront about it!
>
> The reason is, you're a police officer: you can be trusted, you're not a pervert, you're definitely a male, they can see who you really are from your tag, and of course, the glamor of the job's another aspect – the TV helped immensely in this area.
>
> Young cops can't handle that – even some old cops can't handle that. It's like the little ugly duckling, right?
>
> Now say before coming on the department, the young officer met this nice young lady, the expectation of his dreams, and

married her – she's a good mother. Then all of a sudden, he's dating women much nicer-looking than his wife, and some will do anything he wants physically.

Pretty soon, it's: 'Why don't you want to do what I want to do, honey? We *are* married. I got a girl and she'll get down and bark like a fox! And you won't even bring me breakfast in bed.' And after that, comes: 'Screw you, I don't need you any more – I can date these other women.'

It cracks me up and never ceases to amaze me, that you see guys who never, in their wildest dreams, could take out an eight or nine, but here they are, dating all these attractive women – and they think it's *them*. It isn't, right? It's still the little ugly duckling, but now he's in police uniform.

21

The third dirty book store along isn't doing much business either. Three male customers stand widely separated, as though not wanting anybody looking over their shoulders, and flick through books and magazines on the racks. The clerk behind the cash register, adept at blank looks, appears blanked out altogether; rooted there, staring at a patch of real dirt on the opposite wall.

The covers of the various publications lend the drear room its only real color. Some dirty book stores try to be as vividly inviting as a candy store; this one could be selling used tractor parts for all it mattered. It's where Larry Conrad met up with Gerard Viper.

Ric Thomas and George Wilson take a brief walk round the racks, glancing over what's on offer.

Captain La Mott: I'm not a moralist – I don't think anybody on this whole department's a moralist – but we don't like what goes on in these stores, don't like what's being seen.

Going right back, if you had a picture of a girl in a two-piece bathing costume, they marked out her belly-button. Then you could see her belly-button, but you couldn't see the hair on her vagina. That used to be a violation: one hair showing, and you could make a pinch. Pretty soon, it became if you could see her vagina, you could make a pinch. Today, they kinda open up their innards and stuff, but provided there's some 'redeeming social value' – in other words, *any kind of writing at all* with it – that's not an offense!

And it's almost impossible for us – because of Supreme Court decisions, in California and in the United States – to enforce any kind of pornography law, unless the stuff deals with sado-masochism or a person with an animal or with a child. It's very frustrating for us, and in fact, we do very little enforcement any more in pornography.

I think the best thing in our favor is we've reached saturation point, the stuff's not as abnormal to people as it was, and they are beginning to be turned off. A lot of the store owners are saying it's just not worth it any more.

But we do go through these places regularly. Our interest is in the conduct of the patrons inside there.

All three customers look up sharply, having heard an unnatural and possibly unnerving sound for a dirty book store: a laugh. Ric Thomas has just spotted a cover so absurd in its obscene contortions that no sensible man could take it seriously. And at this point, one of the three patrons hastens out.

The clerk carries right on staring blankly, becoming visibly agitated only when George Wilson and his partner turn and approach a row of cubicles at the rear of the store. There are lurid stills on the doors of the cubicles, acting as enticements for the films shown within.

It's time to make the glory-hole check.

'Okay, it must be my turn,' says Ric Thomas. 'Got another quarter?'

George Wilson lends him one, and then they look along the line of cubicles, searching for one that is occupied. That done, Ric Thomas goes into the neighboring cubicle, and closes the door. The back of the door forms a screen, and so he sits on a bench against the wall, faces this screen and drops his borrowed quarter into a slot to his right. There's a flicker, and then the screen shows a naked young woman dragging off a man's pants, grasping his penis and handling it vigorously, showing a great deal of impatience.

But George Wilson isn't watching any longer. His full attention is on the aperture that has been bored through the cubicle wall to his right. This is a glory-hole – and there's another on his left, but it leads to an empty cubicle and therefore isn't of any interest. Any moment now, a total stranger is likely to thrust his erect member through that glory-hole, in the expectation that George Wilson will perform

203

for him an act of fellatio. As an example of blind faith and trust in one's fellow man, even the confessional could hardly rival it.

22

Units from all over the Heights are gathering on the parking lot immediately below the main entrance to Community Hospital.

Carl Brunner is here. The trainee is here, and so is Doug Summers, caught up in conversation with a fellow FTO, an Irish-Mexican who has a gurgling graveyard laugh like the host of a horror show.

Among those also present is an officer who would still have been in plain clothes tonight, working the Vice Squad street detail, had events in his life taken a different turn.

> I was working with a guy who was dating a waitress in a bar, and she had a sister working there too. Well, my partner wanted me to go out to their house after work for a couple of drinks with them. I did it a couple of nights a week for five weeks, then I finally said, 'Hey, I can't be doing this any more – the captain says we're not supposed to.' He's a man for whom I have much admiration and respect. Okay, they understood, and everything was cool. Then one girl got fired from the bar, and her sister told the owners that they couldn't part them if they didn't want hassle with the Vice cops – that they knew a couple of Vice cops and all this. Well, the owners came down and complained, and the lieutenant in investigations called me in. I was honest, upfront with him, the whole shot – the only thing I didn't do was involve any other guys. I got a formal reprimand for 'conduct unbecoming' – that's the worst punishment, it goes in your personnel jacket forever – and I got sent back on patrol. I know I fucked up – I'd no business going to see this girl – and I got my marriage and my head back together. But they never asked me about that, never said, 'Why were you going out there?'

More units arrive, and then Jim Bradford, acting-sergeant tonight, arrives with his ride-along from Scotland Yard.

The squad gets together like this every shift at about nine, so that the supervisor can check activity, answer queries, take a look at reports, and generally assess the mood of the beat area.

So far, for a Saturday night, things have been surprisingly

peaceful. Even down at Chicano Park, beneath the freeway ramps, gang members – senior and junior – are giving no particular trouble.

And indeed, Saturday night, for Second Watch, is almost over.

23

Downtown, what most people call Saturday night is only just getting going, now that enough liquor has flowed and the beat of the music has entered the blood. A time when even small-town visitors start to lose their inhibitions, and it is striking how many of them, the two Vice cops have noticed, end up as the johns on a charge of engaging.

> *Ric Thomas:* I don't know why anyone would pay for it in this town. You go to one of the good-sized nightclubs, discos, and you can have your pick of the ladies.
> *George Wilson:* The majority of the girls (prostitutes) down here aren't as goodlookin', and they don't have the personality.
> *Ric Thomas:* You know, even if you had to buy the lady two or three drinks, you're not going to have to spend anything like you would on one of these.

They are just cruising in their pastel, keeping an eye on – among other things – a petite, elfin blonde with long flowing hair, whom Julie Hofmeyer has drawn their attention to. A casting director would probably snap the girl up to play a wistful college student, quiet in her ways, who reads and writes a lot of mawkish poetry. Julie Hofmeyer has her marked down as a hooker.

> *Ric Thomas:* It's a game, because you're not going to do anything about it – a cat-and-mouse game, and I guess it's been like that since the beginning of time. You try and catch them, and the fine can be as little as nothing.

'Is that guy stopping again?' says George Wilson.

Every other vehicle on the street becomes memorized for a time, while the pastel is cruising, and if one does anything in the least out of the ordinary, then 'mouse' becomes provisionally stamped on its license plates.

'Yeah, same guy as back there,' agrees Ric Thomas. 'And,

hey, is that girl – the little blonde?' He stops the pastel well short of the couple.

'She's getting in the car,' says George Wilson, who has the unobstructed view.

'Is she?'

George Wilson says into his radio: 'Julie . . .'

'Go,' she responds.

'That chick, she's making contact with a silver-gray vehicle in the eight hundred block.'

'What street?'

'Sixth.'

'Was it the one that's just turned the lights on?'

Ric Thomas murmurs, 'There it goes.'

'Yeah,' says George Wilson, on the radio. 'It's got a vinyl half-top.'

'Ten-four.'

'You see it?'

'We see it,' confirms Julie Hofmeyer. 'It's got a bike rack on the back?'

'Yeah.'

'Looks like a Marine or something.'

'It figures.'

'And out-of-state plates.'

The pastel starts rolling. Now come the most difficult phase: keeping track of the two suspects without them knowing it. The best way of attempting this is not to shadow the car by following behind it, but by traveling in tandem along the streets on either side of it, checking at intersections in case a turn is made.

The two Vice pastels keep in constant radio communication, fully expecting the suspect car to keep turning and changing direction, hoping to throw anyone tailing it.

'Now the whores around here are really paranoid,' says Ric Thomas, 'but she's picked a very direct route, very unusual.'

George Wilson says into the radio: 'They've not done any turns or anything – they're just going!'

'We're going to be on Thirty-first and Market,' says Julie.

The destination of the suspect car is already tacitly understood: the Cool Water Motel, up in the Heights.

24

Not all that far from the Cool Water, acting-sergeant Jim Bradford has just been talking to a couple of gang members, mainly as an excuse to show his ride-along from Scotland Yard a few tattoos.

'When you run across one of the older guys,' explains Jim Bradford, once his unit is on the move again, 'somewhere on their arms will be a tattoo of an "M". Sometimes, you've got to look kind of hard, because they'll disguise it in a spiderweb or somethin'. If you find that, or you find "EME", then this guy has been to prison and affiliated himself with the Mexican Mafia.'

'Which is?'

'A prison gang. There's an awful lot of violence in prison. These gangs side with each other, provide protection. You've got your Aryan Brotherhood, which is your whites, and they're affiliated with the Mexican Mafia. The black gangs are affiliated with – ' Jim Bradford slows down his unit to point at some graffiti. 'These gang leaders eventually get out, and they start these little juvenile street gangs we've got. See, after the word "Sherman" is the number thirteen. What is the thirteenth letter of the alphabet?'

'Er, must be "M".'

'Right – Mexican Mafia. There's a direct tie with the Sherman here. Just like the Mafia, once you join you never get out. You can request to, you have to voice your reasons to the council, and they'll take a vote. But you're never free; some day you'll have to look after stolen property, something like that.'

And as they approach the black Christ with missing hands, a Vice Squad pastel goes hurrying past them.

25

Ric Thomas and George Wilson are already parked in a dark back street about seventy-five yards from the Cool Water

Motel. But something has gone wrong: at the last minute, the suspects' car must have taken evasive action, and contact has been lost.

'They're in the complex?' asks Julie Hofmeyer, over the radio.

'They haven't passed on Thirty-second yet.'

'Maybe they're there.'

'Okay,' says George Wilson, 'I'll take a walk up there by the back, and see if I can see the vehicle.'

Ric Thomas waits in the pastel, in case it is suddenly needed. He drums his fingers on the steering wheel, watching the street at right angles ahead, but nothing passes along it.

Then out of the night, through the speaker: 'Car's in the complex. It sounds like she's talking about just maybe being busted, so if anything happens – like her splitting, and him leaving in the car – we'll let these two take her and will follow up on the car, okay?'

'Ten-four.'

Obviously, George Wilson and the other two are now together, because the radio goes quiet for a while. For what seems like a long, long while . . .

'Hey, Ric,' comes George Wilson's voice, hushed.

'Go!'

'Okay, he's just moved the car round – she's got a key to the room. We're going to move in.'

'Ten-four. Give me the room number, so I can join the party.'

'We're going to get a key, Ric.'

'Aw, come *on* – we could tell them we couldn't wait!'

A soft laugh, then silence.

Ric Thomas leaves the pastel, and makes haste to join George Wilson and another officer, who are standing against the street wall of the Cool Water, hidden from the patio inside, while Julie Hofmeyer sneaks in to get a key. The driveway is edged by some small palms that afford a crouching figure reasonable cover on the way up to the manager's office.

A taxi cab comes round the corner, and the driver immediately swings over to the three waiting men. 'You guys want back downtown?' he asks, with the casual air of a man who spends a lot of his time ferrying johns back and forth to the Cool Water.

George Wilson holds out his badge to him.

'Shit!'

The cab literally burns rubber, leaving a stink as it takes off like a toppled sky rocket, swerves wildly to avoid hitting the far curb, and then roars away, frantic and unable to keep in a straight line.

Only with difficulty do the three Vice officers keep their laughter down. Then comes what they've been waiting for, the signal to move into the motel complex, and they turn their backs on a billboard that insists: 'You must ask us about exciting San Diego.'

The patio is brightly lit, the cover minimal. Julie Hofmeyer motions toward the room occupied by the suspects, mouths its number, and as quickly and quietly as possible, everyone gets across there, running on their toes.

The night manager, seated in his office, doesn't bother to watch through his big picture window, but carries right on reading a newspaper, his cigar smoke curling lazily above it.

In sharp contrast is the intensity of feeling outside the blue door to Room Eight: a gleeful, almost mischievous excitement, tempered by professionalism and a need to choose exactly the right moment for piling into the room, and catching the young couple in *flagrante delicto*.

What complicates this decision is the fact that there is a television set on inside, turned up very loud. But then any young whore, with any experience at all, would have thought to take this commonplace precaution.

Finally, when attempts to hear anything else through the door have failed, and Julie Hofmeyer, who alone appears to remain unsmilingly businesslike at all times, has given the nod, the key is inserted into the lock, a silent countdown is made, and the door flung open.

Perfect timing.

Straight ahead is the television set, mounted on a wall bracket and turned to face the doorway. Beyond it, is the unlit bathroom. To the right, on a wide bed, are a pair of naked bodies.

'We're from the police department.'

The crew-cut youngster must be close to orgasm, oblivious, because his pink buttocks thrust forward again, even as the first officer is halfway round the bed on the far side. But the long-haired girl, staring over his shoulder, misses nothing.

That thrust goes into the bedding, as the girl twists from under him, and she flings herself, nails extended, at Julie Hofmeyer, spitting like a wildcat.

There is a brief struggle, much invective, and then the girl dives behind the open door to hide her nakedness. By now, the young man has rolled over on to his back, and is gaping with huge blue eyes at the roomful of assorted strangers.

'Hey, what's – ?'

For a clue, he need only glance up at the television set. At this very moment, by one of those stranger-than-fiction quirks of fate, the screen is showing a detective bursting into a bedroom.

'We're police officers, and you're – '

'Cops!'

The young man scrambles off the bed, stumbles, then stands rigidly to attention beside it – every inch of him.

'At ease, soldier,' an amused voice murmurs.

'You a Marine, son?' someone else asks.

'*YESSIR!*'

And only a Marine could have brought quite that ring to it, although on this occasion the response is robbed of its usual pride and dignity by abrupt detumescence and a falling condom.

Then people start to move again.

Julie Hofmeyer hands the girl something to cover herself with, and then escorts her to the bathroom to dress properly.

The young Marine also gets into his clothes.

They are questioned, separately, out on the patio. Nobody staying at the Cool Water Motel takes the slightest notice.

The girl doesn't try very hard to concoct a tale for Julie Hofmeyer, who quickly establishes that she is a prostitute with eight 'priors'. She admits that the Marine was her 'second date' tonight, and that he'd 'given' her sixty dollars.

The Marine tells Ric Thomas: 'I thought she was a nice girl, just looking for a date.' It had come as a complete surprise to him, he says, when she had asked for fifty dollars. He'd had to give her three twenties, because she hadn't any change.

They are both arrested, handcuffed, and soon the pastels are on their way back downtown.

Ric Thomas and George Wilson take the Marine. He worries aloud about the fate of his car, back there on the patio at the Cool Water. He worries aloud about what the Marine Corps is going to do to him. He worries aloud about what happens next, and says he hasn't even been *near* handcuffs before.

'You're now going to the county jail, Steve,' says George Wilson, 'and you'll be bailed in the sum of two hundred and fifty dollars.'

'Oh, wow!'

'Okay, you can call your friends at the base from the jail,' says Ric Thomas. 'You can make as many local calls as you like – and free.'

'Has this got to happen?'

And he keeps telling them that all he did was take a ride downtown, see a pretty girl and assume she was looking for a date.

Then he comes out with an almost unbelievable line all of his own. 'You got to remember, sir,' he says to Ric Thomas, 'I'm only eighteen and a li'l old country boy from Albuquerque.'

The Vice officers suppress their laughter until he has been handed over to the sheriff's deputies, and they're heading once again for the bars and dirty book stores.

'Just a country boy from Albuquerque!' mimics Ric Thomas, grinning. 'I don't know what it's like in Albuquerque, but you don't drive up to a girl on a corner there, and she comes over and asks you if you want a date! "I thought she was a nice girl, just – "'

'Hey, I mean if it *is* like that,' says his partner, 'I want to go to Albuquerque!'

'That'd be just fine!'

Which makes them laugh a whole block.

I just enjoy the game. It makes no difference to me whether or not we catch them or lose them, and I guess most Vice officers feel that way. It's a kinda fun thing to do. Afterwards? No, I don't want to work Homicide. It's a very grueling type of investigation, it takes a very special interest. And I've seen my share of dead bodies, dead bodies on patrol – dead bodies in Vietnam.

26

With the time just on 10:20 p.m., and Second Watch practically over, Kay Pruitt's prediction for this Saturday night comes true.

Two young teenagers are strolling along a sidewalk in Chicano Park, talking animatedly together, when a white car pulls up beside them.

Someone in the car calls out: 'Where are you guys from?'

'Logan,' replies a junior member, proudly.

'We're from Ysidro,' says the voice in the car. 'You better start runnin'.'

But the shotgun muzzle appears too quickly for one of the boys, a fifteen-year-old.

The blast of shot hits him in the stomach, the chest, and in the arm.

Shrieking, babbling, staggering, stumbling, trying to run, he flees from the park, leaving a trail of blood all the way to a house on National, where he stumbles into the kitchen and collapses on the floor.

The woman of the house, hysterical and terrified, calls the police department. Then she drops to her knees beside the boy, trying to staunch the flow from his shattered arm.

'The kid is probably going to lose the arm,' someone says, as news of the car-hop retaliation gets round.

'That's cold,' says Sergeant Juarez.

Part VI

Sanguinary Sunday

1

Then comes Sunday.

A day when the station down on West Market is quieter than ever. The big iron gate in the watch tower remains closed. Only once in a while does anybody cross the patio, and then they're more likely than not in uniform. Out front, parked pastels form an unbroken line. Patrol has the city almost entirely in its keeping.

Shadows switch direction, lengthening into a drowsy afternoon.

Off Pacific Highway swoops a Viking of a man in blue swimming shorts on a racing cycle, carrying a surfboard under one arm. Big, muscular, with long hair and a sea-raider's mustache, he leaves the street, passes the pastels, goes round the gas pumps, cuts through the vehicle repair shop, and dismounts on the patio, disappearing up to the locker room above the coffee shop. Ten minutes later, in the uniform of a lieutenant, he crosses the patio to take over as watch commander at the start of Second Watch.

Others are arriving, going up and changing. Sergeant Dave Shepherd, Frank Cobb, Kay Pruitt, Carl Brunner, Luke Jones, Lee Easton, Jim Bradford . . .

One of the last to enter the locker room is Officer Phil Maddoc, thirty-two, who has spent the morning at the zoo with his wife and their three-year-old daughter. Not long from now, he will be returning to Balboa Park to patrol in Unit 535 William.

Phil Maddoc is six-three, of average build, and quietly conservative in appearance, notwithstanding his blond side-burns; at a glance, someone likeable and dependable, if on the reserved side. He is an FTO, an instructor at the academy, and in addition, a member of SWAT and a police marksman. He straps on his body armor and remembers to slip his sunglasses into his fresh uniform.

Behind him, a trio of Heights squad officers are discussing last night's shotgun attack on the two Logan boys in Chicano Park, and speculating whether there have been any develop-ments overnight.

215

Their beat area is a world away from Maddoc's own – unless something happens requiring his marksmanship – and there is no telling yet what sort of shift he will have up in Hillcrest. Some Sundays can be very varied before any particular pattern emerges, if at all.

Carl Brunner, making for the door with his tin of Copenhagen snuff, checks the time on his Seiko wristwatch.

> I've had it since my dad was in Vietnam in '66, I guess. He got it for me and brought it back. It's never stopped.

2

Half an hour later, Sergeant Dave Shepherd, with his extra beepers on his gunbelt, and a massive .44 magnum in his holster, leaves the patio in his supervisor unit.

> I do more of the work in the field than I probably should, because I enjoy it. A lot of other sergeants would prefer to sit in the office and handle paperwork and stuff before they come out. My preference is not to do any paperwork that isn't absolutely necessary.

Like Eduardo Juarez, his counterpart in the Heights, Sergeant Shepherd is in his early thirties. He has a military bearing, a ready smile, a neat brown mustache, a youthful unlined face, and tends to speak softly, giving the impression he never utters a careless word. This former airborne communicator in the Coast Guard – the son of a Marine career officer – is one of around thirty SDPD officers who began as unpaid members of the police reserve. He became a regular seven years ago.

The Sunday traffic on West Market is very light. Sergeant Shepherd has barely any need to pause before leaving the station, swinging right on his way up to Hillcrest. The moment carries no sense of transition from 'plain citizen to cop'.

But then he hasn't really any private life. Even when at home in the mountains, with his wife and two children, their kittens and rabbits, he chooses never to be out of earshot of whatever radioed demand may be made upon him as a highly trained police officer, volunteer fireman, or emergency medical treatment specialist. Very confident of himself and of the skills he has been taught, he is almost always the same slightly detached Dave Shepherd, living on serene tenterhooks with one ear pricked and everything apparently at his fingertips, ready for action.

> I've had this squad for thirteen months – one agent, twelve officers and two CSO's. When I first got it, it was made up of three distinct groups and they weren't working together as a team, and I've seen about fifty percent leave. I'm responsible for their work output, their appearance and mannerisms.
>
> I had one guy whose judgment wasn't very good, and he made mistakes that I was afraid were going to get an officer hurt. The final straw was, we had a goodwill box, where people put things to be resold for needy kids, and he took out a couple of books. That was plain and simple theft. I told him I was going to recommend the strongest possible disciplinary action, and he quit.

The safety of his officers, and of the public with whom they come in contact, is also one of Sergeant Shepherd's chief concerns. Nothing alarms him more than a 'fearless' officer.

> You get guys who say, 'Oh, I'm never afraid!' Any officer who says that is either sick or he's lying to himself – and you've *got* to admit your feelings. That's the first thing. When people won't admit the danger is real, they act inappropriately. I'm afraid all the time; the only way you keep from getting hurt is being alert, being cautious, being aware of the dangers there are.
>
> Then we help their courage by building their confidence. I say, 'Look how quick we can get you cover!' – or, if he doesn't feel confident about his ability to handle a handgun, we take him to the range. We're not going to get rid of him because he's afraid, only if he can't handle the problem and his indecision may get other people hurt.

Sergeant Shepherd takes Second Avenue, traveling up past the Plaza and the U.S. Grant Hotel. He frequently uses the phrase 'professional police officer', and it seems likely that, as a policeman, his greatest fascination lies in sheer professionalism for its own sake, with the community at large reaping the benefit.

> I have never had a desire to go into investigations, but I must qualify that a little bit: the big thing that has kept me in patrol has been SWAT, and I've been in it now for six years. SWAT is budgeted for forty-eight officers and twelve sergeants, but it's never that large. We're down to possibly twenty-seven people –

my minimum team strength is ten, usually a pretty good number. Hostage situations, barricaded suspects, they're the two predominant things we deal with, but we also do VIP security work.

And tomorrow his SWAT team will be on standby when the head of the Ku Klux Klan in California, Tom Metzger, arrives at the courthouse in San Diego to take his elected seat on the Democratic Central Committee.

Something of a riot is expected.

3

Pondering the possibility of a different kind of riot, Officer Jim Bradford cruises slowly into the barrio, trying to assess the mood of the afternoon. He notices a familiar sports car parked outside a house next to a church: Sergeant Eduardo Juarez must be paying a Sunday visit to his parents.

Again deputizing for him, Jim Bradford goes farther on up into the Heights, stopping off at a 7-11 store for something to help quench his thirst. Not Perrier water, but a medium fountain Coke, with plenty of crushed ice and two straws. Then he continues to cruise the streets, keeping a watch for white Buicks.

It was a white Buick, eye-witnesses now say, that San Ysidro gang members were driving in Chicano Park last night when the fifteen-year-old was blasted by the shotgun. The Logan boy still has his shattered arm, but according to the latest report, it may yet have to be amputated.

Sipping his Coke, checking out alleys for parked vehicles, Jim Bradford works his way along street after street of jacaranda mauves, bougainvillaea pinks, bright leaf greens, a patchwork harmony of paintwork and living pigments, palms and dazzling whitewashed walls. A droll, slightly overweight man of thirty-two, he is five-eleven, dark-haired, wears an affable mustache, and has almost nine years' service, including some experience as a detective. He is also a Vietnam veteran – 'I spent most of the time in a tank', end of story – and an FTO. Unhurried in manner, his pervading calm can be tinged at times by weary resignation.

I was going to be a probation officer, and I went to college to do the social sciences. After a year, I couldn't accept a lot of it – these social workers and the fancy label they'll put on a problem. Up at Juvenile Hall on an internship, where you get fifteen-sixteen-year-old criminals who've committed robberies and burglaries and nothing's happened to them, it was: 'Don't *call* them criminals! Tell them they've gone astray, and we're going to put them back on the path of righteousness.' So I guess I found out that what I really wanted to do was to enforce the laws.

But all I do now is monitor crime – I don't see where we do any enforcement. Somewhere along the line, we've lost the backing of our court system. We arrest a juvenile out here for robbery or an assault, and the court says, 'Well, we really feel you're going to straighten up like you told us, we're not going to put any pressure on you, so we're letting you go home to mom and dad.' And as soon as he's back, he's doing it again. What's he got to lose? He's heard of so-and-so, who's been cut loose five or six times.

All these years, we've worried about these criminals, never the poor victim. Especially those who have retired, and whose whole life is in the little things they've got in their homes – until some fourteen-year-old goes in and steals them all.

Jim Bradford slows down, but the family up on the porch on the right, waving at him, don't want anything; they're just being friendly. Five years ago, before community-oriented policing properly got going, such a gesture of goodwill was rare.

This area of the city has a tremendous crime problem, but I'd rather work here than La Jolla; the people know what's going on, and you get fewer stupid complaints. It's a good squad, too. Some squads only want to make certain kinds of arrests, and don't want to get involved in chicken-shit family four-fifteens, but these guys are good all-round cops, take everything.

The radio explodes with static. 'Five-eleven-John,' says one of his squad. 'I'll be on foot in the area of Golden Park.'

'Ten-four,' responds Communications.

'Five-eleven-John, go TAC,' says another Heights officer. TAC is the radio channel on which officers can talk directly to each other, rather like using a phone. 'I've checked the east end of the park,' he goes on, 'and it's real quiet, only families. Looks like it's probably going to be a nice day.'

'Ten-four. I've got twenty, maybe thirty Logan boys, all sitting up here under a tree at the west end of the park.'

'Oh, okay. Keep your eye on them – thanks a lot.'

Maybe not such a nice day after all, Jim Bradford's expression suggests, as he finishes his Coke off.

It's got so our whole Sundays are taken up by the park. There's going to be a big fight up there, a big mini-type riot. Sherman think it's their park, and that they're going to run it, but they're sadly mistaken.

4

Rollerskaters are the chief worry of the moment, roughly two miles away across the big green square of the map marked Balboa Park, which includes Golden Hill Park in an isolated bottom corner, cut off by a golf course. Some skaters will persist in leaving the area designated for them, and their antics are hazardous to traffic and especially to young children using the main entrance over Cabrillo Bridge.

Sergeant Shepherd, parked at the entrance just off Sixth Avenue, watches as one of the skaters, a man of about thirty in a red track suit, is given a ticket by Officer Cindy Lewis. He is obviously indignant and waving his arms about, but Cindy Lewis is left to cope with him on her own, even if he does tower above her five-foot-six-and-a-bit.

When female officers were put in Patrol situations, I started to do what a lot of guys did: I started to be very, very protective. But it's not right, it stifles their ability to do a good job and stuff, and so, unlike a lot of other sergeants, I don't any more. I think the idea of female officers is working out very well.

But no sooner has she got back into her unit and driven off, than the skater in the red track suit starts to act sassy by breaking the law again, zigzagging out of the park through the traffic.

The sun catches the red stone in Sergeant Shepherd's ring as he beckons him over. 'I bet you can get out of those skates faster than I can write you a ticket . . .'

'Hey, she's just busted me for it, man!'

'I said, I bet you – '

'Yeah, but I could get out of the park faster than you could get your car turned around.'

'Probably, but I don't think you could outrun my radio.'

Sighing, the man sits down to unlace his skates. It delights Dave Shepherd when he manages to achieve a desired effect 'without expending a lot of energy'. This is possibly partly because SWAT training encourages the idea of conserving one's strength, and not only for the more obvious exertions either. Crouching perfectly still, hour after hour, on an exposed rooftop with a sniper's rifle, can also make enormous demands on an officer's fitness and stamina.

5

The officer assigned to Unit Five-Eleven-John, now out on foot patrol at the west end of Golden Hill Park, is another member of SWAT and, although he's been a policeman for only three and a half years, an FTO as well.

William Conroy, thirty-one, a gangling, loose-limbed San Diegan of Irish-Mexican descent, stands six-two, and has a laugh that could put the wind up a werewolf. What is more, he laughs a lot, and says of police work, 'We might not do much, but we do enjoy ourselves.' His dark hair is long, almost hiding his ears, his mustache is wider than his broad smile, and he wears smoke-tinted sunglasses with pink frames.

Strolling over the lawn in the center of the park, he pauses frequently to talk and joke around. Two boys, possible junior gang members, are shown a couple of arm holds they can try out on each other. A perspiring father, teaching his little daughter to rollerskate, welcomes an excuse to stop and discuss her progress, then William Conroy strolls on.

> When I was a kid, I grew up here in Logan, and during my teenage years, I grew up in Old Town – I won't work that side, because it would involve my old friends too much!

He wanders up to where the thirty-or-so Logan gang members are seated under a tree. There is immediate tension, and somebody mouths off the inevitable mumblings about pigs and their habits. William Conroy draws the group's attention to the litter of beer cans and fast-food wrappers they have strewn over the grass, keeping his tone light and amused.

'You guys have got ten minutes to clear it up,' he says, 'or I'm going to get picky on you – okay?'

'Okay, okay . . .'

> It takes a lot of restraint to take lip and try not to give it back, but I'm just kinda lucky. I was in the martial arts for about eight years, got my black belt, and that helps my self-control. You also find that unless you laugh at certain things, your job can get you down. I've seen it burn out a whole bunch of cops, because they've taken things too seriously, and it's saved me from a couple of fights, using humor. But we've got a lot of young cops who want to make an impression, and to them, smiling doesn't go hand in hand with being professional.

He approaches half a dozen Sherman gang members, who have placed two enormous speakers on the grass, breaking a municipal law by playing their tape deck in a public place. He smiles, talks a while, then tells them to put the speakers back into their cars, and to turn the sound level down. They comply, unwillingly but without a fuss, and he wanders back to his unit.

> Fairness is the basic requirement of Mexicans. If I went round and told everybody, 'Turn that music off!', it would just create unnecessary harsh feelings. I try to enforce by the spirit of the law. If you enforce by the letter of the law, there's really no challenge to it. Like there's so many nit-picking laws, I could stop almost *any* vehicle and enforce the letter, but I let some things slide. You could start a riot in Golden Hill Park by arresting all the under-twenty-ones drinking! The only time we go by the letter of the law, is when you're having a constant problem. I kind of set my own rules. I dislike people who hurt other people. I dislike people who steal from other people. And I do not like people who lie to me.

Back behind his steering wheel, William Conroy notes down some names and the numbers of the cars into which the speakers were returned: he keeps a journal on gang activity. Narcotics are also a special interest of his, and he is a qualified expert in them, putting him on a par with fellow FTO Doug Summers, the lip-reader – whose Spanish, incidentally, is no better than his own. 'I can understand a little bit,' says William Conroy, 'a few words here and there.'

He was in the Air Force, and then worked as a bartender for his brother, before deciding to do something more constructive with his life. He has a sister who became deeply involved in community work in the barrio.

> What's best is that I can basically do what I like, and at times, you can do things that'll help somebody else – you feel good inside you. Half the people down here are scared of the cops, because the ones they used to have down here didn't understand the culture.

Over the radio, he hears Phil Maddoc, the SWAT marksman, being given a call to go to the corner of Meade Avenue and Mississippi Street, where a man's behavior has upset a young woman and is causing a traffic hazard.

6

En route to Mississippi and Meade, Phil Maddoc exchanges a wave with Frank Cobb, who is heading the opposite way with a chunky young trainee beside him. Somebody has mentioned that the youngster used to be in construction.

A promising sign, in Phil Maddoc's opinion, and not merely because he was in the construction industry himself, before joining the department after about a year in the reserves. Both he and Frank Cobb believe that, in some ways, police-public relations have been adversely affected by 'raising standards' through favoring college graduates as recruits, without any regard for their experience of the 'real world'.

Or, in short, it isn't only in the barrio that a lack of understanding of cultural differences can lead to alienation and, in turn, to less effective community policing.

> I remember once I had a trainee, and this guy came up next to me at some lights and said, 'Hey, officer, you wanna drag race?' And the trainee next to me said, 'What's he talking about?'
> It's becoming a class thing, where these kids are getting a bit naive and they don't know how to communicate. What are they supposed to do when they come up against *really* something – and they're supposed to be the mediator?
> I came from a fairly affluent background, my parents were well-to-do, I never had to want for anything, but I wasn't spoiled, per se. I mean I lived on the street, I had a drag race car, I wore the Levi's and the blue jacket like everybody else. I had friends who were grease monkeys – all they did was work on their cars – and I had friends that were socialists, beach bums, so I knew both sides.

But these kids . . . Well, my dad used to say, 'You can lead a horse to water, but you can't make it drink.' The department has all these interpersonal relation classes, they shove it down your throat at the academy, but when they get out here, they don't practice it. It's incredible, I see it every day, and it just astounds me.

Up on the corner of Mississippi and Meade, a wide and otherwise deserted intersection in a residential area of small houses, a man of about twenty-seven is standing on the very edge of the curb. He is dressed in a soiled mauve shirt and soiled beige jeans, has a bag of groceries at his feet, and is looking directly into the afternoon sun, babbling at it with his arms raised imploringly. He teeters, making a passing Oldsmobile swerve out suddenly, almost clipping another vehicle.

Pulling up beside the man, Phil Maddoc gets out and asks him what he is doing.

'I don't know whether this will make you feel good or feel bad, officer – I'm praying.'

'What's your name, sir?'

'Henry Hector Quinn,' the man slurs.

Phil Maddoc tells him he is being arrested for being drunk and incapable of caring for his safety or the safety of others, handcuffs him, and gets him into the back of the unit. Then he picks up the grocery bag, which contains a six-pack, and puts it on the front passenger seat beside him.

'Now we know,' says Henry Quinn, slumping back, 'why the world is so fucked up.'

'This world is pretty bad out, huh?'

'Somebody stop this! Unbelievable!'

'You've been arrested before, Henry?'

'Has a Catholic ever gone to church?'

'That's yes?'

'I just want this to *stop*. I was just standing there, praying away – I was almost home. I live right there.'

Henry Quinn raises himself to jerk his chin at a small white frame house about a hundred yards away, then falls back again, his sweat-dank hair covering his face.

Phil Maddoc carries on filling in his particulars from a driver's license, then taps the grocery bag with his ball-point pen.

'I'll tell you what I'll do,' he says, 'I'll drop this stuff off on your doorstep – okay?'

'You can drop me there too.'

'If I let you out right now, let you loose on society, I wouldn't be doing my job.'

'It isn't that I've hurt somebody.'

'I know, because I found you first. I wouldn't be doing the job you expect me to do.'

'Nice try! Arrest the *innocent* people. I'll remember you the next time someone gets shot – oh, he was out arresting an innocent person! Ha, ha, ha . . .' Then he mumbles to himself, 'But what's *so* unbelievable . . .'

'Pardon me?'

'What's so unbelievable,' marvels Quinn, 'is that I'm just standing there, praying away, *and I'm not even fuckin' religious!*'

7

A couple of young boys in the barrio, in faded tee-shirts and patched jeans and old tennis shoes, run out of a front yard and flag down Jim Bradford.

'Hey!' they yell out.

'Hey, what?' he asks, stopping beside them.

'You got some stickers?'

He has just two left. These card facsimiles of the San Diego Police Department badge have adhesive backs, and come with blank spaces where children can print their names and a made-up ID number.

'You kids,' says Jim Bradford, who has three children of his own, 'are drivin' me crazy – "Gimme a sticker!" '

Two blocks farther down, Jim Bradford slows up when he sees an officer standing at the driver's door of a beaten-up blue Dodge, but gets the Code Four hand signal to say no assistance is needed. Like quite a few others, this particular officer barely comes up to his shoulder; minimum height requirements no longer exist.

> Size doesn't mean anything. A guy can be short, and still do the job. But a lot of your small guys come on here and they seem to have this macho-ego thing – an inferiority complex, is what I refer

to it as. That causes a lot of problems. If you talk to any of these hardline crooks or street people out here, they'll tell you they're very wary of somebody that's small.

A white car emerges from a cross street several hundred yards away. Jim Bradford picks up speed, identifies it as a Buick, and informs Communications he is about to make a hot stop on it, naming the alley into which the car has just disappeared. Red light flashing, and with a yelp of his siren, he pursues the white Buick, which slides to a halt in a cloud of pink dust.

Jumping out, revolver ready, Jim Bradford orders the two men out of the car, just as a second unit arrives to provide cover. The men are Mexican, their English is poor, and they appear very frightened. Then they begin to relax as Jim Bradford, conceding nothing to the drama of the moment, questions them quietly in his usual low tones, asking for IDs and for an idea of where they've been and where they are going. While this is going on, the young cover officer dives into the Buick, roots about under the seats, and searches the trunk.

The two Mexicans give a satisfactory account of themselves, and are allowed to continue on their way, but the young officer finds himself being detained for a severe reprimand. What he's just done constituted an illegal search, and had, say, the Chicano Park shotgun been found, then it would not have been admissible as evidence in court.

Chastened, the young officer backs out of the alley, and leaves, while Jim Bradford makes some notes on an FI pad. In other circumstances, he might not have been as hard on him.

Personally, I think I'd rather see trainees come out and be a little over gung-ho and get into it, because that way you're going to learn, and time is on our side when it comes to crooks. If you kind of work too fast, mess up on a lot of technicalities, he'll get cut loose. But a few years down the road, you'll meet him again, and this time you'll be a lot smarter, a lot wiser, and he's gone for five years. You walk out of that courtroom, and for about a week, you're on a high that's better than any drug or any alcohol could put you on.

8

'Oh, it's much more pleasant now than it was six years ago,
when I first came on,' Frank Cobb is saying to his trainee, as
they respond to a prowler call near Old Town. 'It wasn't
uncommon at all to have someone take a shot at you in a dark
alley, or throw a brick at your car as you go by.'

'How about up in LA?'

'LA's got a lot worse problems, and I think it's in some part
due to the fact their police officers are more trigger-happy than
ours. If you do a stop here, pull some guy over that just gets off
the freeway from LA – some black or Chicano who lives up
there – you always know this, because as soon as the car's at
the curb, the first thing you see is four hands out on the roof!'

'Yeah? So they won't get shot by mistake?'

'That's the way things are, up there,' says Frank Cobb,
before adding, with a laugh, 'It's no wonder the people start
shooting – even the crook has a survival instinct! There's been
some studies done that most officers who die from gunshot
wounds actually die from shock, rather than from being
mortally wounded. They begin to develop this invincible
attitude, and when you *are* actually violated – someone tries to
stab or to shoot you – then psychologically you aren't
prepared for it. It's a heck of a shock! Whereas a crook always
assumes he's going to get – '

They have arrived. Just ahead of them, two little girls, aged
about eight and eleven, in impeccable bright summer clothes,
are waiting at the curb. The older one does all the speaking.

'Me and my friend were crossing the street right here, and
this man was coming along with this dog, and he followed us
all the way to that old house over there, and he hid behind the
bush. When he'd finished hiding behind the bush, we
watched him carefully. He came to this house, and was
watching everywhere, and then went into this alley.'

'What was he wearing?' asks Frank Cobb.

'He was wearing a light-blue Deta shirt, dark-blue pants.'

'And he was Mexican?'

'Yeah.'

'With a mustache?'

227

'Yeah, and glasses – sunglasses.'

'And how old do you think he was?'

'About thirty-five, maybe.'

'You're sure of that? How old do you think I am?'

'Thirty-seven?'

'No, I'm thirty-two.'

'He was really old.'

Frank Cobb smiles. 'At least as old as me, huh? Okay, you live around here?' And when she has given him her name and address, he says: 'Why don't you go home, and I'll come back and talk to you in a few minutes, after we go to look for him?'

The children hurry off, skipping with excitement, and looking very pleased with themselves.

Frank Cobb is pleased with them, too. 'I've been in a neighborhood like this in an unmarked car,' he says, getting back into the unit, 'and I've sat and watched for hours, and you see people look out at you, but they never call the department. It's ridiculous, people just don't call in.' Then he begins the search by turning down the alley.

His trainee, peering at the backs of the houses passing by on either side, murmurs, 'A male Mexican with a blue sports shirt . . .'

'Blues and reds are bad,' Frank Cobb warns him. 'If they say "blue", I always look for red – or, if they say "a red car", I look for a blue one. I've caught the right suspects when the victim has clearly said, "two black males" – and it's been *white* males with blond hair!'

'How come?'

'They go stereotyping, y'know. They start believing that everybody who goes robbing is black, so when they become a victim, they automatically perceive the people as black – and they truly believe they're black!'

9

Carl Brunner, looking purposeful, is on his way up Twenty-fifth Street to Golden Hill Park, having just had a very useful interview with an elderly Mexican lady whose English was fortunately fairly good.

Communication problems, rather than perceptual ones involving stereotyping, tend to complicate police work in the Heights.

> I took three years of Spanish in school, but it's like everything else, you have to practice it every day to remember it – and school Spanish isn't much use in the barrio. I can get by asking their car numbers, where they're going, but I can't carry on a conversation with them.
>
> I wish I could, because it's almost mandatory up here. Plus, when you question a lot of these guys, they'll talk to each other in Spanish, because they don't think you can speak it. If you can listen to what they're saying, a lot of times you pick up good information.

His luck seems in today, however, because the information he's just picked up sounded as though it couldn't be bettered.

> I got a burglary report. I went round to do my witnesses check, and it so happened an elderly lady, who's retired, saw this Mexican guy walk up to the victim's house, and he was peering in the windows, casing it out real good, and he had a harmonica.

10

After dropping off the praying man at the detox, Phil Maddoc has been checking out some of the more remote corners of Balboa Park such as Pepper Grove, a favorite haunt of drug dealers and, after dark, of transvestites who frolic there in long flowing lingerie like wood nymphs. Now working his way back toward the Organ Pavilion, he coasts down the steep curve into Gold Gulch.

Over on the far right-hand side of the picnickers' parking lot is an interesting sight: three young men – probably U.S. Navy, to go by their short haircuts, blue denims and well-scrubbed look – are talking to a biker, swarthy as a pirate, with long unkempt hair, a gold earring, and a blue bandana, who is seated beneath a shady tree, his easy-rider machine beside him.

Noticing the approaching unit, the biker makes a sudden stealthy move, as though placing something underneath him, while at the same time, one of the young men withdraws something in an outstretched hand, and stuffs it back into his pocket.

'Afternoon, gentlemen!' says Phil Maddoc, stepping out of his unit and slipping his baton into its belt ring. 'What's going on here?'

'Sir? Nothing, sir!'

Phil Maddoc was right. The blue-denim trio identify themselves as sailors, down for the afternoon from Balboa U.S. Navy Hospital, adjoining the park. He makes one stand at the rear of his unit, another at the front, and the third an equal distance away, before questioning each one very quietly. Then, satisfied they had been about to buy some marijuana from the biker, he goes over to him.

The biker produces his ID, and opens the canvas bag he has on his lap, showing its contents to be perfectly innocuous. Phil Maddoc asks him to stand up, but can see nothing hidden there in the flattened circle of dry grass. The biker smiles knowingly.

He must have the marijuana in his pocket.

A radio check on the biker and his machine comes back as 'no wants' – no outstanding warrants.

Foiled, Phil Maddoc gets back into his unit, watches the sailors make off hurriedly, and then drives out of Gold Gulch, having at least had the satisfaction of putting a warning shot across the pirate's bows.

I didn't have enough probable cause to search him, so therefore I couldn't search him – and he's been arrested before, so he knows basically what's going on. You can do a cursory search, a very brief, pat-down kind of thing, but only if you have reason to suspect the person has a weapon or whatever, and that you or somebody else is in danger.

11

Probable cause – or just PC, as it's commonly known – probably causes trainee officers more problems and anxieties than anything else.

'Police work is funny,' says Doug Summers. 'You do something that's questionable, you get some big dope deal, and they say, "Good job!" You do the same thing a second time, and someone complains, then they say, "You shouldn't do that!" It confuses policemen a lot.'

Trying to reduce the confusion is part of his duties as an FTO when one of his trainees asks where to draw the line.

A lot of times we create our own problems, simply by the way we conduct ourselves. There's *a very fine line* between police work and criminal activity. You're going to say, 'Hey, wait a minute! That's bullshit! We're like – y'know, night and day.' But it's not like night and day. How many times do you speed coming to work?

Take it a step further. We stop a car. You *know* there's narcotics in that trunk, but you have no reasonable probable cause for arrest or to search the trunk. Legally and lawfully, you shouldn't do a damned thing to the person, but *because* you have this expertise and knowledge, you go ahead and break into that trunk, you obtain drugs. Now you have a choice: most cops won't arrest because it'll be a bad arrest. They'll say, 'Okay, we got the dope this time,' and to their subconscious mind they'll say, 'Well, it's for the good of the world and me and everybody in the community. I did it because I didn't want the stuff distributed all over the place. Yeah, I did the right thing, even though it was the wrong thing.' You moralize it, but it's *still wrong*.

I think you should be an example for everybody. What I've said is, 'Hey, I know what you have – if I search, I'll find it and I can take you to jail. But I don't do that. You continue doin' what you're doin', then I'm going to get you some day.' You play everything above the board, and you'll have a lot more respect – even from the crooks. Because then they'll know when you do get them, that you've *got* them, and there's no argument about it.

Provided, Jim Bradford would add, the trainee – or indeed, fullblown officer – is able to document the case effectively, no matter how probable the probable cause involved.

This is a problem we're having: a lot of guys are unable to justify in writing what they did. They use phrases like, 'the area has a high crime rate', period. A city or district attorney isn't even going to issue if that's all they read. All areas of the city have a high crime rate!

You have to spell out that this certain area has a high burglary rate between two and four o'clock in the morning, and that you stopped the guy at three o'clock. Then the trick is to make the DA see the same thing as you saw at the time of the arrest.

You say, 'He was evasive to all of my questions, he didn't live in the area, he had no friends in the neighborhood, his hands were trembling, his voice was breaking, and he was constantly licking his lips.' Ah, now the DA knows what he's dealing with – this guy was scared!

And if you testify to something that's not included, the defense is going to object, and you're not going to get that little extra piece of information, which may win the case, into court. In fact, we've got a saying, 'If it's not in your report, it never happened.'

The importance of articulate report-writing is often stressed by those who protest at educational requirements being lowered to encourage minority recruitment. Some of the protesters are minority officers themselves, who met the department's previous standards and now feel they are being unjustly forced to share in 'the same stigma'.

Veteran sergeant: I'm not a racist and I don't disagree with equal opportunity but, goddamnit, either you set the standards or you don't. If you want a brain surgeon, you don't hire a plumber. They don't make past tenses out of the verbs, when the whole paragraph is in the past tense, and it reads like some idiot wrote it. I even saw a report where the suspect 'put his penis in the victim's *virginia . . .'*

But minority officers are not alone in finding difficulty with report-writing – far from it, in Jim Bradford's opinion. Just how literate one has to be, and how careful to establish probable cause, may be gauged by this extract from a report on a simple drugs arrest, written to the required standard.

I have been a San Diego Police Officer for approximately (2) years. During this period of time I have received (40) hours of Academy Training in the identification and packaging of drugs and narcotics. I have observed marijuana in excess of (100) times. In a great majority of these cases the marijuana was packaged in clear plastic sandwich baggies. I have noted during my training and street experience that a baggie (lid/ounce) of marijuana can sell for $20 to $80. The sale price is usually dependent upon the naivety of the buyer.

I have been assigned as a uniformed patrol officer in the downtown area for the past (12) months. I have become aware of the problem areas on my beat. I have also become aware of those problem individuals who live on or frequent my beat. 200 'E' Street has been identified as a problem area because of the constant narcotics activity. I have personally arrested over (25) individuals for various narcotics violations over the past (6) months.

I have personally arrested James Douglas (4) times in the past year; (2) arrests were for grand theft and (2) arrests were for sales of marijuana. Both marijuana arrests took place at 200 'E' Street.

On Tuesday, June 14, 1980, at approximately 1200 hours, Officer Keeble and I were on foot patrol in the area of 200 'E' Street. I conduct periodic checks of this area because of the high incidence rate of narcotics activity. Officer Keeble and I walked southbound on the eastside of the Central Federal Building. As we approached the rear patio area that fronts 200 'E' Street we observed (2) subjects standing under a tree on the patio. There was approximately 60' between the (2) subjects and us, and we had an unobstructed view. We both recognized one of the subjects as James Douglas because of prior contacts with him.

Officer Keeble and I observed Douglas for approximately (2) minutes. During this time he continuously looked in different directions while talking to the second subject. Douglas then pulled a clear plastic baggie out of his upper right jacket pocket (brown waist-length jacket) and handed it to the other subject. This subject immediately unrolled the baggie, and then examined the contents by rolling it through his fingers (left thumb and index finger), and then smelling it. I immediately associated these observations with that of a narcotics transaction. I have made numerous narcotics arrests where clear plastic sandwich baggies were used to package marijuana. It is also very common for a buyer to closely examine the marijuana he is negotiating to buy. The second subject handed the baggie back to Douglas, then removed an unknown amount of cash from his left front pants pocket. He counted the money then handed it to Douglas. Douglas placed the money in his right front pants pocket, and at the same time handed the baggie back to the buyer.

And that's less than half what this report comes to . . .

12

Agent Tom Hamilton, on his way up to Hillcrest again from the detox, passes two men acting suspiciously under a sidewalk canopy outside a defunct nightspot. He circles the block and comes back to them, just in time to see one taking from the other what might be a Marlboro filter-tip but is almost certainly a marijuana joint. Both react with a guilty start when they see he has returned. He gets out and goes over to talk to them.

A downtown officer, cruising by, slows down and stops. Agent Hamilton is something of a legend in the San Diego Police Department, having an unrivaled reputation for survival against what are considered impossible odds. And yet, standing over there on the sidewalk, he looks just an average-sized guy, around his mid-thirties, brown hair, mustache, big expressive eyes, some smile lines, roundish face. To the trained eye, he wears no armored vest, and his handgun is a regular Smith and Wesson stainless steel .38, nothing awesome. But most people would just notice his Corfam shoes, which shine like patent leather, and his digital watch, which has an ornate silverwork strap set with blue stones.

Agent Hamilton leaves the two men under the canopy and nods a greeting to his downtown colleague, double-parked beside him.

'Dope deal?'

'Uh-huh.'

'PC?'

'Thought I'd just rattle their cage a little bit, make them paranoid about the paranoid,' says Agent Hamilton, then mimics a street accent, 'My God, the paranoids are after us!'

The downtown officer laughs, and drives on, his expression somewhat uncertain.

Agent Hamilton, the two-striper in Sergeant Shepherd's squad, gets back into his unit and reaches for his cigarettes, which he has a habit of tucking into a different cranny of the car each time he has one. He lights up and pulls away from the curb, singing softly to himself, 'Cupid draw back your bow, and let your arrow go . . .'

A lotta cops go around paranoid. I refuse to be paranoid. I'll walk into a situation where eight or ten cops would hesitate to go, and I've been lucky. I just treat people the way I'd like to be treated – unless they give me reason to treat them otherwise – no matter what they've done. A lotta cops take it personally and their emotions take over. But I'm not the judge and jury; my job is to take them to jail, that's all. I don't care if they've cut their twelve-month-old baby in half with a butcher knife.

And when it comes to armored vests and large handguns, he just shrugs and says, 'I work with hands more than I work with guns. Of course, there's always the unexpected, but it would make *somebody* happy . . .'

Agent Hamilton, who is of Irish extraction, must be slightly older than he looks.

I was a fireman in the Air Force for two years, and when I got out, I

234

needed a job straight away, so I was a fireman for another seven years, here in my own neighborhood in San Diego. I came on the department twelve years ago, and was in Detectives for four years. If you want to shuffle paper and run round in a suit, go ahead, but if you want to be a cop, this is where it's at.

And agent really is a good position. The rank has been around for about two years. It's a nonsupervisor position, but you're still a squad leader. Other officers will come to you for advice, they'll call you when they wouldn't normally call for the sergeant. I handle training for the squad, and if they need anything researched over the weekend, I'll go to the computer and get it all. Agent carries five percent more pay than patrolman, then there's time and a half for overtime and stuff – like today is a twenty-hour day.

Chief Kolender's original intent was to make agent a reward for the senior officer and give him a little incentive to stay in the force. But it had to be a civil service position, and was therefore subject to civil service rules – now the requirement is twice that for sergeant. A sergeant is four years in the San Diego PD and thirty college credits; an agent is four years and *sixty* college credits.

'A jumper,' says Communications. 'We have a report of a possible jumper on a bridge in the park. White female.'

'Five-Thirty-Four from Ash,' says Agent Hamilton.

'Ten-four.'

His face is clouded as he picks up speed. Tom Hamilton may be able to remain emotionally detached when dealing with suspects, but a depth of feeling is something more obvious in him than in most police officers, which may explain how he wins the trust of people so readily. Right now, he looks as though he can already see what lies ahead of him, up the Cabrillo Freeway.

You get these jumpers, and it's almost always the same. You go up to where they jumped from, the bridge, and they've put them all out in a little line: their purse, their glasses, social security card. We need a lot for our senior citizens – that's our most neglected minority. We have senior citizens downtown trying to make it on a hundred and eighty dollars a month social security. They're eating dog food.

13

Agent Tom Hamilton hasn't sung again, not since reaching the bridge and finding everything as he predicted: the pathetic row of possessions on the parapet, the crumpled white-haired body below, further mutilated by being hit by a truck. The truck driver had been beside himself, eyes glazed, talking about his mother.

Fortunately, however, another unit and a car from the California Highway Patrol has got here first, so Unit Five-Thirty-Four is free to respond to a robbery report at the Flowerbed on the Sixth Avenue side of Balboa Park. It doesn't sound too promising, but at least it's a diversion.

Agent Hamilton slows down outside the park, stopping beside a shy-looking man near a pay phone.

'Are you the person who's been robbed, sir?'

'Well, what happened, officer, was me and my friend were over there on the grass, and this black guy came over and he was talking with us. Then he said, "Well, I've got to leave now," and my friend saw that his wallet, that'd been on the blanket, was gone. My friend said, "Wait a minute, buddy! My wallet!" But the black guy just walked away, and I went to call the department.'

'Okay, would you like to get in and show me where this was, sir?'

The Flowerbed looks very peaceful, as Agent Hamilton reaches the scene, parks and goes over to interview the victim. Then things turn a fraction weird.

'The guy came back,' says the victim. 'Talked a little bit, and when he went again, my wallet was right here. You can see it.'

'Where did the guy go?'

'There he is, just over there.'

And he points to a young black man, walking toward a canvas bag at the foot of a palm tree not ten yards distant. Agent Hamilton calls out to him, and he stops. He produces some ID, says he's from Phoenix, and denies having touched the wallet.

Then Agent Hamilton spots a canister of Mace sticking out of his pocket. 'What is this?' he asks, placing his hand on it.

'That's my Mace.'

Taking it from him, which is permissible as it's a weapon in full view, Agent Hamilton says that it is a felony to carry Mace without the proper training and authorization.

'I carry it because I was stabbed and I need protection,' says

236

the young black man from Phoenix. 'I didn't know you had to go to school to carry it.'

He is arrested, and Agent Hamilton picks up his canvas bag to put it in the unit. There is something hard and heavy in the bottom of the bag.

It feels exactly like an automatic pistol.

And conjures up sudden vivid pictures of how different things might have been, had the unit arrived a few seconds later.

Although there's really no telling, and Agent Hamilton doesn't so much as blink. 'Okay, let's go,' he says, resisting the temptation to verify his guess until a legal search of the bag can be made.

> Some curious rookie, reaching in there and yanking it out, he's lost it. That's why the FTO program is so extremely important: the FTO has his trainee's whole career in his hands. There's a lot of officers kicked off the program for various reasons.

14

The most compelling reason being when an FTO's conduct is not only morally reprehensible, but exposes a trainee to the likelihood of death or injury through a lack of proper guidance.

> *Field Training Officer:* I had this female trainee and she's all uptight. I spent two or three days with her, and she's still all uptight. She's not relaxed, and she's not functioning properly. Finally, I got her to talk about it, and I found out that her past FTO had made advances. He told her that if she would do these sexual things, she'd get through her FTO training phase with no problems – she'd be all signed off, and her evaluation would be satisfactory. Whereas, in reality, as a police officer she needed help. She said, 'I guess I'm waiting for you to tell me you want some sexual favors.'

Not that there isn't a reverse side to the same coin, minted when female officers were granted equal opportunity in the department.

> *Officer John Doe:* She was such a nice girl, a really good-looking girl, but she did a one-eighty on me after she'd been on the department a while. What really pisses me off is that when a really good-looking girl comes on, they cater to them so much I can't

believe it – it's like, 'Oh, gosh – they're *gold!*' Then she did a one-eighty. I caught her in bed with one of the training officers and everything. She's got two years on and already she's a ––––, which is a really choice position. The guys used to hate her where she worked patrol because she wouldn't get into fights because she didn't like to mess up her hair.

15

Jim Bradford, reassured that all looks peaceful enough up at Golden Hill Park for the moment, follows William Connor's unit past the tree with SAD GIRL LOMAS painted on it, and then down Twenty-fifth Street. William Connor, on his way to a family fight, turns off left, but Jim Bradford continues right down to Imperial, where Tony's Liquor Store stays: *Open 7 A.M. until 2 A.M.* It is always worth casting an eye over the potential trouble standing about on the sidewalks outside, paper bags around their bottles.

Then Jim Bradford makes his own left turn, and resumes his watch for white Buicks.

Suddenly, immediately to his left, there are three loud reports from inside a complex of cream-painted frame houses. And yet another bang, as he reaches for his hand mike.

'Five-fifteen-William . . .'

'Five-fifteen-William!' comes a cheerful response from Communications.

'A possible eleven-six has just occurred, thirty-one-hundred Imperial in the north alley. I'll be checking on it.'

'Ten-four,' says the Communications operator, solemnly.

Code 11-6: *Discharging firearms.*

Parking his unit out of sight around the corner, Jim Bradford unsnaps his holster, opens his car door, and murmurs to himself, 'Well, maybe I should have worn my vest today . . .'

Then he gets out and approaches the north alley.

16

'Cupid draw back your bow, and let your arrow go,' Agent Hamilton sings softly to himself, as he makes his way back to the station on West Market from the county jail.

Beside him, on his passenger's seat, is a .380 Browning automatic, containing one live round in its magazine clip, inside a zip-up leather case. There is also an impounded canister of Mace.

The automatic, his prisoner from the park has explained to him, is one he has carried since being robbed and stabbed in May. It was bought off a friend of his who belongs to the Piru, a black gang much on a par with the West Coast Crips.

And when Agent Hamilton reaches the station, he is going to run a few computer checks. Not only on the handgun, but on the prisoner himself, who has a distinctive one-inch scar across his chin that someone, somewhere, may just have remembered after an armed robbery or something.

A frantic figure flags him down from the edge of a small park; a gaunt, unshaven man of about fifty in urine-stained baggy pants, a jacket with burst seams and no shirt.

'Officer, I already called the FBI!'

'You did?'

'Said they'll be here in two minutes. Look at this!'

The gaunt man glances up into the sky, then quickly exposes part of his forearm. It's a little dirty, that's all.

'They do that from outer space,' he whispers.

'Okay, just wait for the FBI man then.'

'Just look at my sunburn! That's lasers too! The FBI will come?'

'They'll be right here.'

'Thanks, officer!'

Agent Hamilton pulls slowly away from the curb, taking another look at the man in his rear-view mirror as he returns to sprawl beneath a small palm.

Now that right there is sad. I bet you he has nobody in the world, just loneliness and booze. And just because he happens to be a bum, doesn't look too presentable, there's no reason to kick him out of the park. He's not violating any law; lying there in the day time, that's what the park is for. I make as many arrests – or more – than anybody, but that's of people that have done something wrong.

239

17

Fireworks. That's all those loud bangs on Imperial turn out to be: four silly firecrackers lying in the north alley. But as the sale of fireworks is prohibited in California, and the sound of gunshots not uncommon in the barrio, Jim Bradford can at least comfort himself that his qualified first assumption was a reasonable one, even if it has left him a little high.

But the adrenalin doesn't go to waste. Hardly is he back in his unit, before Communications passes on a Traffic motorcycle officer's report that a riot has started in Golden Hill Park. In seconds Jim Bradford is on his way.

Over the radio, he can hear four other units, closer to the scene, volunteering cover.

Twenty-fifth Street seems to last forever, and then he is through the park entrance, and being waved on by two Traffic officers who have blocked off the driveway. Round he goes to the west end, pulling in behind three parked units, left with their doors open.

A fifth unit is parked up on the lawn near the restrooms, just short of a mob of about forty gang members and their girl friends in confrontation with five officers. One gang member, a stocky youth in a white undershirt, is shaking his fists at a Puerto Rican trainee from New York, and coming out with a stream of defiant obscenities. The air is electric, but nothing seems to have happened as yet.

'This came out as a riot,' Jim Bradford says to William Conroy, who moves down to meet him on his approach.

William Conroy gives a shrug, indicating that police perceptions can vary depending on one's role in the department, but without making any less of a serious situation. The incident had started out as a fight between two gang members, he explains, and the Puerto Rican trainee and a Mexican officer had gone in to break it up. But they'd been surrounded by gang members, and had had to stand back to back, more or less in fear of their lives, until help had arrived. Tempers are running high on both sides, and there could be an explosion of violence at any moment.

The stocky youngster in the undershirt, still yelling at the

240

trainee, starts motioning for other gang members, hanging back under a tree, to come over and join in.

'That really pisses me off no end,' says Jim Bradford, advancing swiftly. 'I've got to contact him straight away.'

Jim Bradford moves into the crowd, and tells the stocky youth to quit trying to incite everyone. The youth lunges forward insolently, and is immediately arrested by the trainee and his Mexican partner, who handcuff him and bundle him into the back of the unit. This obviously gives them grim satisfaction, but the crowd reacts angrily, closing in.

'Hey, what you doin'?' somebody yells out. 'Pee Wee didn't do nothin', motherfucker!'

But Jim Bradford ignores him, beckoning instead to the leaders of the three groups of gang members. 'Hey, can we talk a minute?' he says calmly.

For a tense moment, the mood of the crowd teeters on the brink, and there is no knowing what weapons the girls have concealed. Then, after exchanging glances, the three leaders give grudging nods of assent, and walk with Jim Bradford back down to his unit.

'Okay, Pee Wee was fightin',' says one of the leaders, 'but that – '

'Listen,' interrupts Jim Bradford, 'and I'll tell you what the position is . . .'

He glances back at the crowd. It seems to have quietened down a little, curious to know what its leaders are having said to them, and William Connor is cracking a few jokes, winning a smile here and there. Some of the girls seem to be actually rooting for the trainee, who has started to smile again too.

The position, Jim Bradford explains to the three men in front of him, is very simple: the prisoner will be released on condition there is no further violence in the park this Sunday.

'You gonna cut Pee Wee loose?'

'And we got permission to stay in the park?'

'Yeah, that's what I'm saying.'

Once again, the leaders exchange looks.

'All of us?' asks Logan.

'Right – but I want no more of this. There'll be no more fighting. You can stay here, enjoy yourselves and – '

'You gotta hit somebody if he steps outta line,' cuts in Lomas.

241

'What we're going to do,' says Jim Bradford, 'if we have to come back to the park, we'll start by taking you three out.'

Sherman grins. 'You know what? Let me – '

'We'll take you out *first* – and to jail. People have got families and kids around here, man.'

Now all three leaders are smiling, plainly flattered to have their own authority recognized in this way.

'Everything is fine, man!' exclaims the Sherman leader, nodding hard. 'If they fuck up again, you can do anything you want, man, because we don't want people hurt and – well, we understand, man, you're doin' your job, man, and we'll not make it hard for you, man. And if anyone fucks up, you take him, man, and I'll help you do it, because I don't like people fuckin' up myself, man, because I love my brother, man.'

'Okay.'

'Right *on*, man!' says Lomas.

'Thank you, man, thank you!' says Logan. 'We fuck up, you come back, okay?'

'You fuck up, we'll be back.'

'I'm cool, man,' says Sherman, 'I'm cool – you *know* who I *am*. Thank you, man!'

And off they go to disperse the mob, which relaxes its mood almost instantly, but the trainee's face is like thunder when word reaches him to release his prisoner. It's a look that suggests this whole affair could have been settled far better by rushing in extra manpower and clearing the park, even if that would have meant filling up half the county jail. ·

'Oh, shit, I should've gone over to talk to him,' Jim Bradford says to William Conroy. 'I never liked it as a patrolman when the sergeant would intervene – I disliked doing it today, but at least we've maintained the peace.'

Chief Kolender: The name of the game is the officer asking himself: 'Will my solution have a more negative effect on the community than the problem I'm trying to solve?' That's the philosophy I want to see in this department. You can't allow criminals to run loose, you can't allow people to get hurt, you can't allow property to be damaged, but you've got to look at the big picture through a wide-angle lens, pal. And when my officers do that, I love it – I love it!

18

And suddenly it isn't afternoon any longer. Things have begun to look different. There has been an almost imperceptible shift from clean remorseless sunlight to a slightly bluish haze that brings with it a hint of unreality, like soft-focus scenes in early three-reelers.

'Five-Thirty-Five William?'

Phil Maddoc reaches for the hand mike. 'Five-Thirty-Five William . . .'

He had been thinking of taking another ride down into Pepper Grove. But in seconds he's plunged instead into the world of Ross Macdonald – or indeed of Raymond Chandler, who once lived and wrote in nearby La Jolla.

Not that there is much suggestion of this at the start. All he has is an address in a rather dull neighborhood of rather dull, modest homes, and some idea that the garbled message received by Communications had touched on child-stealing.

'The man says he'll meet you up there,' adds Communications. 'He's by a pay phone.'

Phil Maddoc makes his way across Hillcrest to the address given, and finds himself at a small general store that is closed on Sundays. There is a pay phone on the parking lot, however, and beside it are parked a yellow Bentley and a silver Mercedes Benz. He approaches them, stops and gets out.

A dapper little man in his mid-fifties, wearing a black blazer and with his hair brushed flat, emerges lightly from the Mercedes. From the Bentley comes a brawny six-footer, manicured and fleshy-jowled, leaving behind him a wide-eyed silent child on the lap of a hard-faced woman who looks very out of place.

'Jesus Christ, is it good to see you, officer!' he exclaims, quickly introducing himself as Mr Tony Tomacelli, the father of the child in question. 'Jesus Christ, you gotta do something *right now!*'

He is dressed casually in several hundred dollars' worth of open-neck shirt, pants, fancy belt and fancier shoes. His wrist watch would probably buy a family car, and his gold identity

243

bracelet, a speedboat to tow behind it. He has a lot of gleaming black hair, some sprouting from his chest, some from his nostrils, some from the backs of his hands, which he waves about a lot and uses to keep pointing to an abrasion at the side of his neck.

The gist of his complaint isn't too easy to follow at first, probably because of his agitation and because he can't keep an imperious ring from offsetting what would otherwise be a humble cry for help.

'The harassment!' he says. 'You see my neck? Where her mother broke my gold chain off? You shoulda heard the language she uses! I can't take any more.'

'Okay, so you said you were the ex-husband or something?'

'Jesus Christ, they tried to take my baby away from me. You know how much I had to pay some guy to find it? Twenty grand, officer – *twenty grand*. So I want you to come and arrest these people, take them all to jail!'

'The mother of your baby is – '

'She wears a big cross, but she curses and screams! Please, officer, you gotta help me.'

'She's your ex-wife?'

Tomacelli shakes his head. 'I just want my baby. These people aren't fit! I can't take the harassment! You know where the baby was that time? Montreal!'

Gradually, with some help from the dapper little man, who smiles somewhat enigmatically most of the time, Phil Maddoc pieces together a rough idea of what this is all about. Tomacelli is the 'natural father' of a child born to an unmarried mother of twenty-two who lives with her parents. As the father, Tomacelli has 'Sunday rights' to the child, expiring at six o'clock in the evening, and so earlier, at five-fifty, he had turned up at the parental home to return the child to its mother. But this was when everything had gone wrong, he alleges. According to his story, the child's grandmother had come out to the car, had said her daughter was at church, and had tried to claim the child. Tomacelli had refused her custody, and had been sworn at and assaulted, having his gold chain ripped off in the process. He had then gone round to the church, where the child's mother had also cursed at him, attacked him, and had tried to drag the child out of the car, but he'd decided she was unfit to have it. Now he wants

244

both women arrested for assault, and the grandmother for attempted child-stealing.

'Okay, you'll do that?' says Tomacelli. 'You follow me in my car – the place is just a few blocks away.'

Noncommittal, Phil Maddoc says he will look into the matter, and returns to his unit.

But the place isn't just a few blocks away. It turns out to be over in the next police division. This intrigues Phil Maddoc, who can't help wondering why Tomacelli drove all the way into Central to find a pay phone.

19

Even in the fading light, the colors of the *Barrio Sherman Mural*, as it's entitled, are astonishingly vivid.

Better known, perhaps, are the murals down at Chicano Park, which have been painted on the giant T-sections of reinforced concrete that support the freeway ramps curving above it. One shows three excellent portraits of Ché Guevara, each from a different angle, above this quotation: *Let me say, at the risk of seeming ridiculous, that the true revolutionary is guided by great feelings of love – Ché.* Another, less sophisticated mural, using symbolism and a comic-strip technique, purports to tell the story of *The Undocumented Worker*, beginning with a scene where a U.S. Border Patrol is hunting illegal aliens, and ending with a wall being smashed down to signify the destruction of all social barriers. Not all the Chicano Park murals have a political bias, however: some simply celebrate everyday life in the barrio, while others appear inspired by Aztec mythology, resulting in some very strong and complex designs. Among this type of work is a panel of writhing serpentlike monsters that must be one of the finer sights in San Diego.

But just as worthy, in William Conroy's view, is the Sherman mural that he is passing right now, up in the Heights. It is a remarkable composition, covering one side of a building, and has unity as its basic theme. Set against a backdrop dominated by the bridge to Coronado, its various other elements range from Aztec temples to a church and the white dove of peace, from rural life in Old Mexico to contemporary street life in the United States, and just off center, creating a violent discord, is a shrieking death's head. It was begun by an ex-con who was trying to rehabilitate the local ex-cons. There have been at least two stabbings over it.

Then the mural vanishes from sight, and William Conroy's attention switches to a low-rider that looks all set to run a stop sign.

But the radio intervenes, coming alive with a burst of urgent voices. It's all fragmented.

A fight.

Lomas members outside some stores.

Sticks and chains.

Young white male attacked.

Two white males in rifle counter-attack.

Rifle pair escaping in gray Ford pickup truck.

Already hastening toward the scene, William Conroy spots the pickup careening into a cross street out of an alley. He grabs his hand mike, radios the locality, and gives chase.

The next two minutes or so are pure, exhilarating Hollywood corn: roaring motors, screaming tires, big dips and bounces, the gap closing every second. The pickup blows a front tire, veers wildly, and dives down a steep alley. The unit gets right on its tail, peppered by flying pebbles and small rocks, still gaining. The fugitives must be allowed no respite in which to turn and fire, no time to think of a good escape route. Desperate, the pickup makes a sudden right – taking it straight into a cul-de-sac, where it plunges under an avocado tree in somebody's back yard.

Cut.

It's no longer Hollywood.

Real bullets, no blanks—and if William Conroy makes a mess of it, there'll be no Take Two.

And yet the cloud of golden dust around the pickup truck seems to hang there forever and ever, trapped in slow motion, catching the final rays of the sun. Pickup doors opening and opening and opening. Two gigantic shaggy-haired men, bare-chested, built like Li'l Abner, emerging, growing taller and taller.

'FREEZE!'

They freeze, solid.

Muscles bunched.

Trembling.

It wasn't a shout, a command, but a ferocious roar.

And if they thought they'd moved fast, SWAT-trained William Conroy had moved even faster. Shielded by his open car door, his magnum steadied against it in a double grip, he had been out and poised to shoot before either truck door flew open.

The dust vanishes, gone in a twinkling.

William Conroy unfreezes.

Dogs bark and kids come running.

20

Phil Maddoc, standing in a palatial livingroom, carries on listening to the Capistrano family, standing there before him.

Miss Capistrano, who looks the kind of young lady that might well interest JR if she ever went to Dallas, has the floor at the moment. 'He pulled up behind me, and I went over to his car. I said, "Tony, just give me the baby!" – and then he said – you'll excuse my language – "You fuckin' cunt!"'

'He called me an *F* and a *S*,' interrupts Mrs Capistrano, clutching a gold clutch-bag. 'I do not like to say the words.'

Mr Capistrano, a small, tired-looking man in floral casual wear, says nothing.

His daughter goes on: 'And I said, "Listen, just let me have the baby – I don't want any problems." He started cursing at me, "You fucking bitch, you fucking cunt! You're this, you're that!" He said I've got to come across here before I could have my baby. So I grabbed his glasses, I tried to get the keys from the car. What do you do? And the baby's flopping about – he slapped me on the face.'

'He said,' says Phil Maddoc, quietly, 'you dragged the baby out of the car.'

'Wait! He – '

'He has visitation rights on Sunday until six o'clock. Okay, if he's meant to be turning the baby over to you, why weren't you here at six o'clock? If I was him, I probably wouldn't turn the baby over to your mother either.'

'Wait, wait, wait! *It's the women with him!* Every time he comes, he brings a different one – and he tries to get them as cheap as he can – to take *my* daughter! I can't take the harassment.'

'He says the same.'

'Tomorrow, we're going to court,' says Mrs Capistrano.

'He said we did this to set him up again,' says Miss Capistrano. 'Listen, I just wanted to go to church. We just wanted everything calm and peaceful.'

'We don't use abusive language,' says Mr Capistrano.

'Well,' says Phil Maddoc, 'it just seems to me that if you're the mother of the baby, you should be here at six o'clock.'

'I want to file charges against him for child-stealing *now*,' says Miss Capistrano.

'No, I want to file charges for slapping me in the face!' says her mother.

'And he wants to file charges against you and your daughter,' says Phil Maddoc. 'The problem is, everybody's going to jail.'

'Fine!' says Mr Capistrano. 'We'll all go to jail!' And he takes a step toward the hall door.

'But if you all go to jail, the baby will have to go to Hillcrest Receiving, which is not a nice – '

'But nobody's going to call my wife a whore and a slut so the neighbors can hear! It's the second time he's knocked my wife down.'

'The last time,' says Miss Capistrano, 'he beat me up, I couldn't even walk. I've turned Christian – I can't commit adultery any more. I can't live like this. The last time, I called my parents and they said, "Leave!" He called everybody I know, told them dirty lies about me.'

'This is no way to live!' says Mrs Capistrano. 'He won't marry her – he's got four other children already.'

'So what's going to happen tomorrow in court?' asks Phil Maddoc.

'He said he was going to kill her,' says Mrs Capistrano. 'All he wants is her body. He – '

'What's going to happen tomorrow?'

'I can't take any more,' sighs Miss Capistrano.

And her mother says, 'He said he was going to get the Mafia to kill me – he was paying them a contract to kill me.'

'Shhhh!' says Phil Maddoc. 'Just a simple question: *why* are you going to court tomorrow? Has the court asked you to – ?'

'No, no, no!' interrupts Mr Capistrano, with a wave of his hands. 'Let me explain this, please! We are going to court tomorrow because he assaulted two police officers right here. They had to put him in irons and haul him off to jail. I mean, I could never repeat what he said to the police officers! My wife has been subpoenaed as a witness. He broke a window and smashed his way in, and he started – '

'Right here?' echoes Phil Maddoc.

His question is rhetorical. Now he understands perfectly the mystery of why the man had gone to such lengths, quite literally, to avoid contacting the local police and to cunningly engage the help of an officer from Central Division. Then Mrs Capistrano adds something that makes it difficult to keep a straight face any longer.

'We've already called the police,' she says. 'They're coming right now to see what he's been doing this time.'

21

The scene of William Connor's 'hot stop' on the Ford pickup truck in the barrio is beginning to resemble an early-evening performance at an impromptu festival of folk drama.

Tier upon tier of enthusiastic spectators, many of them flat-chested little girls in bikinis, nail polish and bright lipstick, are perched on the high banks surrounding two sides of an open-air stage, suggested by the bare dirt of the backyard with the avocado tree placed almost dead center.

Downstage, at the tailgate of the pickup, tower two huge bare-chested brothers, handcuffed, rather drunk, loudly proclaiming that they're 'a couple of good ol' hillbilly boys', who had been obliged to undertake the heroic rescue of a friend in dire peril. And the setting sun is just right for heroes; its last rays are slanting in, accentuating rippling muscle and giving each head of shaggy yellow hair a fiery halo.

Before them stands the tall lean figure of William Connor, who has taken quite a liking to these two prisoners, all the more so since hearing that they had apparently only threatened the gang members with a rifle, which could be construed as a mere misdemeanor. He laughs when the younger of the brothers confides to him, 'Hell, I'm a *peaceful giant, officer . . .'*

And it's such a villainous laugh in its way, evocative of wicked men with long black mustachios, much given to tying hapless blondes to railroad tracks, that it could easily cause confusion along the back rows as to who exactly *is* the good guy down there.

But, even given the barrio's ambivalence over La Placa, nobody in the audience seems to be in the least bit confused about whose side they're on, and appear to be enjoying every minute of it.

A couple of young police officers, one fair and one dark, arrive to join the police extras.

'Starsky!' cries out a young barrio beauty.

'*And* Hutch!' Carl Brunner reminds her.

Then a back door opens in the house beyond the avocado tree, and from it stalks a husky young Mexican in black shorts and a green sweat shirt. Expressionless, he glances at the crowd, at the police and the prisoners, at the vehicles parked just about everywhere. Without pausing, he picks up a heavy set of lifting weights, turns, and stalks offstage again, like a long-suffering props man who can't always keep pace with Acts of God in the barrio.

22

Now only a murky half-light remains before night finally comes to San Diego. There is a warm wind rising. Palm fronds rattle and scraps of litter swoop like bats across El Cajon Boulevard, twisting and diving. A dog runs on three legs across an intersection. Shadows have no proper shape to them.

And it's shadows that Officer Cindy Lewis is interested in, as she searches an eight-block area for a face to match the photograph she has seen of a suspect wanted on an attempted rape charge.

> He's strange, but he's not a registered sex criminal. He's got a
> tattoo of a spider web on his penis – and, this is gross, he's got 'Let
> me come on your face' tattooed on his stomach.

Not a man to do much sunbathing in public, presumably, but
certainly someone known to venture forth at about this time, if
only to buy some cheap wine and cigarettes.

Her smile could make a pessimist walk under a ladder. Her
face is open and friendly, needing no cosmetics to improve it,
and her glasses have frames the same shade as her very fair
hair, which she wears up in a roll on duty. Young looking,
Cindy Lewis is in fact twenty-six, and has the sort of
five-foot-six build that caption writers would dither between
calling 'cuddly' and 'outdoorsy', making much of the fact she
enjoys water-skiing. Her own view of herself is characteristi-
cally down-to-earth.

> I'm a little stockier than most girls. Some female cops are so *dinky*,
> and I don't know whether it's because they've got a complex or
> what, but they're so sullen. They all seem to be in a depression of
> some sort. They don't talk to me – I don't know why. And I don't
> know if it's just me, because I notice that hardly any of them are
> close. They have male buddies – I guess that's why.

It's very true that the majority of female officers do appear to
be on edge while on patrol, and seldom display the
exuberance of their male colleagues, out there 'having fun'.
Back at the station, there isn't much evidence of them being
totally relaxed either, discounting attempts at clipped macho-
type humor: prodding a policeman in the legs with a baton,
and growling, 'Okay, spread 'em, bud!'

Perhaps recruiting officer Billy McGuire offers some insight
into this phenomenon, when he says: 'All the things I'm
hearing now about what women do and can't do, I once heard
it about blacks. The Caucasian officer isn't watching me now,
because he's got something else to watch: he's watching that
woman. And he's sort of saying to me, "Boy, am I glad you
showed up! – 'cos I'd much rather have you here than have a
woman."'

Billy McGuire further believes that it takes a 'special quality'
to overcome this form of prejudice, and to feel accepted by
both the public and by the police community itself. Like most
special qualities, it isn't easy to define, but recruits who start

251

off older, having developed their personalities, and who have few illusions about police work, seem to display it more often than those who are young, immature, interested in the 'glamor', and who delude themselves that there are easy ways of gaining at least peer acceptance. Worldly Cindy Lewis isn't one of them.

> There's a lot of sexual harassment by co-workers. If you won't go to bed with them, it bothers their egos! I had a talk with a sergeant once, and I've often wondered if sexual advances would have got me somewhere. I never know what men think. But I felt the affair – or whatever it was going to be – wasn't going to be worth it.

A native Californian, born and raised in Los Angeles, Cindy Lewis has been working as a police officer for about eleven months, having had a wide assortment of jobs in the past, ranging from high-speed deliveries to hospitals on a 'blood run' to bookkeeping for a small industrial firm. She moved to San Diego when sixteen, and became interested in policing while working in a bank.

> Some officers came into the bank one day to take a report, and I got talking to them, went on a ride-along, and got into the reserves. I changed jobs, got fired – some red tape, it was quite dramatic! – and took a temporary job. I was bored, really bored. But now I'm never bored; this job doesn't give you a chance to be.
>
> It's an entire way of life, and I've had to adapt to so many different things. But change excites me – I've moved perhaps 20 times in the last six years! And this sure is an extreme type of occupation. Sometimes I think I'm just a glorified secretary, because of the amount of paper we have to write to combat what we're up against. At other times, I *wish* I was just a glorified secretary – because it's scary, believe me.
>
> Most of my big shocks came in the reserves. The *violence* . . . I was so scared. I hadn't been scared, really scared, since I was a little girl, and that's something you have to get used to, I guess. I was shot at my third day as a cop.

The wind is still rising, the light fading fast. Tail-lights glow feverish.

'Five-Thirty-One John . . .'

It's a call to a motel, where someone is trying to hold two black males caught ransacking a room. But by the time she gets there, although it is only around the block, the two intruders have escaped. Three male officers arrive to give cover.

They won't take your arrest away from you, but sometimes they do interfere. I want to do my work myself. In every bad situation I've been up against, even when I've been there first, they've either gone, 'Hey, move over!' – or they've got right in front of you anyway, and you think, 'What's goin' on here?'

The motel guest is able to give her a fairly good description of the two men he found in his room, and she leaves to search the area, saying she will come back and take details for her report later. This sudden activity has left her looking very lively and filled with wellbeing.

As long as I don't think about death and dying on this job, it's fun. I know there's the stigma of carrying a gun, but it's really nice because there *are* people who still respect the police, and a female officer is a kind of oddity or whatever, so it's enjoyable in that way.

23

The wind whips away a whispered name in the barrio.

The kneeling police officer leans in closer, hoping to hear the name repeated. But the fifteen-year-old, lying there on the sidewalk, thinking of dying with four stab wounds in the chest and two through his upper arm, is staring up at an airliner passing low overhead, its monstrous cruciform shape just darker than the sky, and its navigation lights flashing like cheap gemstones. Another whisper, lost in the roar of the slipstream, and then a sudden cough, leaving frothy blood on the officer's forearm.

But before the boy's head drops to one side, the whisper comes again, 'Little Rabbit . . .'

The paramedics have him. Practiced, expert, they check, assess, take measures to insure he stays alive on the high-speed dash to Community Hospital. Three units go with them, followed by the boy's parents.

His mistake had been to go to a school friend's party in a different neighborhood than his own, and then to come back on foot, right into the clutches of a rival gang just short of home territory.

The ambulance yelps up the ramp and stops outside the hospital entrance. A blonde in white slacks, with SUPER

NURSE printed across her white tee-shirt, is already hurrying out. A doctor is there, too, and the boy is swiftly borne through the lobby, passing the windows of the waiting room, and offering a fleeting distraction to those within, who are watching a comedy on the television.

Doctor, nurses, paramedics and EMT-trained policemen work on the boy together, curt with haste, deft with sheer familiarity, grim. At the door of the emergency room, the parents stand watching, dressed gaily in their Sunday leisure clothes, tears brimming and falling. The mother starts crossing herself, over and over, and the father takes that hand in his own, closing workman's rough fingers around it tenderly, then squeezing. Gusts of canned laughter come from the waiting room. Someone else joins the intent group around their son, a pretty redhead in white slacks and an orange tee-shirt which says, X-RAY TECHS SEE EVERY-THING.

That whisper has become almost a shout.

The boy's parents hear it, being repeated loud and clear by a handie-talkie to their left in the coffee-break room.

'Little Rabbit . . .'

24

Cindy Lewis hears it, way over at the intersection of Florida and University, as she responds to an armed robbery call from a gas station.

She also hears someone offer positive identification of the barrio suspect, and say he'll make a search for him.

The radio has turned raucous with activity. Her whole squad seems tied up, nobody is volunteering cover for want of something to do, and Sergeant Shepherd is going on calls that supervisors don't normally bother with, unless they're checking on work quality or being just plain nosey.

Alone, she arrives at the gas station, where a really scared-looking woman of about her own age is standing behind an empty cash register, waiting to be asked exactly what's happened.

But Cindy Lewis's first words are typical of her. 'Hi, are you okay?' she asks.

Outside, in the bluster of the wind, a pickup draws up, and the big, bearded man at the wheel looks across at Cindy Lewis, framed in the gas station window. He gets out and stands beside his vehicle, still looking at her, watching her carefully. He glances round, then back at her.

There is now a wildness in the last moments of the day. Dark cloud, bruised and torn, scuds across the purple sky behind the big man, and in the dim valley far beneath him, where traffic moves in a mindless roar, the lights have begun to shine more brightly, jittery and garish. His mind teems with terrible images of sudden death, of injury and mutilation. He can recite in a rush from a litany of lurid clippings, quoting details of wanton killing after wanton killing, and is aghast at how many heartless people there are out there, ready to stop at nothing and to allow nobody to stop them.

He sees Cindy Lewis raise her handie-talkie, ready to radio in a quick description of the suspects.

I'm her boyfriend. I've got a scanner in my pickup, and I heard her take this call. I know most of the codes. In a way, you worry, y'know. I mean, you put the shoe on the other foot! – it makes you stop and think. The worst of it is you know their weak spots, and that's what you're afraid they're going to get caught at. Cindy is super cautious, but she's too eager.

25

The fifteen-year-old, rushed to Community Hospital with stab wounds, lies dying, hearing nothing of the harrowing sounds being made by his parents. In the coffee-break room, a cluster of handie-talkies chorus that the wanted suspect is already under arrest, and on his way down to the Gang Detail at the station.

Picking up one of these handie-talkies, Officer George Ramirez, a great bear of a man in his late twenties, makes his way out to his unit, down the main hall past the waiting room. Broad-faced, with a small mustache and his hair semi-Afro, his manner is dedicated, very direct, supremely confident and breezy, almost light-hearted. He is a member of the 'power squad', experienced officers whose shift starts about halfway through Second Watch to deal with late-night problems, and

wears the bilingual name-strip. On an average night, George
Ramirez handles twenty-five calls.

I grew up in the barrio and my family's still here. They wanted the
best for their sons and daughters, they wanted me to achieve my
goal, and I've done that all on my own – I had nobody to help me.
Sure, they're scared – I've been hurt, been in hospital – but they're
still backing me a hundred percent. A good feeling.

I know most of the families here. A lot of people come to me,
needing help. 'I've had my car repossessed – what can I do?' Or,
'My boyfriend is bugging me – what can I do?' I give advice but I
never take sides; most Mexican American families, they're very
tight. Seeing their faces, I think, 'Wow, I'm glad I chose the career
I did.'

I've had a lot of rewarding experiences. Several times I've had to
do CPR – cardio heart massage – and the doctor has told me, 'They
were dead for two minutes, and you did that and they've revived.'
And it makes you feel, 'Did *I* do that?' I've surprised myself.

But I've gotten so many negative views on me, here in the
barrio. It's, 'Oh, here's a Mexican who's bustin' his own race!' –
that kind of stuff. Most people tell me we've been whitewashed,
we've gone over to the Anglo way of thinking. I also think the
people project the image of the real Mexican police on us, the
police in Mexico. You can't compare them with us, they're corrupt
– it's 'who you know' down there.

That's one of my really pet beefs, when they start throwing you
this racial thing. I remember when I first started out, I asked this
inspector who told me I was hired, 'Sir, I'd like to know, seriously
and honestly, was I hired because of my qualifications, or because
you had to fill a quota?' And he kind of laughed.

The relationship between the department and the barrio is very
uneasy. Gangs are the main problem. It's the same with the black
community: we've had several quote-unquote 'incidents' where
the black community leaders have said we over-reacted, but they
don't see the whole story – the officer getting beat up, the officer in
danger. They only see the final result: this black citizen got hurt.
They don't know he's a dope addict, that he's been arrested many
times for attempted murder. I don't like this racial excuse.

I think it's a little easier with the Anglos. I've worked up in the
North Park area, and they're really, really citizens. They want to
talk to you, they're interested in how to protect their homes. I had
meetings. Whereas I try to organize things here, and nobody is
interested, nobody cares. They say our idea is just to get into
houses and look for stolen stuff.

I'm going to ask our sergeant about maybe letting me and
another Mexican officer walk house-to-house, talking to people,
getting them to trust us.

As he slides behind the wheel of his unit, George Ramirez gets a call. More car windows are being broken at a very familiar address in the black community. He takes off hurriedly.

> I know them, they're very hard core. One of the brothers went to prison last week for armed robbery, and I've arrested him before. That was the one time I've fired my gun. A robbery in progress. Another officer followed the car until he could get some cover – I was his cover, five miles away. I finally caught up to him, and we had a high-speed chase before they finally went crashing into a cul-de-sac. I'd never been scared until then – I'd never had anybody shoot at me before! – and I was shaking. I got out and two bullets hit my car. I missed. I hope I never have to fire again, I'd hate to have that on my conscience, but I want to survive. The other officer used a shotgun.

And it wasn't, as Daniel L. Jackson recalls, at all like shooting at rabbits.

26

The barrio stabbing suspect is through in the innermost of the Gang Detail's suite of three very cramped offices, where he sits handcuffed to a metal chair, looking very much at his ease. He is a lazy-eyed, curly-haired Mexican of sixteen, who came in chewing gum, and is still chewing it.

Sergeant Glen Crawford, who leads his six-man team from a small, cluttered desk in the middle office, gives a nod, and one of his officers goes in to interview the prisoner, closing the door. The muffled exchange that follows has the sound of a very ordinary conversation.

Another interview is being conducted in the front office, barely more than a cubbyhole opening off the hall across the way from Captain Walker's area command room. Sergeant Crawford glances in there, and sees a diminutive black boy, aged about fourteen and around four-foot-three, speaking animatedly to two smiling officers in brightly colored shirts.

The walls of the room are covered in garish, rather morbid artwork – tombstones and human skulls being a repeated motif – and in various examples of gang graffiti, including some 'Olde English script', painstakingly executed on sheets of paper.

There's this kid we know real well. He knows where we come from, we know where he comes from, and we get along. He said, 'Hey, if I write one of these up, will you put it up in your office?' Then guys from rival gangs see it and they figure, 'Why shouldn't we have some stuff up there?' So they all bring it.

One of the two officers follows Sergeant Crawford back into the middle office, and says of the small black boy with beads braided into his hair, 'We picked him up at his grandmother's house. They just gave him up, no trouble.'

Sergeant Crawford gestures toward the closed door. 'This kid, under arrest for assault with a deadly weapon, comes in here without any handcuffs on.'

'He did?'

'My first question was, "Is this a prisoner?" The officer goes, "Yeah." "Then why didn't you handcuff him?" "Well," he says, "I know the guy pretty good." So I said, "But what if he's just taken some kind of pills or somethin', and in another ten minutes, the guy's going to go bananas in the back of your police car?" He said he'd searched him – let's hope he did search him, because we find a lot of things in cars.'

'Right.'

'I said to his supervisor,' Sergeant Crawford continues, ' "Now this officer hasn't been stabbed yet, or had a gun put to his head, which is nice, so maybe he's done this before." It's nice to have rapport with people and to know what's going on, but it's a small world.'

Then Sergeant Crawford breaks off to answer the phone: it's an informant with something new on the Piru. The Gang Detail is primarily an intelligence-gathering unit, and has on its files gang members' names, their nicknames (or 'street names'), girlfriends' names, mug shots, Polaroid close-ups of tattoos, and information concerning social activity and occupations. Identifying suspects and victims is one of the detail's main roles, and sometimes weapons too: 'Sticks, bats, they'll always put their street name on it. Street names are based predominantly on what a person looks like – Night owl, Rabbit, Bear, or Chino, say, which is for Chinese.'

Assimilating cultures alien to his own is nothing new to Sergeant Crawford, a broad-shouldered, slender man in his thirties, with a large mustache and longish brown hair. He has spent four and a half of his twelve years' service 'working dirty' in undercover narcotics. Quick, assertive, clearly someone who brooks no nonsense, his humor tends to be dry and laconic.

Sergeant Crawford makes a note of the information phoned in by the 'snitch', and then adds it to a card which warns that this particular member of the all-black Piru is 'into karate and kick-boxing'.

> Black gangs, as I understand it, aren't as territorial-bound as the Mexicans and aliens, and they're in it primarily for the money and for the sense of power and wellbeing—when you run around with a group of guys, it makes people get out of the way, and within a gang, everybody takes care of each other.
>
> But Mexican and alien gangs are basically territorial. Apparently when Mexicans came into the LA area, way back in the 1800s, they would go to certain areas and seek out people from their portion of Mexico, and that's how the gang thing sort of got started. If you talk to people in the barrio, they'll always talk about their Mexico as the village where they lived.
>
> The gangs stick to certain neighborhoods and very seldom leave it, except to go to parties or maybe the beach. Some will come into the downtown area, but you don't see them committing many crimes away from the gang culture – there's always some involvement. Most of them work, but you have a hard core in every gang, twenty to twenty-five percent who're always involved in the stabbings and shootings.
>
> We're finding that they're getting in younger and leaving when they're older, twenty-four, twenty-five. With the younger ones, there'll often be an older guy, and they'll look up to him. A lot of times, this can happen with officers who work the Gang Detail. You may run into a kid who lives with just one parent, and you'll run into him on a very, very constant basis, and he'll almost look up to you to provide him with some kind of leadership.

The small black boy is still talking away animatedly in the front office, keeping the two officers amused and probably, he hopes, in awe of his exploits. But silence has fallen in the innermost office, and a moment later, the interrogating officer emerges in his jeans and two-tone blue shirt.

Officer Mando Apodaca is a very striking-looking Mexican-American of thirty-two, just under six feet tall and weighing a lithe one-seventy. He has the head of a Florentine noble by Raphael, curling black hair and piercing green eyes. His seven years' service is very evident in his quietly confident, good-humored manner.

'Did he cop out?' asks Sergeant Crawford.

Mando Apodaca nods. 'I said, "Did you stab him?" And he said, "Yeah. He challenged me to a fight, and I said, 'Okay, just me and you' – so I fuckin' stabbed him."'

All as simple as that; Mando Apodaca just shrugs.

It's like the old cliché: 'Shovelling shit against the tide.' I arrested one guy, not too long ago, who'd been arrested twenty-one times for burglary, and he'd never once been sent away. Like this kid I've just been talking to, he was arrested for possession of a switchblade *two days* ago – and he's got [priors for] other crimes of violence, stabbings and gang fights. The kids know the laws are so lenient for juveniles, so damn ridiculous, that they don't give a shit – that's why they cop out.

Sergeant Crawford doesn't change expression. The confession hasn't surprised him in the least either. He just listens to the rest of what the boy has had to say, and then watches Mando Apodaca return to clear up a few points. The sixteen-year-old is still chewing his gum, and has a look of smug amusement on his face. He knows that even if this becomes a murder charge, very few prosecutions for murder are even attempted when it involves gang members. Sergeant Crawford turns back to his paperwork.

I think the thing to do in this country is to throw out all the law books and to start again with the basic Ten Commandments: Thou shalt not kill, thou shalt not steal. They have so many laws now, they can't make sense of them.

There was a recent case where a man pled guilty. It's in a court of law, and they said, 'You don't have to talk to me, and you do understand that if you plead guilty you can get ten years in prison?' 'Yes, your honor, I understand. I robbed the place. I put the gun into her face. I took the money.' 'You definitely did this thing?' 'Yes, your honor.' And he got sentenced. Now he's appealing – *how can he?* Does that mean everybody we arrest is stupid? That they can't even talk like a man or woman, and say, 'Yeah, I did it.'

Lawyers believe they are the only ones who can solve the problems all over this country, but to me they're probably the most inept people who've just got themselves in a big position.

I remember that when I first came on, twelve years ago, I thought an attorney was about next to a doctor as far as greatness. Then I arrested this attorney for receiving stolen property – him and a big football star were in it together. This attorney I arrested was apparently making a hundred thousand dollars a year – if not more than that – and he had a nice big law firm and everything else. *He* knew what he was doing: he was president of the San Diego Bar Association.

The telephone rings. It's a message from Community Hospital. The young stabbing victim has just died. His self-confessed killer, upon hearing the news, simply shrugs, leaves his smile where it is, and carries on chewing his gum.

27

Officer George Ramirez drops what he's doing and heads the rush of units to a halfway house, where a fight is reported.

One reason he's hurrying is that he feels the fight at the halfway house needs someone with the right background and experience, lest things become blown up out of all proportion.

When you're new, you're shaky and you're scared, especially in an area like this, which is not the greatest. Most of these younger officers probably grew up in upper-class white neighborhoods, and to them the barrio means everybody's got knives and chains, they confuse low-rider clubs with gang members. Some people like photography, these kids make the car their hobby.

The rich don't know what it's like to have to really, *really* survive – and God, not to have money! I'd say less than twenty-five percent of the kids looking for jobs find jobs, then they're mostly menial with, I believe, a minimum wage of three dollars an hour now. That is bad, very bad, and it's why we have so much crime rate: to get money they steal, burglarize. Some people hate it, but they have to steal.

Two months ago, I went to court on a guy, and I was listening to the cases ahead of me. One guy got two years for stealing a loaf of bread – two years in jail! I'd never heard of that. And here we have murderers that are out on parole in six months, maybe a year.

Right ahead, on a street with a poor surface, stands the halfway house, a single-story dwelling set back on a plot of graded dirt with a few trees in front. All the lights are blazing.

They can't have foster homes for these kids. Nobody wants them – they're too hard core.

They don't have a father, they don't have a big brother, they don't go to baseball games, they don't have anything – *nothing* – they never will, except at a place like this. And if nobody steps in to help them, they're going to be our next murderers, robbers, and that's what we don't want.

George Ramirez gets out of his unit, and starts across the uneven front yard, accompanied by three young officers providing cover. They go straight into the house, and into the very sparsely furnished front room. A broken chair lies on the floor, and beyond it, a gray-faced black youth of about seventeen is clutching at his midriff with one hand, and holding his neck with the other. Six or seven other residents of the halfway house are there too, keeping in the background, and watching over them all is a concerned-looking black man, dressed no better than they are in the cheapest of clothing. He gives George Ramirez a weary smile and a welcoming nod.

'You been having a fight here?' asks George Ramirez, turning to the youth with the apparent injuries. 'You started it, Roy?'

'I didn't start it, man, no way!' replies Roy, with a pathetic wailing intonation that he never lets drop. 'I said I needed a doctor, man, and this dude said he wanted to play, man, and I told him I didn't want to play, man, and he started talking crazy, man. So I went over to the corner, man, and he grabbed me by my arm, man, and the other one grabbed my neck, man, and he's pushing me one way, and this dude's pushing down on my neck.' He winces and snuffles.

'You said you had to go to hospital – for what?'

'Yeah, man, I think I got a stomach pain, and I was there the other night,' wails Roy, weeping for himself, and no sound could be lonelier. 'But they told me to come back, and every time it's another doctor and my schedule was messed up or somethin', and they had to take me tonight. But then in the emergency ward, the lady said it'd be forty-five minutes to an hour before they could see us, and so Mr Braithwaite said we must come back here again. Then he called her and she said it would be two hours before they'd see us. And I've got this pain in my stomach, man, and I think I'd better go, man, 'cos I think I've strained my neck or somethin', man.'

Having heard him out, George Ramirez turns to Mr Braithwaite, the supervisor.

'We have, er, a security problem here,' says Mr Braithwaite, with another weary smile, 'and in our judgment, it doesn't make sense to go and sit at the hospital for two hours. This man is the aggressor in the whole situation, and – '

'No, man!' whines Roy. 'I just said I didn't want to play – '

'Mr Braithwaite has no reason to lie about the situation,'

262

says George Ramirez. 'And this isn't the first time it's happened.'

'This man was pullin' me and stuff, man, and – '

'Hey, we don't want to come back again, okay?'

'So behave yourself,' says one of the cover officers.

'Understand?' says another.

George Ramirez takes Roy aside for a quiet word, leaves him looking less self-pitying, and then quits the halfway house, after assuring Mr Braithwaite that he'll be right back if anything further happens. Plainly, from the way Roy and the other hard-core juveniles have reacted to him, Officer Ramirez is a man they respect, and whose presence is sufficient to make it unnecessary to do a whole lot of talking.

> I try to come out here as much as I can, and we have meetings and stuff. If you can help *one* kid – well, that's my goal as a cop. I had a kid here come up to me and say, 'Hey, I want to become a police officer – how do I go about it?' So I brought him all the literature, brought him books to read, the whole bit, and now he's passed all his tests and he's waiting for an interview. Isn't that great?
>
> Me, I also grew up being streetwise. I've been arrested for burglary, auto theft. That was in my younger days, around fourteen-fifteen years old, when you do it to prove you are macho. I got caught, I learned my ways! That's why I work with these young kids here today – y'know, I was once them. I was a Logan gang member.

28

'Five-Thirty-Five, there's a four-seventeen on Beat Five-Thirty-Two, Fourth and Palm, armed with a knife. It's a white man with a red bandana around his head, a possible ten-ninety-six. He's been threatening people with a knife.'

'Ten-four,' again acknowledges Agent Tom Hamilton, making a sweeping U-turn.

Up here in the real world, the wind has died away, night has fallen, stars prick pinholes in the sky, and it has turned out to be a balmy Sunday evening. Not to be entirely trusted, of course, even though the tempo of calls has slackened off a bit, but certainly a good match for the mood he is in.

> That guy I arrested with the Mace and the gun in the park. I got ICAP checking through their computers for any robberies he fits

the description of, and they've come up with a couple. I've also learned he's a suspect in an assault-with-intent-to-commit-murder case, where one woman was shot in the face. I imagine the crime lab will love to do some ballistics tests.

Approaching Fourth and Palm, there is no sign of the possible ten-ninety-six – suspected mental case – allegedly armed with a knife, but two young men in their twenties are standing outside a gay bar, looking toward the unit expectantly. Both are middle-class at least, and very tidily dressed.

It takes only a couple of minutes to get their story. An unprovoked attack had been made upon them by a tall man as he left the club. Adopting a martial arts stance, he had struck them both in the mouth, and then had threatened them with a large sheath knife. Their injuries are slight, but their fright and their concern for the safety of others isn't.

'Okay, which way did he go?'

'Down this street.'

'He had a red bandana on his head?'

'A red bandana and a camera and a case.'

Agent Hamilton takes a quick look for their attacker. Less than a block away, down the same street, a tall lean man is sitting on the curb at the foot of a telephone pole, dressed in a bright floral shirt, glittering gold pants, cowboy boots, and a cream Stetson.

It can't be, not so soon.

Then a glimpse of red bandana under the Stetson, a glint from a camera worn around the neck, the corner of a leather briefcase, coming into view just beyond him.

It has to be.

The unit coasts to a gentle stop, its lights pinning the man against the night. He remains motionless. And then, as Agent Hamilton steps out, the man rises slowly to his feet, compelling an immediate association: Goofy, on a visit from Disneyland. The same slouched, hollow-chested lanky body; the same big nose, the same big eyes with white showing all around them; the same underhang of shorter lower jaw, canine.

Agent Hamilton strolls over. From progressively closer up, that first impression of an essentially comic figure begins changing. Those huge eyes are fixed in a menacing stare; that lower jaw has narrow, yellow teeth; there is a panting sound, soft and lupine, getting quicker. For a long bristling moment, lasting perhaps a split-second, the stare intensifies, searching the calm face before it. Not a blink. If Agent Hamilton is afraid, it isn't showing.

The moment passes, the eyes drop, there is a slight submissive movement backwards. 'Oh, man . . .' sighs the suspect.

The two victims, watching from up at the corner, see Agent Hamilton ask a couple of questions, and then their attacker raising his hands in the air, turning, and leaning against the telephone pole, feet well apart. He has a ten-inch knife taken from a sheath worn in the small of his back, is patted down, and his hands cuffed in front of him. More questions, and he is allowed to have a cigarette.

He is still smoking it, staining the paper with sweaty hands that seem all knuckle, when the victims are asked if one of them will make the arrest, as Agent Hamilton wasn't there to witness the two misdemeanors of battery and displaying a weapon in a threatening manner. It needs only three words to be spoken.

'You're – you're under arrest.'

'So are you!' booms the prisoner, startling his victims. Then adds, his voice breaking, 'Now I go back inside for about fifteen years . . .'

'What did you do time for?' asks Agent Hamilton.

'Armed robbery in '64. I robbed a cab driver, because I was hungry.' The prisoner fixes his stare on the two victims. 'Have *you* any *idea* what *it* is *to* be *hungry*?' And he weeps, watching them out of the corner of his eye.

'Now listen to me,' says Agent Hamilton, his tone still conversational, 'let me ask you again: what's your name?'

'I don't know.'

'Jimmy Smith?'

'I don't know.'

'Jimmy, have you ever been in a mental hospital?'

'I know I'm not crazy! I was going to sleep in Balboa Park, but the sergeant said I couldn't sleep there. So what can I do? I go in the goddamn bar and I didn't know the goddamn booth was taken!'

'Jimmy,' says Agent Hamilton, opening a rear door of his unit, 'get in here.'

'Get out?'

'Get in.'

Another long moment, then prisoner flicks his cigarette aside and obeys. His curious submissiveness seems to tremble on the brink of its exact opposite, filling the air with a quivering tension, and the clunk of the door closing is a sweet, sweet sound. The victims react to it as though they've just stepped off a high wire after crossing Niagara Falls in a Force Ten.

'Oh, wow . . .'

'Phew! He's so scary! I thought he'd – '

'A very shaky guy,' agrees Agent Hamilton. 'Talks like he's possessed. You could tell he could go either way real quick.'

'What I don't get is why he – '

'I need to ask some questions for my report,' says Agent Hamilton, fetching his clipboard.

Ten minutes later, he gets back into his unit, turns it around and heads for the station. The prisoner in the back is crying, sobbing his heart out.

'That's good once in a while, buddy,' remarks Agent Hamilton, glancing over his shoulder.

'My – my female psychology told me.'

'And it doesn't hurt your macho image?'

'No, it builds it up – it's a way out.'

'There ain't nothin' wrong with a man cryin'.'

'The females have set this on me.'

'Yeah.'

'Look, man, I don't care if you give dope to kids, but never do it in San Diego!'

Just the sound of the motor, the murmur of voices on the radio, the sob and suck of more weeping. Other people in other cars pass by, each wrapped in their own intimacy; quite a few of them seem to be laughing. Monday isn't until tomorrow.

'Sir, I didn't do it!'

'Why should those two guys lie?'

A great sob, then: 'I don't know!'

'You didn't take a karate stance and smash both in the mouth? Are you proficient in the martial arts?'

Silence.

'I participated,' says the prisoner, loftily.

266

'And you didn't pull your blade on them?'

'No, sir, I didn't.'

'It'll all come out in court, I guess.'

'Yes, it will.'

Agent Hamilton stops at a red light. 'I don't think,' he says, 'specially being an ex-con, you should be walking round the streets carrying a knife like that.'

'I don't like queers, hippies, and that stuff . . .'

The green shows.

'You taking any kind of medication, Jim?'

'I take Dalman. It makes you sleep. I keep talking to a baseball.'

'How long have you been in town?'

'I just got in. I believe in freedom.'

'You think you're ready for the streets, Jim?'

'Yessir, I do. Look at these smokers out there, weedsmokers, LSD, PCP, angel dust – am *I* ready?'

'There's a lot of people on the streets who aren't ready for it.'

'Are they ready to be in prison?'

'How much time you got hangin'?'

'I'm off! Got off parole April 24th.'

'I'm glad I got to you when I did, or you might have been in a lot more trouble in your frame of mind tonight.'

'I feel pretty good.'

'Well, I think you'd have wound up in big trouble before the night was over.'

'I want to know what you get for raping women in San Diego.'

'Jimmy – '

'I'd like to ask for protected custody, because you don't know what's going to happen when you get inside the jail. Not that I'm scared, but I enjoy freedom.'

'You can take it up with the deputies.'

'Will you ask the deputies? For my own safety? Because I'd like to get married some day and have some children, and you know how it is . . . When will I go to court?'

'Well, Monday or Tuesday,' says Agent Hamilton, crossing the street where he made his joke about the paranoids.

'Do you know which judge I'll go before?'

'No.'

'I don't want protected custody! If I'm getting killed, I'm gettin' killed. If they jump on me, and beat me up, then I'll show the judge. And if I'm dead, I'll do the same. When your number's up, it's up.'

'Yuh?'

'You can kill me, because I'm not scared of death any more. But I do have fear.'

'When you get to the – '

'And if anybody has fear, well, *you'd better kill them quick.*'

Agent Hamilton glances into his mirror. The prisoner is leaning forward, his nose pressed up against the steel-mesh divider like a snout.

'You said I'd have been in big trouble before the night was over – who would've died with me?'

'Don't know, Jimmy.'

29

Carl Brunner looks at his Seiko wristwatch. It could be a good time to make another circuit of Golden Hill Park. Although not a bad night so far, what with his prompt arrest of the lazy-eyed stabbing suspect, there is no reason why, with a little luck, it couldn't get even better.

He turns up Twenty-fifth Street.

'Five-Thirty-Five William and Five-Thirty Sam, an eleven-forty-five gunshot, thirty-twenty-four Iowa, on Beat Five-Thirty-Four.

'Ten-four,' comes Phil Maddoc's acknowledgment, and a few seconds later, Sergeant Shepherd replies from Unit 530 Sam.

Then a footnote from Communications to say that the paramedics are also on their way to the scene of the attempted suicide by gunshot.

'Ten-four,' says Phil Maddoc.

Ghosting into Golden Hill Park, Carl Brunner follows the circular drive around to the left, peering into the shadows on either side of him.

30

Phil Maddoc and Sergeant Shepherd arrive at almost the same moment outside the small, cheaply-built dwelling on Iowa. It could be a house; it's more likely to be two apartments, one behind the other. From the front, all the lights seem to be on. A woman is waiting on the path at the side entrance, hugging herself as though chilled to the bone this pleasantly warm evening.

'Mr and Mrs Forsyth?' asks Phil Maddoc.

'My husband's in there with them,' she says, opening the nearest front door.

Immediately the babble of two police radios mixes with the loud complacent voices coming from the television set in the corner. It's a small room, cluttered with bric-a-brac, cheerfully sentimental, yet oppressive with the sense of something momentous lying just beyond it. Awe shows in the face of the short middle-aged man turning toward the door; dread in the face of the young woman in green, twisting at her wedding band.

'Help us, it's my husband! I can't believe it! He just said – '

'This way, please, let me show you,' says the man, waving at a doorway to make his meaning clear despite the din.

Sergeant Shepherd and Phil Maddoc follow him out into a tiny hall and into a front bedroom.

A heavy-set, full-bearded man in his mid-thirties, handsome as a king, is reclining in an unbuttoned shirt and denim shorts against the gold-quilted headboard of a half-made double bed, his glazed eyes fixed on the bureau. The top of the bureau, like every other flat surface in the room, is piled high with trinkets, tools, cardboard boxes, magazines, lotions, ointments, jars, bottles of this and that. Tidy, almost absurdly neat, is the small round hole that gleams in his chest, just about where most people imagine the human heart to lie.

'Five-Thirteen William!'

The sudden stereo effect, produced by the pair of handie-talkies, jerks the man's head round.

Sergeant Shepherd moves swiftly to begin emergency medical treatment, while Phil Maddoc hurries out to help the paramedics with their equipment, passing a big tank of tropical fish, serene amid the emotional turmoil of the livingroom.

31

'Five-Thirteen William,' responds acting sergeant Jim Bradford, breaking off his explanation to the Puerto Rican trainee of why his prisoner had been released in the park this afternoon.

'What is your location?'

'Five-hundred on Twenty-fifth.'

'Stand by . . .'

'Okay, I'll stand by right here,' he says, replacing his hand mike before adding with some foreboding, 'She's gonna give me something good, I just know it . . .'

This isn't entirely a matter of intuition: when a supervisor is asked to stand by, Communications can often have a nasty little job up its sleeve.

'You're still pissed, Paul?' asks Jim Bradford, returning to the subject of the park incident.

The trainee shakes his head. 'Hey, you know all the girls were on my side?' he says with a laugh, pointing to a love-bite just visible above his collar. 'They saw my hickey!'

Then the dispatcher comes back on the air with a message for Five-Thirteen William that confirms Jim Bradford's worst suspicions, and within seconds he's on his way, grim-faced and driving fast.

Not deeper into the barrio, but out of it. Up into a pleasant middle-class area of quiet residential streets, quiet law-abiding people, the kind of folk who readily turn to the police department when they have a problem or feel they ought to report something unusual. A man called Mr Truscott has just called Communications to say that he feels the police ought to know two things. Firstly, that he has killed his wife. Secondly, that he will have died by his own hand before anyone can reach his address.

It's just that he doesn't want anyone not used to this sort of thing, to find the bodies.

32

'What have you got on my nose?' asks the bearded man in the crowded bedroom, his voice deep and gruff.

'Oxygen.'

'Who are you?'

'Paramedics,' says the petite blonde. 'This is my partner Martin, I'm Tracy. This is an air-tight dressing, okay?'

'It hurts.'

'It's starting to hurt now?' inquires Martin.

The bearded man smiles slightly. 'This isn't the first time I've been shot,' he says.

'This isn't the first time?'

'I had two years in Vietnam.'

There is an exchange of looks in the room. From the bathroom, down the short hall, comes the sound of the man's wife spitting into the handbasin. She keeps spitting and spitting. Maybe she has already done all the vomiting she can.

Phil Maddoc, his face stern, moves over to where Tracy the paramedic is setting up some equipment. 'He was cleaning his gun?' he asks softly.

'Uh-huh.'

'I don't see any cleaning cloth.'

'Well, that's what he said – I didn't notice.'

The paramedics connect their patient to a portable electronic monitor, so they can keep a continuous check on his vital signs, and then begin to prepare their radio link-up with the hospital.

Phil Maddoc walks round to the other side of the bed and confronts his suspect. 'What were you doing, sir?' he asks, mindful of the fact that attempted suicide is a criminal offense in California.

'Cleaning my gun – m'pistol.'

'Didn't you unload it first?'

'I usually do, but the other night a guy came by, and he was a kind of weirdo-type person . . .'

'Okay, go ahead,' says the hospital.

'We're at the scene of a gunshot wound,' reports Martin.

'A gentleman was cleaning his gun and it discharged. A twenty-two caliber through – '

'Magnum hollowpoint,' interrupts the patient.

'A twenty-two magnum hollowpoint, so it spread out a lot,' continues the paramedic. 'Entry wound is in the anterior portion of the chest, about the third intercostal region, midline on the left side; exit wound is just around the scapula, about the same height, a little bit more lateral. Approximate blood loss at this time – it looks about a hundred CCs. We have a blood pressure of seventy-six. Patient is compos; skin is normal in color, and moist and warm.'

'His weight?' asks the hospital.

'About one-sixty pounds in weight.'

'One-fifty-four,' corrects the man with a bullet-hole through him and a piece missing from his back.

'Excuse *me*, one-fifty-four,' Martin relays back.

The hospital issues a string of instructions, and Sergeant Shepherd helps with an IV drip.

The bearded man frowns as Martin sticks something over the needle inserted in his arm. 'What are you doing?' he demands.

'I'm putting a bandage on it so you won't bleed to death,' quips the paramedic.

A touch of humor is just what the room needs at this moment. The young woman in green is back from the bathroom, looking distraught, and a lot of unspoken things are passing between her and her critically injured husband. Above his tousled head is a wall plaque that reads:

> *Be Patient . . .*
> *God isn't*
> *finished*
> *with*
> *me yet*

33

Still grim, visibly preparing himself for the ugliness that awaits him this star-spangled night, Jim Bradford pulls up outside a dark house on a very quiet street indeed. Not a soul to be seen anywhere. The house is a Spanish-style-bungalow set well back from the sidewalk. An ordinary enough house, except for one thing. A stunted tree has been allowed to grow hard against the main front window, which is almost totally hidden behind dense foliage as black as a blindfold.

'What a bucket of worms this is gonna be . . .' he sighs, reaching for his flashlight.

The cement path runs straight and wide across a well-kept lawn. Up two polished steps, and on to a long veranda. *CRIMINAL BEWARE* warns the orange Community Alert sticker on the frame of the screen door, and the silhouette of slit-eyed Boris the Burglar looks back shiftily over his shoulder.

The screen door is unlatched.

The front door stands slightly ajar.

A clear invitation, or maybe nobody within is worrying too much about burglars any more.

'Mr Truscott, sir?' Jim Bradford calls out.

There's a groan from inside.

Cautiously, Jim Bradford pulls open the screen door, and then prods the front door with his flashlight. When people make what sound like crazy calls, it is impossible to be too careful. The front door swings inward to reveal a dim livingroom, lit only by a spill of light from somewhere beyond its gray walls.

'Police department, Mr Truscott – you okay?'

Another groan, cut short by a thick choke.

Jim Bradford steps inside and makes for the light. The livingroom is immaculate and reflects refined tastes in decor, furnishing and ornaments – Royal Doulton's famous *Balloon Lady* is among the porcelain displayed. A pair of men's slippers, kicked off beside the couch, strike the only wrong note.

Reaching an archway, Jim Bradford gets his first glimpse of a back bedroom; the immediate impression is of drabness, old furniture, faded fabrics. He takes one more pace, carrying him into the hall outside the room, and stops, if only for an instant.

There, stretched out on the far side of a high bed, as though asleep in her frilly nightdress, with a plump of pillows beneath her silver tresses, is a very definite corpse – the skin color alone makes this obvious: processed cheese, with a faint bluish tinge to it. No visible signs of violence. But on her motionless chest lies a hammer.

'Oh Jesus,' murmurs Jim Bradford, 'I'm not going to look the other side of that . . .'

Then, sprawled on the floor on the near side of the bed, facing in the direction of the dead woman and completing the tableau, is a gray-haired man in a short-sleeved shirt, slacks, and a pair of socks. He is groaning and trying to peer round. A pool of very bright red blood has spread out from under him, and is already the size of a cheerful new scatter rug.

Jim Bradford hastens forward.

> I get a mental block. I don't *look* at anything. I give quick glances, see what there is, but I don't concentrate on it. If you concentrate, then it's going to stay with you.

Kitchen knife.
Two wounds.
Elbow sliced into, joint almost severed.
Virtual disembowelment, hara-kiri style.
Blood and other bits pouring out.
A face looking up.
Still very much alive.
Eyes that shriek *I don't want to be!*
Oh Jesus . . .
'Set up the IV.'
'How old are you, sir?'

The paramedics have arrived, as single-minded as ever, showing no dismay at what they see before them. Theirs is not to reason why, of course, which must make something of a difference.

34

Up in Golden Hill Park, under the moonlight, things are quiet. For the third time in less than an hour, the same unit comes ghosting in to take the circular driveway. This time, however, it slows right down and then stops.

That can't be a shadow over there on the grass, there isn't an azalea bush or palm tree close enough to throw a shape like that. And another thing: it wasn't here earlier.

Carl Brunner reaches for his baton, opening his car door at the same time. The night air is very still, cooling slowly.

It smells good for the first few paces he takes across the grass. Then, a pace or two farther on, the air becomes slightly sickly, too sweet by far.

Sweeter still.

Must be a glue-sniffer.

And so it is, passed out on the grass with paint all over his face. Not just any old glue-sniffer though, but one who enjoys making his own music with a harmonica.

35

Death brings sudden life to the quiet street where Jim Bradford's unit and the ambulance stand parked.

First, the back-up units arrive, and then a whoop of young boys, stunting around on their bicycles.

Porch doors start opening. Neighbors drift out. Passing cars stop and people alight from them. An inquisitive crowd begins to gather on the opposite sidewalk.

It isn't long before a sunburned man in a yellow sports shirt ventures across.

'How you doin'? he asks a pair of young officers.

'Pretty good,' one of them replies.

'What's going on?'

'You live around here?'

'Yes.'

'It's a police investigation – we can't reveal it right now.'

'Investigation for what?'

'I don't want to sound rude, but that's all I can tell you.'

The man cocks an ear at the message being blurted out by the radio in the nearest unit, then notices the look he's getting. 'You want me to get away from your cars?'

'Well, we'd like you to go back across the street.'

The two officers watch his reluctant retreat, and then the more talkative of them takes a nibble at something concealed in his hand.

'It's kinda gross, I guess,' he remarks, 'standing out here on the sidewalk, eating smoked ham at a homicide.'

'Oh, I dunno . . .'

'My first really upset me.'

'Yeah.'

'And I was at one of those auto-erotic hangings, y'know.'

'You were?'

36

Hitting a lull, Cindy Lewis returns to her hunt for the spiderweb man.

> You know, I haven't seen any dead people yet – except for the morgue, and I've only been to two accidents.

It must be the spiderweb man's lucky night. Only about a minute or so goes by, before Communications again interrupts the search. A call has just been received from a fourteen-year-old girl in a state of great distress. She says her father is drunk and firing off a gun in the house. She's afraid somebody may get killed.

Eagerly, Cindy Lewis slews her unit around and puts her foot down. 'Come on, Volkswagen!' she mutters, as a meandering Beetle fails to get out of the way fast enough.

37

'We're packaging for transport,' radios one of the paramedics in the back bedroom of the homicide house. 'Code Three.'

They have achieved the almost unbelievable: not only is the old man still alive, but he's now ready to be moved to hospital with at least a fair chance of survival.

Jim Bradford organizes help with carrying their things, and they leave in a rush, the IV bag held high. Within what seems like seconds, the ambulance doors are closed, its lights come on, and it takes off up the street.

'Hope that old guy doesn't make it,' one of the watching police officers remarks. 'Can you imagine?'

276

'He'll just do it again.'

'Yeah, cut his stomach open from one side to another – well, he wasn't foolin'!'

Jim Bradford's sentiments exactly. He goes back into the house for a final glance round, just to make sure nothing has been disturbed. The body of the dead woman lies there, exactly as he first saw it, but at least the hammer is now more of a mystery than anything else: there doesn't appear to be a mark on her far side either. Some form of asphyxiation was probably used.

Glancing away from the body, and from the slithered pool of blood now turning drab, Jim Bradford goes thankfully out into the night.

38

Phil Maddoc, whose own unfinished business with the bearded Vietnam veteran has been set aside for the moment, pending recovery, is once again in his unit, patrolling the streets of Hillcrest.

'Five-Thirty-Five William,' comes Sergeant Shepherd's voice, sounding urgent, 'go TAC.'

Phil Maddoc switches to Frequency Seven.

'Ten-four.'

'Hey, Phil, there's a guy, has a gun – he's shooting it off!'

A statement bound to bring a quick flashback to the chest with the small neat hole gleaming in it – although this time it could be one's own chest, above where an armored vest reaches.

'I'm gonna be the first one there,' says fellow SWAT officer Phil Maddoc, as soon as he has the address.

I don't *want* to be the first one there! If the guy's really drunk, he's not going to be doing what we tell him to.

Unit 535 William leaps forward, siren yelping, and for the next few minutes, as various other units join in the exhilarating race to bring help, Frequency Seven is staccato with excited exchanges.

'I'm University and Park!'

'I'm Cajon and Utah!'

And then, nearing the address, Sergeant Shepherd warns: 'I don't want any sirens or any loud screaming tires.'

Phil Maddoc's siren is already turned off, and he's coasting down a steep narrow street into a small canyon. The moon has clouded over, but there is still enough light to see plenty of trees growing on either side, providing good cover. The canyon also has a fairly high concentration of residential properties of one sort and another, which makes warning people to stay indoors – and away from their windows – a first priority.

Equally important will be establishing whether the man is alone in the house. Because if things go badly wrong, and it seems that the only solution lies in a full-scale assault, shooting through the walls and all the rest of it, then this sort of information will be vital.

Right ahead of him now, flagging him down from the opposite sidewalk, is Cindy Lewis, standing shielded by a garage with a young girl at her side.

39

Outside the homicide house, the quiet street is almost back to normal.

Ever since the ambulance's departure, the onlookers have been drifting away into the night again, leaving only a few diehards to eye every move the police make – not that they appear to be doing much at the moment.

In fact they're doing nothing at all, apart from standing on the sidewalk and making sure nobody puts a foot on the property until Homicide and the deputy coroner arrive. Departmental regulations are very strict in this regard, insisting that, once any immediate problems have been dealt with, every murder scene is secured against any possible 'pollution'. Or, to use the words of one young officer, 'They kind of turn it into sacred ground'.

And if this begins to conjure up fanciful notions of an inner chamber, blood sacrifice, acolytes awaiting the high priests of death to begin some dark ritual, then it may, at a subconscious level, be contributing to the very decided aura that now seems to surround the house.

It's certainly hard to think of it as being totally empty.

'Apparently, she had a terminal illness.'

'Uh-huh. I guess the old guy just wanted to put her out of her misery.'

'I heard he was sick, too. Could've been medical bills.'

'Sure, they were retired – right?'

Jim Bradford has moved his unit a little way down the street, to where he can keep an eye on things without becoming involved in small talk and idle speculation. He has his report to start getting organized. *The skin was cold and stiff –*

'Hi, officer! I'm with the Sheriff's Department. What went on here? I live right around the corner.'

Expressionless, Jim Bradford runs an eye over the man approaching his car window. 'You're with the who?'

'The Sheriff's Department.'

'As in "deputy"?'

'Yes.'

'A homicide-cum-suicide.'

'Oh, okay. Is that all it is?'

'That's all it is.'

'You have a good one!'

'You too.'

40

'I'm facing a window on the upper floor – I've got all those covered,' comes a low voice on the radio.

Nobody sounds excited any longer on Frequency Seven, down in this dark valley where fear has a taste, chill and metallic, like an old coin slipped under the tongue.

'Ten-four,' responds Sergeant Shepherd, his tone hushed yet briskly confident, a man in his element. 'Cindy – are you in position?'

'Confirm. I'm in the entrance to the garage. I can see the door with the twenty-eight-twenty-four on it. Is that the home?'

'Affirmative. I'm just going to slip into this next-door apartment and get out of your line of fire.'

'Ten-four. The daughter stated that he has at least three shotguns, handguns, and lots of ammunition.'

'Ten-four.'

Fortunately, the daughter has also been able to confirm that her drunken father is alone in the house, which has simplified a lot of things.

Communications breaks in: 'Apparently somebody else wants TAC now – is it possible for them to get it? We're getting a big build-up here.'

'Well,' says Sergeant Shepherd, measuring his tones, 'the reason we wanted TAC is we have a shooting going on, which over-rules your TAC. Let's say it's more important at this precise moment.'

'Ten-four.'

'Soon as it's over, we'll give it back to yuh!'

Then a long silence. The small duplex in a row of four is now covered front and back. Sergeant Shepherd radios for two more downtown units and for the SWAT alert to be broadcast.

The low voice says, 'I just saw him, near a closet – bending over.'

'Okay, just stay out of his line of sight.'

41

The first member of Homicide Team One arrives and is briefed by Jim Bradford, before taking a tape-recorder out of his car. He waits outside the house, however, as protocol demands this until the full team is present.

Jim Bradford goes back to his unit.

There's four Homicide teams. Each team has got a sergeant, three officers and a lab guy. Every investigation gets the full treatment. Each officer has certain things to do, and there is a check list they constantly look at, no matter how many homicides they've done.

This guy will start walking around out here, talking into a recorder and describing the neighborhood, the street, the house itself. Another guy will draw up a diagram of the actual scene; he'll draw a master plan of the house, and then he'll draw all the individual rooms – hallway, bathroom, bedrooms. Another officer will go through this neighborhood, contact every house on the block, building up background on the victim. Lab will go in and start taking photographs of everything – probably around 100, 150 photographs.

When they get done – and it's a clear-cut investigation – the paper work will probably be about five inches thick.

Next to arrive is the deputy coroner on night shift, a big, jolly-looking man in a bow-tie and light-weight jacket, who steps from his car brimming with bonhomie and wellbeing.

Nobody can touch that body, only I can. The police investigators might check its temperature, but *I* examine that body, with them watching me.

I'm retired from the Navy – I was a hospital corpsman for twenty-six years. I came here five and a half years ago, had a month on-the-job training. I love it. I'm an investigator – I'm the ears and eyes of the pathologist in the field. I never call him out; he doesn't visit the scene.

We average about three thousand deaths a year; two or three deputy coroners on during the day, one at night. In Californian law, anyone who is found expired becomes a coroner's case. With a Rosicrucian, if it's a natural-type death, we put that body aside and we do not touch it for 72 hours – they believe there is a gold or silver thread attached to it until then.

I make notifications. When I leave here, I might get a traffic accident, and then I'll go to that house and notify the next-of-kin. I don't tell them I'm a coroner. I identify myself as a county officer, and I go in and tell them a little story leading up to it. By using psychology, I try to make *them* break the barrier and say that the person is dead. If I said it to them, maybe they wouldn't accept it. Then we counsel them, tell them what to do, and how to go about it. I get help in, family in, the clergy. We try to leave somebody with them.

The two hardest parts of the job are the notifications and the children, crib deaths – child abuse, more so. It's not easy, I don't care how many you do. Children upset me terrifically, anybody that's young.

42

Hiding in the entrance to the garage, revolver in hand now for almost half an hour, Cindy Lewis keeps watch on that very ordinary front door, illuminated by a unit's spotlight from the street.

It is becoming harder and harder to maintain total

concentration. Yet concentrate she must, because if that door suddenly jerks open, and the drunk comes out with his shotgun, there might be only a split-second's difference between either being a dead body or looking at one in the field for the first time.

A dog barks in the distance.

And it's not as though the drunk is still unaware of the police presence, now they have him properly surrounded. He knows what is expected of him: to come out and give himself up before anyone gets hurt.

A whisper on the radio.

And another voice saying, 'I can barely read you, Dave.'

'I'm right near the suspect,' says Sergeant Shepherd, 'I can't talk any louder.'

Which is something else that builds up the tension: the difficulty of working out just where everyone is in the dark, and sometimes of recognizing who is speaking. An edge of anger has sharpened some of the voices. People have had an opportunity to reflect on how totally absurd this is, risking life and limb because some idiot has apparently had an argument with his girl friend, and now wants to take it out on the world. There might be a certain glory in going down, riddled with shot, at the scene of a bank robbery, but dying here in the canyon tonight would be almost embarrassing.

'He's bending down near the closet again.'

The strain of waiting mounts. In some ways, it would be almost a relief if he started shooting again, making it essential to take drastic action. But department policy is that the suspect is given plenty of time, and that nothing is done to precipitate unnecessary bloodshed.

That dog barks again in the distance.

The picture changes.

Flick-flack, quick as a slide show.

And Phil Maddoc says softly on the radio. 'The front door's open.'

Cindy Lewis can see a silhouette looking out.

Straight at her, only yards away.

Then it crouches.

She hears Sergeant Shepherd say, 'The door's open?'

'Affirmative,' she whispers back. Then adds in amused amazement, 'Hell, we are *naked*!'

And out he totters, hands held high, not a stitch on him, and what is more, he's a ridiculously small man when measured against the looming hulk imagined only moments ago.

'Freeze!' bellows Sergeant Shepherd. 'Stop! Put your hands on the back of your head! Interlace your fingers! Kneel down! On your knees! Get down on your knees!'

The drunk's smile is mocking.

'On your knees!'

Slowly, he lowers himself to kneel on the stone patio, like a haughty squire about to receive a knighthood.

For an instant, it all seems a little unreal, like a ludicrous game, excessively melodramatic, that everyone is being manipulated into playing. But there is a cure for that. In the next instant, he is grabbed, handcuffed and hauled to his feet, as his daughter rushes towards him.

'Take that girl out of here!'

43

The deputy coroner comes back out on to the sidewalk, having been inside the homicide house for a cursory look at the body. His cheery disposition hasn't altered one iota; if anything, he appears more buoyant than ever, as though having just called in on a favorite aunt for coffee and cookies. No doubt, in his scale of things, an unmutilated corpse of advanced years must occupy a position close to that.

And besides, he is a man who takes an innocent delight in his apparent expertise, which has enabled him to confirm that the body has been dead for many hours, probably since the early morning.

44

Already teetering on the edge of a sense of acute anti-climax, and the depressive effects that can bring, nobody is really in the mood for the little drunk's sneers and high-handed manner.

From the moment of his arrest, his complaints have continued unabated. He demands to know what right the police have to be on his property. He demands to know what right they have to put him in handcuffs. He demands to know who dared report him for something he was doing in the privacy of his own home.

Peering down at him in their midst, the feelings of one and all on the patio are perhaps summed up by the stoney-faced officer who mutters, 'All that – for this *asshole* . . . ?'

'Ha!' he jeers into the nearest face. 'A lot of guns get fired! So why should you care what I do? Which gang is supposed – '

'Listen – '

'You dumb bastards think you can do what you like! You wait! You just wait!'

Around two minutes of this, however, have proved long enough, and so, without further ado, he is bundled into the back of a unit, and left there to scream and holler.

'Jesus, will you look at this?'

The staircase just behind the front door is littered with handguns. The sight of them certainly livens things up again, and with excited curiosity, the trail of discarded weaponry and ammunition is followed up to the landing.

'Look what I see,' says Sergeant Shepherd, pointing. 'I see a hole in the door – I see a hole in the wall!'

Bullet holes.

And that's only the beginning. Soon it becomes almost impossible to properly comprehend what they have walked into. For a start, the two bedrooms look as though they've been ransacked by burglars, doped to the eyeballs. Clothes, papers, books, lie strewn ankle-deep, closets yawn, drawers have been yanked out and upturned. On the table in the back bedroom lies a paperback copy of *The Holcraft Covenant*, flipped over so that the blurb on the back can be seen from the doorway: *The Fourth Reich is about to be born. The only man who can stop it is about to sign his death certificate . . .*

More ammunition, lying everywhere: cartridges, shotgun shells – a hall closet that is packed from top to bottom with more than one hundred thousand assorted rounds. All sorts of paramilitary equipment: emergency kits, rations, flares, lifesaving jackets, holsters.

'Hey, Phil, look at that – a three-fifty-seven!' says Sergeant

Shepherd, picking up the magnum revolver. 'And over there, an M-16 . . .'

'He had a lot of guns, huh?'

'And I would suspect he's got more handguns – there's holsters that don't fit these.'

A Remington Wingmaster, a regular shotgun, a folding shot-gun, a Colt .45 automatic . . .

Cindy Lewis comes bouncing up the stairs. 'I was scared to death,' she says. 'Then all of a sudden, he's coming out and it's so *funny*, he's got no clothes on – stark-assed naked!'

'Look at the guns he's got,' says Sergeant Shepherd.

'Jesus . . .' she says, her jaw dropping.

'I'd say he was a gun buff,' Sergeant Shepherd adds drily, 'and that there's going to be more.'

There is. The front bedroom looks at a glance like the corner of an army supply depot after an artillery attack: a chaotic jumble of survival gear and small arms fills the space between the bed and the walls.

'Why does somebody have to have all this stuff?' asks Cindy Lewis, wonderingly.

Nobody volunteers an answer.

'It reminds me,' she says 'of a typical flashback situation – war veteran.'

Then one of the other officers, edging his way into the room, points and says, 'What's that?'

Everyone looks toward the table in front of the window, and at the thing on it, directed out into the night over the patio.

It's a moment that halts any sense of an anti-climax dead in its tracks, and provides total justification for Sergeant Shepherd's low-key handling of the incident.

'That's some kind of machine gun,' he replies. 'I'd say an H&K Ninety-One.'

45

Sunday, for Second Watch, is almost over. Two officers, an FTO accompanied by a recent recruit to the department, drive by the scene of the murder on their way back to the station. There isn't much to see, though, just Jim Bradford talking to the sergeant in charge of Homicide Team One, and a couple of bulky young men in crumpled uniforms waiting by the morgue van.

So the two officers carry on down to West Market, their thoughts preoccupied by the riot predicted by Criminal Intelligence for tomorrow, when Tom Metzger, Ku Klux Klan dragon in California, attends his first meeting, as congressional candidate, of the county's Democratic Central Committee at San Diego County Courthouse.

Like his FTO, the recent recruit is a veteran officer and has also been involved in riots elsewhere, including one when 25 bikers tried to expel 500 Chicanos from a park.

> In the end, we had to call in about 24 other law enforcement agencies, and it was 6½ hours, I guess, before we put the riot down. For two weeks we had big articles in the papers about people gettin' abused and beat up. That's the problem with outside agencies; they realize it's a kind of freebie for them, that they can go in there and wham the daylights out of people without writing paper on it.

'Okay, and so tomorrow,' says the recruit, 'there'll be us and who else?'

'The deputies,' says the FTO.

'Uh-huh.'

'Basically, we'll do token things – moving in a wedge or a scrimmage line. We had a rule in Orange County: you break that line and you get thirty days off – no matter what the reason. We got hit with bottles and shit, but that was the rule.'

'Sure, it only takes one guy to drop out to take his revenge on somebody, and – '

'You've lost it.'

'Yeah,' says the recent recruit, looking a little tired but very contented.

> I've only known Doug for two weeks, but he's a hell of a guy, I enjoy being around him, and I know if it came down to it tomorrow, I don't think I'd hesitate to, y'know, give up my life for him. I think it would be mutual. Basically, what it amounts to is an old saying that's kind of humorous and I get a lot of meaning out of: 'You can fuck with Saint Peter, you can fuck with Saint Paul, but when you fuck with a cop, you fuck with us all.'

286

46

The first shocks over, the time has come to start imposing some form of order on the chaos surrounding the officers in the upstairs bedroom.

Phil Maddoc moves the H&K 91 machine gun from the window table and adds it to the stack of firearms to be impounded. 'All ready to bring death and destruction to the neighborhood,' he remarks.

'A jack of all trades . . .' muses Cindy Lewis, picking over the mess on the floor. 'Photography, too. Turkish cigarettes? I wonder if these are dipped. Boy, those are ex-pen-sive cigars! You want all the ammunition?'

'Right,' says Sergeant Shepherd, who is making sure all the firearms are unloaded.

I wish this would disqualify him from gun-ownership, I really do. You could say he'd violated the trust once, and hence we're not going to trust him any more. But the bumper sticker you see around really epitomizes it: 'They can have my gun when they pry my cold dead finger off the trigger!' That's what we're up against.

Immediately below in the livingroom, the prisoner, who had been brought inside to be helped into his clothes, doesn't like something about the underpants he is being offered, and is refusing to step into them.

'Listen, Mr Scott, I strongly suggest you start trying to be cooperative,' says one of his escorts.

Utter disdain is the only response; what seems very clear is that the prisoner wants it recognized that he's a lot more civilized and intelligent than any of the beings surrounding him.

'Hey, aren't those the same goddamn underpants he just took off?'

'Yeah, must be – they were right here, along with the rest of his stuff.'

'Mr Scott . . .'

'They're *green* – can't you see that? And I'm not into green.'

That does it. He's into green underpants faster than he can raise his voice in another protest, and then straight out into the night again, dressed in nothing else but a pair of handcuffs. Told to get into the rear of the unit, he perches on a corner of the seat.

'Put your feet in!'

Loftily, he obliges, as if expecting a laugh from the semi-circle of watching neighbors, and the door is slammed shut.

'Hey, look at this!' says someone upstairs in the front bedroom, turning back the mattress on the bed and disclosing a tin box hidden there.

47

Jim Bradford has now dealt with them all: the groaning suspect, the inquisitive neighbors, the deputy as in sheriff, the family pastor, Homicide Team One, the deputy coroner, the television news crew that came and shot, among other things, the Boris the Burglar poster on the telephone pole, over there across the street.

A quiet street with little to show for the night's activity, apart from the pattern of tire marks left by vehicles braking to a suitably dramatic halt outside the house of death.

He takes his leave, indifferent to what the investigation will reveal, simply glad to be on the move again. Gladder still, to be on his way home, although with his paperwork yet to be completed, it could well be Monday before he gets there.

Klan Monday . . .

> I honestly, truly, in my heart, don't care what happens to Metzger. He advocates white supremacy, and that's anti-democratic because democracy is based around the philosophy that everyone is equal. There is no way I'm going to risk my life and safety for him. If they came up to me and said, 'You've got to work it', I would say, 'I'm not' – and I'd tell them why, I feel so strongly about it.

Just as he felt strongly about the way the near-riot should be handled in Golden Hill Park this afternoon. But anyway, having spent the weekend as acting sergeant of the Heights squad, Jim Bradford has the day off tomorrow.

48

'Hey, damn you! Hey!'

The bellowing is coming from the unit, where Reserve Lieutenant Buck Masters is grappling with the prisoner, for reasons not immediately apparent. What is clear, however, is that the man is berserk with rage, and thrashing about violently.
So violently, that the officers hurrying over have to end up hog-tying him, while he screams abuse at the part-timer.

An officer asks Buck Masters, 'Did he come across to you?'
'Yes.'
'He try to fight?'
'Oh, he was kicking the door.'
'What happened to his arm?'
'Ow, ow, ow!' whimpers the prisoner, as the hog-tying brings his hands and feet together in the small of his back. 'Ow, ow, ow!' he yells.

He is replaced on the seat and the door is slammed once again.

Buck Masters smiles in at him. 'You're happy now?' he asks. 'Oh Jesus Christ – stay away,' he adds, catching the stink of vomit. 'He's barfed in the car!'

Then everyone goes back to what they were previously engaged on, and the reserve lieutenant, looking very happy, goes sorting through some of the firearms, earmarking the ones he plans to buy for his own gun collection when the police department offers them for sale.

Meanwhile, in the front bedroom upstairs, the tin box found hidden under the mattress has been opened to reveal what looks like a quantity of marijuana, so Cindy Lewis had been right when she'd suspected drug involvement.

Sergeant Shepherd isn't sure, however, that the charge will stick.

We'll probably never get it in court, because this is a search for weapons, and we shouldn't have been looking in places where there weren't weapons – even though you and I know you could get a weapon in that box. And a lot of times they'll give the guns back, because they'll say it was an illegal search. You'll say, 'But the weapon was probably used in a crime,' and they'll say, 'It doesn't matter – illegal search.' The *idea* is good – it's my rights, the same as anybody else's – but the unfortunate thing is it makes it very difficult for us to get guns off the street.

'All I'm really concerned about,' he tells Cindy Lewis, 'is that we get all the guns and ammo.'

'All the ammunition?' she sighs, imagining the job she is going to have in making the inventory.

Sergeant Shepherd looks at his watch. 'My wife probably thinks I crashed on my motorcycle going home,' he says, realizing how late it is.

49

The station patio on West Market is deserted.

Phil Maddoc, who hasn't had a chance to eat since coming on shift close to ten hours ago, feeds quarters into the vending machine outside the darkened coffee shop, and gets himself an apple pie – and then a can of something cool to wash it down.

He crosses back over to the watch commander's office, passing the hog-tied prisoner in the back of Unit 535 William.

Silence.

'I'm trussed up like a – oh!' says the prisoner, grimacing.

More silence, moonlight, and the reek of his own vomit.

The driver's door opens, and Phil Maddoc slides in behind the wheel, ready for his last official ride of the day – up to the county jail and back.

'Mr Scott,' he says, holding a slip in his hand, 'you've been arrested for possessing a dangerous weapon, for firing a firearm within the city limits, and for possession of hash.'

'I think you're terrific,' says the prisoner. 'Pardon?'

'You'll be told *all* about it later.'

'You had PC? You think you had enough probable cause?'

'More than enough probable cause,' says Phil Maddoc, putting the charge slip aside.

'I see . . . And someone is going to complain about that little thing?'

'Yuh,' says Phil Maddoc, starting his engine.

50

Cindy Lewis has the look of somebody who, having wished in a weak moment tonight that she were just a glorified secretary, now realizes her wish has been granted.

Having been named as the arresting officer, which means the report on the shooting incident is her responsibility entirely, it's up to her to go on compiling detailed lists of the weapons and ammunition to be impounded and taken back to the station. Some of it has already gone, but what still remains, in the sordid mess surrounding her, is enough to make anyone wilt.

On top of which, it is difficult not to feel like someone who has been left alone to clean up after a party from which one's fellow guests departed the moment they stopped having fun, but then, a lot of police work is like that.

It takes Cindy Lewis five and a half hours to prepare the report. She has to write it twice, because she isn't too clear at first about the exact sequence in which things happened.

An exercise in futility, as it turns out.

The police should have applied for a telephonic search warrant because, in the heat of the moment, something vital had been overlooked. Having been told by the daughter that her drunken father was alone in the house, they'd had no right to enter it after he came out and surrendered himself – they could have done so, without a warrant, only had they had cause to believe someone else might be inside, possibly in the need of their help.

And so, early on Monday morning, all the charges are dropped, the prisoner is released and allowed to reclaim his arsenal, although he prudently doesn't ask for his machine gun back – nor for the tin containing vegetable matter.

Then he goes home, and so does Cindy Lewis.

> This job makes me want to almost clam up at times. It makes me more aware of what the nice things *really* are – not all the material things, but the nice things. I'd like to buy myself about five acres, give myself a little ranch, grow my own things. I think this job has a lot to do with that. I find solitude important now, and staying in my own little shell.

Part VII

The chicken's head

1

Monday, 12:57 p.m. and counting.

With the confrontation between demonstrators and Klan leader Tom Metzger now only hours away, the coffee shop down at the station on West Market is crowded this lunch time by an unusual number of patrol officers in casual clothes. Along the line at the service counter every other word seems to be 'riot'. There is nervous banter, excitement. People are already on a high, aware that some very different demands are about to be made on them.

> Y'know, we're supposed to be community-oriented, right? All that anti-macho, low-key stuff: no hollowpoints and just the twenty-four inch baton. But like today it's the thirty-six-inch riot baton, gas mask, the helmet, and they're going to have to psyche the guys up for this – at three, there's a crash course on riot control. Jesus, the only riots I've ever even *seen* were on the TV, and if this thing turns to hell . . . Well, the Chief's ass'll be on the line, I guess – which is kind of funny, when you think what kind of guy he is, and why we're doing this.

2

Chief William B. Kolender, even when seated behind his desk, is a strikingly big man. Big build, big hands, big handsome head; big in the trim way a fully grown lion is big, and every bit as nonchalantly self-assured. His strong features, bracketed by dark sideburns, are mobile and expressive; an Identikit portrait would probably find his double among the leading baritones at La Scala. Wholly uninhibited and unpretentious, bluntly passionate in his beliefs, Bill Kolender exudes, above all, the confident air of a man well used to being liked – and not giving much of a damn if he isn't.

> I grew up in Chicago, and came here when I was eleven. I had problems in school, not so much academically as attitudinally. I flunked out of high school. I went to summer school, got my diploma, and went in the Navy at eighteen. That kind of got me

295

squared away; for some reason, they picked me as leader of the squad at boot camp.

But I was in the Navy only two years – I got married very young. God, I was twenty! I went to work in a surplus store downtown, and I enrolled in community colleges. A friend of mine was a cop, and I thought, 'Why not go to school in the daytime and work as a cop at night to feed the family?' That's exactly what I did, and I graduated from City College with a degree in criminal justice. Then I read at State University for a degree in public administration – in 1973 I was Alumnus of the Year there, which was kind of pleasing.

When I came on here, I was just barely twenty-one. I walked beats and worked all over the town for about four years. I was the youngest person ever to be promoted sergeant in the department: I was twenty-six. I stayed a sergeant for about four years, and then went into Community Relations to help the lieutenant in there. When he retired, I became acting lieutenant, and then lieutenant when I was thirty.

I started to really get the community relations program going. I had a very unfortunate first marriage. Some guys go bowling, some guys get drunk – I became a community-involved cop. I became involved in everything in this city: racial groups, civil rights, labor – all of the strikes at the time – and I started getting awards. I was Young Man of the Year for the city, I got the Human Rights Award from the Mayor – oh, I got all kinds of things. I've been president of all the Boys' Clubs, I've been head of a lot of boards, set up the (schools) integration program, I've taught community relations at both the University of California, San Diego, and at State University. I also taught for a long time a course called 'Selected Topics in Criminal Justice' at the State – it was very interesting, bringing in the radicals from each side and having a discussion.

And when I was thirty-two, I took the captains' test, and by God, I got that – and I went on up the line.

That was during the 'bad, bad sixties' – in July 1968, to be exact. A militant in Southeast San Diego, one of the most troubled minority areas, went on record as saying, 'For a pig, he's not bad. We're glad for him he got promotion, but we hate to see him leave Community Relations.'

Four years later, Bill Kolender was still finding time to attend community meetings and to address various groups almost daily, while also taking a graduate course in literature. He had by now risen to the rank of inspector and was in overall command of the Patrol Division, taking charge at any major disturbance.

'When everybody's throwing rocks at you,' he told Robert P. Laurence, of the San Diego Union, 'you definitely think, "What am I doing here? Why am I here? Why are they taking out their problems on us? We're not responsible for this society."

'Many times the balance of liberty and responsibility, for example, is put on our shoulders when it's not ours, it's the total community's thing. We all have a responsibility to eliminate these negative conditions, whether it be housing or unemployment or education.'

And with this as part of his credo, he went on to become San Diego's youngest ever Chief of Police in February 1976.

> I can brag a little bit! They did surveys in 1976 as to who the most influential people in this city were. I was Number Seven – they'd never had anyone in law enforcement before.

Never had the police department known a chief quite like him either, and not only because he made it soon known, 'I personally will not tolerate a racial slur.'

> I think authority is a very poor substitute for leadership – and you can do without it. With leadership, you can be just as forceful, and hold people just as accountable, if not more so.
>
> What's helped me is that for ten years I was a member of the Police Officers' Association, and for two years I was president of the POA. *I* used to come in here and see the Chief, *I* used to go before the city council for salaries and benefits. Now I've a different perspective, but I think we've got a very good relationship, because I've been there. It's kind of unique – not many police chiefs have been president of the union!
>
> Also, I'm pretty young; that helps, I think. I'm forty-five now, and I was forty when made Chief. I was the youngest ever by far, but I was not resented, which was great. And being a Jew, which I'm very upfront about, I've never felt any anti-Semitism, never felt any prejudice at all.
>
> It's a fun job. If you love your city, this is where it's at. As law enforcement goes, so goes this government, so goes this town – I believe that. We're the first bulwark against any kind of corruption, and we have a very direct effect on the quality of life here.

Beside his blotter, lies a photocopied page of newspaper clippings collected over the weekend by the information office. The largest headline reads *Cops report crime decline.* Below it is another story: *Police Officer Is Charged.* This begins,

'A 30-count felony complaint was filed yesterday against a six-year veteran San Diego police officer in connection with a series of burglaries of East San Diego business establishments.'

> It used to be if a policeman did something, then you wrote a report and he was suspended or fired. I prosecute them just like anybody else – that's the way I think it should be. I believe it was Johns Hopkins University did a study on ethics last year, and we came out Number One in law enforcement.

3

For a police department that places such emphasis on ethical conduct, the officers of the San Diego PD appear remarkably free of the 'IA paranoia' that haunts members of many other departments. In fact, it's very seldom that anyone ever mentions Internal Affairs, other than in a jocular context, and it is plain that the thought of complaints from the public is not one which weighs heavily.

There are at least three possible reasons for this. One is that San Diego police officers would seem to be genuinely proud of a reputation for keeping a 'clean house', and are prepared to endorse any measures necessary to maintain that reputation. Although the Second Watch officer arrested on 30 charges of burglary is said in the Press to have been experiencing 'domestic and financial difficulties', the reaction of his colleagues has been singularly unsympathetic. A typical comment being, 'I don't feel sorry for him – no way! I don't care what his problems were. People see that in the paper, and it makes the job a lot tougher. What I care about is what he's done to the department and to *me*.'

Another reason is that, unless a complaint is of a serious nature, it is dealt with by the immediate superior of the officer concerned, thereby avoiding what someone has termed The Molehills-into-Mountains Syndrome.

And thirdly, it would appear that anyone involved in an Internal Affairs investigation expects to be treated fairly.

> *Lieutenant, Juvenile Division:* The IA unit of ours has never really had the bad reputation that some other units in other places have

had. Y'know, where it's all bangety-bang, and they really screw people over and screw them around. Units where, if there was an officer who felt like he'd like to cooperate and really be helpful, they destroy that feeling.

Sergeant, Homicide: Our Internal Affairs operates differently from any other that I've seen. I've heard it happen where officers have asked that Internal Affairs investigate a complaint against them, and not their own commanders, which would indicate it's a pretty fair and unbiased organization.

Inspector J. L. Kennedy is the officer in charge of the Internal Affairs Unit, as well as the Inspection and Control Unit, which places on him the basic responsibility for the 'quality' of the department. He is a distinguished-looking man in his forties, very reserved in manner, with a slow, almost reluctant way of speaking, verging on the morose.

The department averages about eight-hundred to nine-hundred complaints a year – not a large number. The public is satisfied about our accountability, very much so. I think we've proved over and over again we're much more objective, and will probably take much more serious action, than a civilian review board.

We have nothing whatsoever to do with the discipline in Internal Affairs. Sometimes we hear what discipline was taken, sometimes we feel it was too severe, sometimes not severe enough – mostly the latter.

And that's where the other side of the business comes in, the Inspection and Control. If we conduct an inspection where the command is constantly too soft, or constantly too hard, we point it out to the Chief. No rank is immune from quality control. In the first inspection I carried out myself, they found that the Chief had erred, the Number Two Chief had made a mistake, and right on down the line.

Random checks are carried out continually. The Inspection Unit may pick on a burglary case, say, and make a 'backwards investigation', contacting everybody involved in it, including the victim and any witnesses, to assess the quality of the work done. The complaints handled at command level are also subject to review, and here again everybody concerned is contacted.

Turning to the more serious complaints handled by Internal Affairs itself, Inspector Kennedy shows the same degree of equanimity.

I would imagine the most common would be to do with an allegation of false arrest or excessive force. The great majority are found to be unfounded – or we can't sustain the complaint, because it was a one-on-one situation. Self-defense is a defense to resisting arrest or an assault on a police officer – a defense attorney would be derelict if he did not file that allegation, or at least attempt to do so.

4

Over in the coffee shop, with the time now approaching one-twenty, much of the talk is still revolving around major disturbances and the unsettling prospect of standing in the middle of a mob that's throwing things. Some club sandwiches and bowls of salad are being only picked at.

At other tables, however, appetites remain unaffected even by topics that could readily deter those with less seasoned stomachs from their lunch. 'When I was in Sex Crimes before,' remarks a detective, continuing a conversation about the curious requests sometimes made by the public, 'one guy had a woman call who said she wanted to talk to him about a problem she was having with her husband – she wanted to know if there was anything we could do. "What's the trouble?" he said. "Well," she said, "the trouble is that my husband puts wieners up his butt, then he puts them back in the refrigerator. I have to keep throwing wieners away all the time, and we don't eat them any more."'

'Oh, *gross* . . .' exclaims another detective, delighted.

'Hey, there's more. "I could put up with that," she said, "but the other day I went to the refrigerator to make a salad, and I found a head of lettuce in there. This lettuce, he'd punched a hole in it – "'

Another burst of laughter, which briefly attracts the attention of Sergeant Eduardo Juarez who is seated with two Mexican colleagues working liaison down in Tijuana. He will be leading one of the three riot squads this afternoon.

The moment passes. Patrol officers and detectives slip back into their separate worlds again, each with its own pressures and anxieties. Not that they are entirely divorced from one another, because thanks to Patrol, Kim Benton and her fellow Burglary detective, the impeccable Joe Cronin, lunching in the corner, are having themselves a very good Monday.

300

Joe Cronin came in this morning to discover that his prime suspect in the stolen firearms case, the fourteen-year-old known as Zizz, had been arrested last night by the Gang Detail at his grandparents' home, and is available for questioning. Zizz, incidentally, has also indicated he might have been the supplier of the shotgun used in the Chicano Park gang-retribution shooting.

And as for Kim Benton, she has had no need for a mood elevator today either. Carl Brunner's glue-sniffer, arrested in the park last night and subsequently also charged with being in possession of stolen property, has turned out to be the missing accomplice in a case of burglary over the weekend. While questioning the burglary suspect about his accomplice, she had asked, 'Okay, what does he look like?' – and he'd said, 'Well, sometimes he has a harmonica.'

5

The number of reported burglaries in San Diego has dropped by 5 percent over the last quarter, according to the clipping headed *Cops report crime decline* which lies beside Chief Kolender's blotter. Homicides and robberies are down by 15 and 16 percent, respectively, and there has been a 1.7 percent decrease in the number of crimes reported overall, when compared to the same period last year.

Comforting reading at a time when the Los Angeles Police Department is reporting a 16.7 percent increase in homicides, and further rises in other major crime for the first six months of the year. Robbery, up 20.4 percent; forcible rape, up 6.2 percent; aggravated assault, up 5.2 percent; burglary, up 13 percent; theft, up 9.1 percent; and motor vehicle theft, up 10.1 percent – making a total average increase of 11 percent.

Not that Chief Kolender feels able to account for why his city has escaped so lightly.

> I don't know why crime went down, I don't know . . . Violence is down, property is down – property crime, I can understand, with the advent of these neighborhood alert groups and getting the public involved. Maybe the quality of life here is higher than many other places – the climate, the newness of the community, plenty of things to do. I think that helps to keep the crime down.

And as of Friday, we will have the most people ever on the streets in the history of San Diego. We *always* had less policemen, per thousand population, than any other city in this country, because by the criteria the (city) government set up for judging the quality of law enforcement – response time, the amount of case cancellations, all those things – we were tops, and there didn't seem any need for more policemen. But in recent years we found ourselves very undermanned, and so we went to the council with what we thought were sophisticated rationale for an increase, and they bought it. Over the past couple of years, we've gotten over a 100 more police officers a year, and we're also going heavy into civilizing jobs – the training director, public information officer, range master, the people in Communications.

There has of course been a controversial side to the recruitment undertaken in recent years, with allegations being made, within the department, of a decided bias toward women and minority candidates.

Chief Kolender doesn't deny this. But what annoys him is that his critics seem wilfully ignorant of the position he finds himself in with regard to recruiting. He is also profoundly irritated by accusations of unjustly favoring this group with 'preferential treatment', by way of unmerited promotions and special assignments.

Five years ago, the city was investigated by the Department of Justice, and to make a long story short, they felt that the police department was in fact discriminating against women and minorities.

That's true. We had black slots and brown slots and all that kind of stuff, and women were only detectives and never in Patrol. When I became Chief, there were only twenty-eight women in the department.

But these guys that bitch are stupid. It's nothing like in the Sheriff's Office. He promotes because they're black – he's going to have a black list, a Mexican list, and a white list. Never happens here. Where we have quotas, it's at entry level.

We must hire, according to a mandate, twenty percent women, fifteen percent Chicano, and ten percent black – and we're barely making those numbers. These are not goals, they are quotas set for us by the Federal Government. I don't like it. I think it's terrible. But the Federal Government did it.

And they hold over the city's head the cutting off of millions of dollars if the city doesn't comply, and so the city complies, because they've gotta.

You've heard the three greatest myths in the world, haven't you? 'The check is in the mail' – 'I won't make you pregnant' –

and, 'Hi, I'm from the Federal Government, and I'm here to help you!' Bullshit. They get you by the balls, and you've had it.

That's where we are in that thing.

And we've tried very hard not to lower our standards in the training of the women and the minorities. We've done very well, judging by their success rate, but we're not perfect – we have made some mistakes. In many cases, we're not hiring as high a caliber of people as we should, as evidenced by the fact that some of them leave. Most are being terminated by us because they couldn't cut it, because they weren't qualified.

It's a very very complex issue when you start to talk about the educational system and the socio-economic conditions these people come from – about their attitudes. You know, they have to be nondiscriminatory also, and just because you're black or a Mexican, it doesn't mean you're free from prejudice. There are a whole lot of problems.

Special treatment? *Nobody* becomes a sergeant because they're black or because they're a woman. There's a written exam, an oral interview, and a grade by a review board. Could they give a woman or a minority a higher grade? – Yes. Do they? – I don't think so. I give them no orders either way.

But I have appointed minorities and women to positions of leadership because they are minorities and women in an effort to set them up as role models. It is not an officer becoming a sergeant. We've also got groups that deal with the minority community – like the School Task Force – and I've given those jobs to minorities because I thought they'd be more effective.

Some of the role models are outstanding. What we have to do is encourage them, let them know we want them to get promoted and so forth, but that we can't lower our standards or make people a rank because of their ethnic background. And anyway, the good ones wouldn't take the rank – it would piss them off. If you were black, would you want to be a lieutenant because you're black, or because you're a good cop?

And that's the way it's got to be. So it's up to the administration and to me to see that what we do is fair, and that we have a humanistic approach to the way we treat people in this police department – then we can worry about the community later. Start from within. Meaningful change in law enforcement, or in any institution, has *got* to come from within and not from without. You can't force it.

Tucked away in the fifth paragraph of the clipping on San Diego's latest crime figures is a decided change in the number of reported rapes in the city: they have risen by no fewer than 33 percent.

6

'There's no one reason why rapes are on the increase – if in fact they are,' says Sergeant Mike Dalton of the Sex Crimes Detail. 'Maybe the reporting of rape is on the increase because of groups like the C.W.S.S. Rape Crisis Center who encourage victims to come forward and to contact the police department. They're no longer our adversaries, they're our allies. They'll say, "You can go to the police, they won't mistreat you, you'll be treated properly."'

The Sex Crimes Detail has two sergeants and nine investigators, plus a secretary. They work in a bright, cheerful-looking office, the walls of which are kept free from the usual humorous 'mood elevators' cherished by detectives. There is, however, one very droll, oblique comment on the nature of the detail's work – a poster that shows and describes the characteristics of various sharks.

The two sergeants have their desks in a glassed-in cubicle on the far side of the room. They also share a warmth of personality and an open-minded attitude that is immediately apparent to any caller.

Sergeant Susan Astaire can recall when standards of rape investigation were very different: 'Fifteen years ago, you would have been horrified!' A quietly attractive woman of forty-seven, unauthoritarian in bearing, she seems to have a core of tranquil maturity.

I was twenty-nine when I came into the department after a bad marriage. Ninety percent of the time, I thoroughly enjoy it. The only time ninety percent I *hated* was when I worked Internal Affairs. That I happen to fully believe in, but I came closest to getting an ulcer I've ever done!

I've only been back in Sex Crimes for about three months. A lot of young officers say, as they bring in a victim or a suspect, 'Boy, I couldn't work this all the time!' But when they've been around a little longer, they'll find yes, they can. There's a great deal of satisfaction, and a lot of frustration – and sometimes with a suspect you have the feeling (*she shudders*), but it's imperative you don't show this. Let's face it, we're not all *that* good.

Sergeant Dalton is a two-forty-pound six-footer who describes himself as a 'family-type person'; he has been married

eighteen years, and has three teenagers. His original ambition
was to be a veterinarian, but he soon followed his father into
the Philadelphia PD. He has a broad, engaging face, a ready
wit, and radiates a jolly yet profound sense of contentment.

I was a motorcycle officer in Philadelphia and that struck fear into
the hearts of everybody, and I loved it. I loved it! And it
accomplished something: you put guys like that in where you
have trouble, and it stops the trouble. But I matured and got that
out of my system.

That's why we don't take people into Investigations until
they've had some experience, because otherwise they can't relate
to the crooks. You've got to be around for a while, raised your own
children, seen them get into trouble with your best friend, had
your mother or father arrested for drunk driving, all that kind of
thing – and to have realized: 'Hey, to err is human!' It makes you a
much better police officer.

I came out here to San Diego because I heard it was more
professional, and worked a lot of different assignments, including
Homicide. My goal was to be a supervisor in Sex Crimes and I've
been back about a year. In spite of the fact I'm not in love with the
way courts do things all the time, they still take rape more
seriously than they do just about any other crime, and so the
self-satisfaction you get is much closer to being equal to the
amount of effort you put in. I've worked Vice where you arrest the
prostitutes and they reduce to disturbing the peace and fine them
ten dollars. It wasn't meaningful. *This* is meaningful: the people
we take off the street, need to be off the street – and with the
victims, you can help people.

I still think about some of the heavy cases when I go home. My
wife's a nurse, a night supervisor; we both see death, we see
tragedy, we see fantastic disappointment – we have a hell of a lot
in common, talking about work and things like that. But, for
reasons of mental health, you've got to be able to divorce yourself
from it. I learned long ago that people I arrested would spit on me
and call me a rotten, no-good, son-of-a-bitch pig and that what I
had to think, was, 'Well, you're still a crook, you're going to jail,
but when I go home tonight, I'm "Mommy and Daddy".'

I've found my own little niche. I accept those things I can't
change, and I change those things I can. It's not bad for a
bald-headed guy of forty-two.

A detective, just back from lunch, puts his head round the
door. 'She doesn't want us to come and get her, but we're
kicking around the idea of going out there and just talking to
her, trying to convince her to come back with us.'

'Did she say for a fact she didn't want to come down?' asks
Sergeant Dalton.

305

'No, no – she said she didn't want to testify.'

'We've got to get that guy off the street.'

'He could kill somebody, because he's smart enough to realize that we catch him every time now, and so if he did it that way, there'd be no evidence.'

Sergeant Dalton ponders a moment. 'Okay, if you want to run up there, go ahead,' he says.

Sex offenders have the highest rate of recidivism. I think I know one of the reasons. Unfortunately, from my own narrow point of view, the system in California is that, upon being found guilty, they are all sent for evaluation as to whether they are amenable for treatment in a psychiatric hospital. In the hospitals, they learn from other rapists – who've been there longer – how to play the game, how to say the magic words the doctor wants to hear, and they all become like parakeets. We've heard from some of them that, when they sit in these rap sessions and groups, they'll talk to each other about, 'What do I do next time, so the cops won't get me?' And somebody says, 'Cover the victim's face, so she can't identify you – do this, do that.' So what it is, it's a trade school on how to become a better rapist!

And it used to be super, the courts could sentence them from three (years) to life. Then the social bleeding hearts said, 'It's not fair for a person to go away and never know when he can come back to society.' Well, that's tough shit, in my opinion, lump it! But now they've come up with determinate sentencing: for rape, it's six, seven or nine years, they'll be eligible for parole at one-half of their sentence, and they automatically get one-third off for good behavior. What's happened is we've lost the ability to put the rapist away for a long period of time – he could be out in a year again.

The victims are terrified, absolutely terrified, that the suspect is going to come back to them – you know, before we catch them, at the time of trial, and after they're put away. It's part of our job to explain that rarely if ever happens.

Juries are also a major source of frustration to Sergeant Dalton and his colleagues in the Sex Crimes Detail.

There are some areas where we're still in the Dark Ages as regards rape. We've had hung juries where we've talked to the jury afterward, and we've asked, 'Why did you vote for not guilty? Was our case that weak?' – 'Oh, no, you had a good case, but he was too good-looking to be a rapist! That guy could walk in any bar and pick somebody up – he doesn't have to rape anybody.' We even have some judges of the old school who also figure nobody can be raped unless there's a little bit of guilt on their part, so you never know how the heck a jury's going to go! All that physical evidence, the confession and the rest of it, out the window –

because they don't understand that a rapist doesn't do it for that.

With most rapists, the victim's not a sex object – *it's a revenge object*. They want to degrade and humiliate as much as they possibly can, that's the whole purpose of it. It's basically they've developed a hatred for women. A great many of them had domineering mothers or grandmothers, or were the only male in a family with three or four daughters. That's why you have some who rape old women, because they represent maybe a grand-mother who raised them and was very strict – or perhaps there was a sister who got nice party dresses while he had to wear old clothes, and he'll seek out victims who'll represent her.

We also deal with forced anal sex, and I've seen, over the past two or three years, an enormous increase in that. Maybe the rapist has turned to sodomy to degrade and humiliate his victim because he thinks that regular sex is so free and easy now that it won't degrade a girl who's had five or six boyfriends.

Positive changes have been happening as well, however, much to the satisfaction of Sergeants Dalton and Astaire.

Before, the defense attorney could cross-examine the victim about her previous chaste character – how many times she'd had it, and with how many different people. But after a lot of pressure from police organizations and women's groups, the legislature realized it made no difference what the woman's previous character was. Now the only thing they can still bring in is her relationship with the suspect. And there was another law just passed, thank God, that says the victim doesn't have to prove any longer that she resisted. Well, damnit, a robbery victim has never had to show he resisted being robbed! But up until last month, a rape victim did, and why the hell should she be singled out? Because that meant she had to resist and maybe get physically hurt. Statistics show that of the women who resist, about eighty percent don't get raped – but seventy percent of them end up suffering severe physical injuries. It wasn't fair.

And among the positive changes the police department has itself introduced, two are of special importance. The first is that patrol officers are trained to treat alleged rape victims as *bona fide* victims, no matter what doubts they may have about the veracity of the story told to them. The other change concerns the medical examination of such victims.

They used to be taken to the jail hospital and then put up on the cold table, where they'd be given the physical. Then we realized that this was adding to the trauma of the victim, and so now we have four hospitals contracted to do these examinations in their emergency rooms. Our lab people have trained the doctors and nurses in the physical evidence that's needed for court, and there's a rape protocol book the hospitals follow, developed by some of the rape advocate groups and our department.

Included in the contract with the hospitals, is a psychiatric consult with a social worker, and they also give victims these CWSS and REAL (Rape Emergency Assistance League) brochures, so everyone has somebody to talk to. The advocate groups will go with them to court, kind of give them moral support, and help them with their problems. They're trained counselors – we aren't.

The very fact that the San Diego PD and local rape advocacy and support groups collaborated on the protocol book lends extra weight to Sergeant Dalton's claim that they enjoy 'a good rapport', and work together in the interests of rape victims. Ironically, however, such cooperation is sometimes thwarted by the high standard of empathy and professionalism that the Sex Crimes Detail aspires to.

If the uniform officer has his act together, then he's the Rock of Gibraltar, and that contact can start bringing the victim back to reality. Then they meet our investigators and they find, 'Hey, these people *understand* what happened – they know what's going on inside my head!'

When a victim is raped, she feels face to face with death, that she is not in control of her destiny – somebody else is. You know, some maniac with a knife or gun, or maybe just somebody much stronger than she is, has total control of whether she lives or dies, turns left or turns right, stands up or sits down. That is very very traumatic. And so our investigators are trained to put them back in control of their lives. We say, 'We would like you to do this – but it's your decision. We would like you to prosecute – but it's your decision. We would like you to come to a line-up tomorrow morning – but it's your decision.' What we're doing is restoring them to what life is all about: making your own free choices.

And when I was an investigator, I'd say, 'I know because I'm a male, it's difficult to talk to me, but talk to me as you would your own family physician. I've heard these stories before – nothing will shock me. Believe me, I'm on your side.'

They start to feel comfortable with you, they bare their souls to you, they lean on us. We have trouble getting them to go to other agencies for follow-up work, because they feel that these other organizations are maybe just snoopy people, and that they've already done enough, talking with the investigator. Not nearly as many of our victims go to the other agencies as we'd like – and they should go, because they need counseling. Mothers and fathers also need counseling, husbands too. Some husbands want to immediately have sex with their wives after they've been raped, to re-establish they belong to them. But the wives don't need to have that Everest reconquered, they may not be ready for sex with love for a week or a month, and when the husbands push the issue, that creates more problems – some real severe mental ones.

But I guess it's a kind of a pleasing problem that a lot of our victims really rely on our investigators for a long time after the crime occurs. It's very difficult not to get emotionally involved with them, when you see the mental problems they have. They call us *years* after to tell us: 'I'm engaged' or 'I'm getting married' – or, 'I've just had a baby, and I've named him after you.'

7

It's rising two o'clock.

Pushing aside the remains of a belated lunch, Sergeant Henry Caswell gets up to leave the coffee shop and to return to his office. Two young patrol officers stand aside deferentially at the entrance. They seem alert to an aura of sorts surrounding him, and this brings an echo of what was said last night at the scene of the old woman's murder, when someone compared it to 'sacred ground'.

Sergeant Caswell heads Homicide Team One. He is forty-seven, has a wife and two teenage daughters, and his interests are land investment, sailing, camping, mountains and old guns. His hair is short, his suit and necktie suggest a bucolic conservatism. In fact many might mistake him for a farmer from some dustbowl district – he has that same lean, rather melancholy and introspective look – and for once, such an assumption would not be completely wide of its mark.

> My mother and father had a farm in Michigan where I was raised, and they sold it around when I graduated from high school. We moved out here, and my dad went to work for an aircraft firm. I worked as a lineman for a telephone company, in the aircraft industry, and I was in the Navy for four years. I joined the department twenty-one years ago – I can't really recall exactly why. My father'd worked for the Buffalo PD, and I had an uncle who'd been a policeman.

His progress was rapid. In three years, from walking beats in the black and beach areas, he'd risen to first-class patrolman and been chosen to work Vice. A spell in Burglary followed, another in Homicide (which had only one team in those days), and then came promotion and three years in Patrol.

Before returning to Homicide, he was in Internal Affairs for a while.

> I believe it's a good check and balance in the system, but it was hard to adjust to. It's a tough thing to sit down with a fellow officer and say, 'You're wrong. You shouldn't have hit that guy a second time with the cuffs, once was enough' – when he thinks he was right.

Sergeant Caswell steps from the shade out into the dazzling heat. The patio is brisk with activity. Second Watch officers are bustling about, readying themselves for line-up, and the Narcotics Street Detail has just arrived with some prisoners for fingerprinting and mug-shots. A pair of SWAT officers, looking very military in their combat boots, dark-green pants, dark-blue tee-shirts and caps, are crossing over to the armory. As he passes them, he catches a snatch of earnest discussion about the predicted riot this afternoon. A few years ago, Sergeant Caswell was himself in SWAT as a supervisor, and knows what a countdown period like this can feel like. But right now his mind is preoccupied by last night's homicide-cum-attempted suicide, as he has a message to pass on to one of his team.

> Many times you'll find a husband and wife lying next to each other and dead. Both very willing to go along with what has been planned. A person has terminal cancer, the family deep in debt because of the medical bills, that kind of thing. She'll be in her nicest nightgown and her hair made up, her face made up – and the house will be spick and span, everything in its place. There will be a very precise and detailed note of what people must do. She'll have a hole in her head, and he'll have a hole in his head, and the gun will be in his hand.
>
> I don't think it was money (last night). He had five hundred bucks in his wallet, and there was a big thick wad of World War Two savings bonds. I think it was probably – I'm just guessing now – that if you look into their story, it was just they were lonely, both of them ill and not getting any better.
>
> I'm a deacon in the Church of Christ. I often find myself in the position of trying to reconcile my faith with what I see. But child homicides bother me most. I think it's probably the waste of the whole thing: they're snuffed out, they didn't get a chance. I can understand – I *try* to understand – the Lord taking a child, but for someone else to go out of their way to strangle or mutilate, cut up, shoot or burn to death, that bothers me. It always has.
>
> It's part of why I think Homicide is the ultimate in investigative work – sex crimes don't interest me, and I've never wanted to

work Juvenile. In everything else, you usually have a victim that can talk to you, but in Homicide you're working with a phantom. Your victim's dead, and there really isn't anybody else to look after that person's rights, to defend them and bring the suspect to justice.

Andy Stapleton, the evidence technician or 'lab guy' attached to Team One, also has strong religious convictions. He is a mild, very personable and friendly man in his twenties, with a degree in industrial photography. Occasionally, he takes the photographs at friends' weddings, but for the most part his pictures are confined to violent death.

The first one I went on, it was an elderly lady, a burglary. Somebody broke into her house, and they killed her while she was sleeping for no reason at all. That got to me – it's the kind of thing that happens a lot now. But you get used to it real quick; not knowing the people, you just don't get personally involved.

It's just the way things are. I'm a Christian and I believe in the Second Coming of Christ, and that things aren't goin' to be any better until that happens.

What gives me most satisfaction is being able to catch the bad guy – I love everything except the paperwork. There's four evidence techs in the department, not enough to go round. We'd like to have more – it'd sure help out the investigators if we went out on burglaries and rapes – but we just stick to homicide, unless something special comes up.

The first female Homicide detective in California, Officer Marianne Flynn, is a twenty-nine-year-old lapsed Catholic with 'no particular philosophy' and a brisk, confident way of speaking. She joined the department from Pacific Telephone at twenty-one, wanting a job that was 'different', and was in Criminal Intelligence before joining Team One roughly two years ago.

It was quite by accident. I was working for Pacific Telephone, and my room-mate was going for an application – police work was something she'd always wanted to do. I'd never thought about it prior to then, but I said, 'That's interesting – pick me up one.' It so happened I got the job and she didn't, but she's happy now she didn't, I think. My family reacted shocked, I guess: my dad, kind of troubled; my mother didn't believe it. But it was something different.

Smartly turned out, with medium-length dark-blonde hair and a pleasantly strong, slightly remote face, Marianne Flynn reminds one of a successful sportswoman – a Wimbledon player, perhaps, on her way to a charity luncheon.

> My first year in Homicide was spent doing crime scenes, now I'm interviewing. All ours have been mysteries this year; we've had only a couple of suspects in custody. You get so many, you lose track. People will say names in the office, and I go, 'Huh?'
>
> There's no kind of homicide that bothers me. Dead bodies have never bothered me – I prefer that, I suppose, to having live victims. I found Sex Crimes, where you deal with a live victim, very difficult. And I don't get involved with any of the families – or even with the victim, where we're on an attempted murder. I just do the best I can up to the point where I turn it over to the court.

Responsibility for the crime scene in Team One has now rotated to Chuck Davis, thirty-four, who has spent almost half his twelve years' service working Homicide. He is a tall, lean, dark-haired, good-looking man, wholly American and yet curiously European in some way – it could be there is simply an 'Old World' graciousness about him.

> Whether it's a report I've read, or a suspect I've interviewed, somehow I feel tainted. I go home and take a shower, go over to a friend's jacuzzi. I want to be cleansed of all this ugliness. That *is* the job: it's ugly. And I guess you say to yourself after that, 'Okay, it's gone for a while. I don't want to get dirty again – but, damnit, soap and water will get it off.'
>
> Sometimes, going through everything at a scene, like last night's, you find charm and nice things. In a lot of other cases, you open a refrigerator door and you're taken aback by a graveyard of cockroaches. Or quite often you go to one of these downtown hotels, where drunks get in a fight and one of them keels over and dies. You've got a room about eight feet by ten feet, the stench, bugs, the unkept bed, the matter vegetating in the corner. It has a way of affecting the psyche: you want to get in there and then get the hell out – you don't want to be methodical, you know what happened. But you do your job and you're methodical.
>
> And it's still as glamorous in a sense, I guess, as it was when I first came on. I didn't have any aspirations, I just needed a job to maintain my security after being drafted into the Army, but you get that bug. Then, you know, you've reached this division – Homicide, the epitome of investigation – and you have to be creative, to be continuously mentally involved in a case.
>
> Some people can cut off, most of us can't. You lay in bed thinking, 'Jeez, did I do this? Did I do that?' And you hear your mate say, 'The children need new shoes.' 'Don't bother me right now, I'm thinking about something important . . .' 'But they *do* need shoes! They've got holes in the soles of –' 'Sorry. Just take

some money and go buy them.' You never discuss things. I take my hat off to the wives; they take a lot of mental abuse.

And I can't tell you what the rewards are. After maybe two and a half days without sleep, diligently working on a case, and the person you're working with is a very dangerous person, you nab the guy, and you get like a load of lead off your back. You feel relieved – you've got rid of one evil of society. For a day or so, you get that self-satisfied feeling, the pats on the back, the laurels, the accolades, but the next day, you're back in the old rut again, and people will continue to kill each other.

In this particular job, you strive to think that maybe there is a Supreme Being, and that when your number's up, your number's up. But it has made me more cynical – callous, to a certain degree, when you have to look at whatever somebody has decided to do to a body that isn't his.

On the other hand, it's made me appreciate people a little bit more. In almost every case, when you talk to a suspect, you see that goodness in the person, and you cannot really understand why that goodness went wrong, why it created whatever it was that made the person take another human life.

Sometimes it's not difficult to understand the motivations. I guess the classical situation is a husband and wife who've been married, say, eight years – seven of them tumultuous, with ever-violent confrontations. Finally, it gets to the point where the woman, beaten short of death, can't tolerate it any longer. She takes a gun, and while he's laying on the bed, cold-bloodedly shoots him in the head. If you look at the underlying features of the case, you can maybe feel for the person. But you can go one step further and say, 'Jesus Christ, why have they lived like that for eight years? They could've taken care of it seven years ago!'

Murder is very related to social conditions, to cultures – and American society is based on the freedom of the dollar to impress. It's very competitive, and the competitive conditioning we all go through is a big factor, I believe. Whether you've got baseball or football or whatever, you've got winners and you've got losers – and sometimes the losers can't cope with that idea, with the abuse from playmates or from the coach or from the managers. 'Why did you strike out? Why did you miss it?' They go off and continue to lose, until they decide they *will* win something – by maybe killing somebody.

I forget about the cases that've been; I just get on with the next one. But I do think about, anticipate, the kinds of killings I don't want to work. They are the children, the cop killers, the mom-and-pop grocery stores – people who've worked all their lives, then some jerk goes in for a couple of dollars, and in the heat of the anxiety, shoots them. In the last five years, I've had to work on three cop killings – it's very difficult when you see the fellow lying there on the slab, and you went drinking with him maybe

313

three weeks before. They're the hardest ones, but all three are very, very hard to accept.

Probably the most frightening experiences I've had in talking to suspects has been with cop killers. It's a challenge in itself. You have to approach suspects objectively in order for them to be cooperative, to set up rapport, and with cop killers you have to compromise your values, your subjective conditioning about what's good and what's bad. But you do it, then you spit it out, cleanse yourself, and go on.

My closest friends are police officers. I had a family – past tense, *had*. That's one of the problems with this particular job, the divorce rate is *so* high. I was married for eleven years, and I had three lovely children – I still see them quite often, as much as I'm allowed.

In my first year or so, I began setting goals for myself, and I've accomplished every one. Now I've got to start thinking of going into other areas – you get burned out on this job.

And somebody will replace me. Somebody else will get into the same syndrome that I've been involved in, and it'll continue to ruin marriages, just for a day or so of selfish feelings. That's all it amounts to.

The job of crime scene officer in a San Diego homicide team is extraordinarily demanding, and the results account for a large chunk of the huge 'book' prepared on each case. 'When you're in that house,' explains Matt Svenberg, the fourth member of Team One, 'you describe it in its entirety, down to the flower vases, what types of flowers are in them, the books, the authors . . .' And this despite the fact that the old woman's murder has every appearance of being completely straightforward.

Just as last night's other killing, that of the young gang member who died of stab wounds, had been a 'slam dunker' too – to use Matt Svenberg's expression.

The biggest problem you have with the gang situation is that under our system of law someone accused of a crime has the right to be faced by his accusers in a public trial. If those people are unwilling to go into court, and to go on the stand to establish a corpus, then you have no crime. You can't force witnesses into court; there is a ruling that says we can no longer impeach.

And there is another problem. Say we get a witness into court, and then they get to him. Once he is under oath, he can say he can't recall, can't remember what happened, and then even though you have a twenty-page statement from him and a tape-recording, you can't introduce them. That's it.

Matt Svenberg is very much a professional. His is a friendly face that could win respect for its quiet toughness among Hell's Angels, for its alert intelligence among university intellectuals. About average in build, with fair coloring, he was in Sex Crimes for six years before switching to Homicide thirty months ago.

Everybody wants to be a Homicide detective. The uniform guys joke with you, call you the Lighter-than-air Squad – y'know, the ability to walk on water without getting your cuffs wet!

But it is one of the better jobs, and the satisfaction you derive from putting together an extremely complicated case is hard to explain. With a homicide investigation, you start at the moment of death and you work backward in time. That's all you're doing. You're rebuilding that person's life from everything you can find out about him, and through the reconstruction, you can usually find your answers, although it's a very slow process.

And it's not just you, it's the whole unit, the whole team, and you're just a part. There's no showboating. Showboating doesn't work over here – there are no superstars.

The configuration of a team is different from team to team; personally, I like a working sergeant. It's a tough job for a married person to be in – I'm single – because the hours are feast or famine, and we alternate on a week's call to take the first victim.

I think the highest number of cases we've ever handled has been five in seven days, and that's just one team. Our call-out rate is increasing. At one time, you could be in here and know every case that went down, every case that every team was working on. Now they're coming down so fast that we have to have meetings to bring everybody up to date, because sometimes cases overlap. Last year we had a hundred-and-one, a hundred-and-two – I don't count them any more.

You get some premeditated murders, and they're extremely difficult to figure out, but most of it is spontaneous, and more and more, they're narcotics-oriented. The problem there is getting into the subculture of the narcotics world. They're between the devil and the deep blue sea; they can help you and they can't help you – like if they snitch, it means cutting off their own source of income. You're fighting crime, *and* you're fighting millions of dollars.

We're also starting to see a lot of multiples, two deaths and one suspect. People are now just so much more willing to use gross forms of violence to solve their differences. I don't think you can blame the gun laws or anything else – you can go into your kitchen and make a bomb with just basic kitchen ingredients and the Anarchists' Cookbook! But I once did a paper and the premise I used was that, 'This nation was born and bred on violence'.

Literally, from the time of the colonists and all the way through,

315

we've fought and fought – we've fought other nations, we've fought ourselves. The whole idea to *achieve* – One, is aggressive; and Two, being aggressive one must sometimes use violence – has been really a kind of keynote in our birth, and people work within the system they grew up in.

I'm glad victims' rights are starting to be recognized. We've been so concerned with suspects' rights, we have tended to forget them – but I saw the change quite a bit in Sex Crimes. With homicide victims, it's a switching device: you just have to think that what you're seeing isn't a person, it's just a lump of meat. And unfortunately, that's true: any life force has long since gone, although children get to you. We don't see that many, but you often wonder what their ultimate destiny could have been. A child has started, and it makes you wonder, makes you wonder . . .

And when I leave here, again I like to think of it as a switch at the side of my bed, and I shut it off. My social life isn't police-oriented. I'm not in the subculture, I don't go in for a heavy head-trip on police. I do things that are light and easy, where you can just gear down. I enjoy opera, I enjoy the Starlight Theater – I'm a big fan of Walt Disney. On vacations, I just totally disappear. I have a large touring motorcycle, and I just load it up and I'm *gone.* That's my escape.

Sometimes people ask what my job is, and usually it creates a morbid fascination and I don't like that. So I say, 'I work for the sanitation department.' And if they say, 'What do you do?', then I say, 'Well, I deal in human waste.'

But not entirely. Matt Svenberg also deals in cheating death where possible, and is on call as a highly trained hostage negotiator. It's a 'positive area' of his expertise that is shared by his two fellow officers in Team One. In fact all three of them were present when SWAT was tricked by a murderer and kidnapper – a Nigerian student named Millham Augustine Ossaba – into shooting him dead in a freeway confrontation. And the shots had rung out when Ossaba pointed a pistol at them.

Art was the primary on that, Marianne was the second, and I was the supervisor. It was really a classical suicide – he didn't have a round in the chamber or anything.

I've done about fifteen of them, and they're each very different. The basic philosophy is, if you get past the first thirty minutes without a death, you're going to win. We're prepared to be there for an hour or a month. You try not to lie, in case you lose credibility, and you make it very clear to the person that you are not a decision-maker. You're simply their only link to the outside world.

316

I did a seven-hour one where I had to convince him first not to shoot me, because I had to stand outside a window to do the negotiations. And then he wanted to test-fire the gun, so I convinced him he should shoot the coffee-pot – which he did. Then he shot the light fixture, wanted me to buy him drugs to overdose. I told him I couldn't. So ultimately he said, 'Will I feel it?' I said, 'You may – there's a chance you may linger.' There is a transference effect. He shot himself, and it was like I got shot.

Sergeant Caswell leaves the patio and makes his way to Homicide, where he finds Marianne Flynn at her desk, writing up a report. She has been to both the morgue and to the hospital today, following up on the 'slam dunker' murder-attempted suicide case. The suspect is already on the road to recovery.

What's sad about it is, the first chance he gets, he'll commit suicide – that's how I see the outcome of this. It wasn't as if he was 'crying out' last night; he obviously made a very good job of it. Why there was water in the bath tub, I don't know . . .

'She died from strangulation,' says Sergeant Caswell, delivering his message.

Marianne Flynn looks up in astonishment. *'She died from strangulation?* You're kidding!'

'That's what Dr Gardiner says.'

'What did he strangle her with?'

'That's what he was wondering.'

'I just noticed lividity through that area, but there wasn't any bruising I could see. Interesting . . . I *wonder* what he used to strangle her with.'

'That blow to the back of the head,' adds Sergeant Caswell, in his slow, somewhat mournful voice, 'there weren't any fractures or hemorrhages.'

'Oh, really?' Marianne Flynn frowns a little. 'Both the embalmer and myself felt there, and it was obvious that there was something – naturally, we didn't do any X-rays or anything. Strangulation? Hmmmm.'

Sergeant Caswell moves towards the doorway. 'I don't remember seeing anything. She was on a pillow. Some bruising to the muscles of the throat.'

'When I was up at the morgue, I felt the head,' Marianne Flynn repeats firmly. 'There was a crackling.'

Puzzled, still with a slight frown, she watches Sergeant

Caswell leave for his own office, and then takes down a textbook on forensic pathology. Turning to the section on strangulation, she first studies the color plates.

> Autopsies fascinate me. Not so much autopsies on the homicide victims, but the other people. Really, it fascinates me how people let their bodies go, what age and smoking and things like that can do, cancer. And of course, layers of fat fascinate me!

8

Close at hand, clack-clack, clack-clack . . .

Then a yelp of siren, rabbit-chopped short.

Over the last hour, Second Watch has been moving out on to the streets of Central Division again. By three, the last of B Squad should be ten-eight from the station, leaving behind a motley collection of fellow officers, all brandishing riot sticks, on an improvised drill ground behind the 'back lot'.

About half a dozen are in uniform. The rest are wearing a wide variety of casual clothes: brightly-colored tops, jeans and running shorts, striped ankle-socks, desert boots and sneakers.

They joke around, waiting for the SWAT lieutenant to begin his crash course in riot control. Right now, he's having a quick word with Captain Walker, who has been at the station since seven-thirty this morning, checking and double-checking the contingency plan for today.

Then comes the order to form ranks. Sergeant Juarez has eighteen officers in his riot squad, including two policewomen. There are another pair in the twenty-strong squad led by FTO Doug Summers, the bane of Billy Johnson, but none among the sixteen officers led by Agent Jack Lipton, also of Second Watch, a quiet, very reserved man.

It is at a moment such as this that many male officers feel particularly doubtful about the wisdom of allowing female officers 'equal opportunities to end up in hospital'. Lieutenant Rae Chassam, of Tinkerbell fame, who has accompanied Captain Walker out here to help with the marching, is unequivocal in his views.

The women can handle virtually all police work, there's no

problem there. But when push comes to shove, once they are attacked, they lose – which is a shame. And not only do they lose, they tend to be retired because they take a lot of damage. A male officer can be whipped, sure, but he'll come back again, and a little scar on a man's face might be interesting – a scar on a woman's face is disfiguring. What the hell, we've around a hundred-and-fifty women on this department, and I bet you that I could whip any one of them in a fist fight, and I'm forty-seven years old.

And it would be difficult to accuse him of being simply prejudiced about female officers, as his delightfully funny and vivacious wife is a former policewoman herself.

The marching is a bit of a shambles to begin with. It is very plain that most people have half-forgotten whatever they might have been taught about close-order drill, which hardly has much place in day-to-day community-oriented policing.

Sergeant Juarez, unjaunty and serious-looking for once, calls out, 'No, your other foot, Jorge – your *other* foot!'

A downtown beat officer glances up from the trunk of his unit, into which he is putting his helmet and black attaché case. He watches the marching for a few seconds.

What do we really need now in a cop? We don't want a robot, but we do want the efficiency of a robot. That conflict causes more problems for an officer, I think, than anything else. We want the chicken's head, but we don't want his looks!

9

Then Ben Williams closes his trunk lid, and gets behind the wheel. He starts up his unit. His ignition key is attached to a brass key-ring stamped with the word 'MACHO'.

The unit is moving, leaving the back lot.

Ben Williams is thirty-three. He has a young son and daughter. He does not own a car, but rides buses. He reads a lot and subscribes to *Time* magazine.

Market Street.

'Ten-eight from the station . . .'

The 'MACHO' key-ring swings as the unit dips crossing the gutter. Private joke, private laughter. A wry rumble of amusement is very much part of Ben Williams. Cindy Lewis has noticed: 'He's always really cordial.'

319

Market Street, the four-hundred block.

And sometimes he invites people to laugh out loud with him. He has this habit of saying sudden, pithy things. Like: 'I'm outnumbered by *one* person . . .'

There's a heat shimmer over Market Street, a puddling of light. The radio is having one of its rare silent spells.

Ben Williams rides with his shotgun in the trunk.

> Whenever they call for a department shoot, there I am. I'm accurate, in that I hit the target in the 'deadly' area, and they say, 'Hey, you're a really good shot!' – and all this good noise.
>
> But guns just don't . . . If at all possible, I would much rather not carry one. I'm perceived as a threat just to look at me, and my ability – or inability! – to carry out that threat does not affect it, I'm a threat.
>
> I had to shoot a man. The four-hundred block on Market, 1978, I had to shoot a man.
>
> Two card players. The loser became quite upset. He threatened the winner, and said he was taking his money back. The winner pulled out a revolver and said, 'Oh no, you're not . . .' The loser said, 'You're right – I'm not!' And ran outside.
>
> I'm driving along, minding my *own* business, and: 'Officer, officer, officer! A man's pulled a gun on me!' I get out of my car and go inside. The winner sees me and he runs into a room at the back. I didn't see a gun, but I believed the loser, so I drew my weapon.
>
> Then the door to this back room opens, and the winner steps out. He looks at me and draws down on me. That was *it*. I shot him. I didn't kill him, I hit him in the arm. It was enough for me to shoot a person. I was off work for three weeks and two days.

Way up, two hundred and more feet above the bay, a bread truck breaks down on the swirling curve of the bridge to Coronado, and the radio comes to life again.

10

Fiery-cheeked, rawboned and with a voice like a whipcrack, the SWAT lieutenant surveys the ranks of solemn faces drawn up in front of him on the dusty square beyond the back lot.

Lee Easton, with his military-police bearing; former Lomas gang-member George Ramirez; Luke Jones, who has in his pocket a poem written specially for him by the drunk who shares his enthusiasm for Samuel Taylor Coleridge.

'The clavicle, the cartilage here, the groin . . .' recites the SWAT lieutenant, running through the riot-baton target areas once again.

He has the three squads repeat the defensive moves. Longer batons certainly afford better protection than the COP variety.

Then comes the 'psyching up'. He warns everyone against staring vacantly into the mob facing them, lest this helps to weaken the line. 'You pick on some asshole and *you look right at him*, into his eyes. You look at him so that he just *knows* there's nothing you love better'n to kick ass and break bone!'

Next, comes the briefing in the coffee shop at half-past four. Time to change into body armor.

11

Four-thirty finds Ben Williams dropping off his second downtown drunk at the detox.

> I didn't want to be a policeman. There's a fear I've still got of the police. I had some negative, negative experiences with the police; through relatives, through being from the South and the attitude of the police there. I was scared as heck of 'em.
>
> But I met a black officer here who was actively recruiting black officers. I was really bored with my job of electronics tech, watching traces on an oscilloscope. I thought about the life-style, the excitement. This was in 1969, and I kept the application until 1970, and sent it in after a lot of discussion – I was married then, the job takes a lot from you.
>
> My family was *shocked*. They thought I'd flipped, because of my fear. I would wet on myself when contacted by the police at the teenager stage. To this day, we still talk about it: the only one out of five boys ditchin' in this field.
>
> It's an interesting job, but I don't really see it as serving its original function, 'to protect and serve'. It's go, go, go – you're into more of a secretary than a protector. Do I have a value? Yuh, I do. I fulfill a condition delegated by the Federal Government that you will have *x* number of blacks!
>
> Hopefully, I am able to come forward with this power that I feel, which is larger than it really is. There are times when I want to come on like King Kong and his troop of Tarzans, but most of the time, I want a good rapport.
>
> Being black gives me the advantage in the field. I'm a threat –

321

I'm a threat to this individual because of my color. I know it. When I get out of my unit downtown, 'Oh my God, here comes a big black gorilla – *and* he's got a gun!' Blacks are mean, blacks are dirty, blacks are untrustworthy. All things black are bad. The good guy always wears a white hat. So how do you make people believe in a black policeman, a black cowboy?

Getting back into his unit, he informs Communications that he is 'in service' once again, and is immediately sent on a four-fifteen call to one of the five-dollar-a-night hotels downtown. According to the hotel clerk making the report, it's some form of family disturbance.

Ben Williams leaves the detox parking lot in a hurry. This private, complex man, seldom keeps his public waiting. Moreover, in his view, a family disturbance carries a high priority.

If your life's going to be taken, the chances are it's not going to be by a stranger. It's going to be a relative, a person that knows you. So our job is protecting poeple who know each other *from* each other. It's really similar to the Vietnam War, where the North and the South are the same people. It makes the job easier, it makes the job tougher.

12

Big Bill Kolender leaves his Chief's Office and strides down the long hall leading to the main entrance and the patio, heading for the coffee shop.

He passes the Gang Detail's door. The duty roster on the wall reads like graffiti:

> *Italian gelding*
> *JR*
> *Kah*
> *Roco*
> *Sad Sax*
> *Sleepy*
> *Piru*

Nobody at home; they must all be over at the briefing. Specialists of many descriptions are a help when a major disturbance threatens.

Out on to the patio, with its criss-crossing figures; a straggly line of relatives accompanying a robbery victim to an interview; young Mexican children huge-eyed at the sight of so many holsters, envious.

> Our biggest problem today is not the public, not the government, but the handling and the holding of jobs of accountability. When you've got thirteen-hundred people, and most of them carry a gun, you've got a problem. The power there.

The coffee shop is crowded. An easel has been set up, and on it is a street map showing the county courthouse and the area immediately surrounding it. Now only plainclothes officers are in casual clothes; everyone else is in uniform, and some have their visored helmets with them.

> When they wear helmets, they look pretty ominous – you can't tell one from another. It dehumanizes. With this Metzger thing, it's a good idea.

Faceless mob meets faceless force.

13

The elevator in this downtown hotel has no buttons, just a lever poking out of a dented metal box. Perhaps one of these dents was made by Gary Gilmore's frustrated fist.

Very slowly, the elevator creaks its way upward, carrying Ben Williams to the four-fifteen family disturbance.

> 'Oh Daddy, what do you do?'
> My son realizes I am involved in a dangerous job, and he'd rather not involve himself in constant threat. He defers to his mother's teaching, 'You can lose your life at any time, and the black people don't like you.'
> He wants to be liked. I think most people want that. But if you need people to like you, to think kindly of you, this is not the job for you.
> All I want is for people to leave each other *alone*.
> And if they're going to engage in confrontations, then fine, let them engage *me*. I want to be the person that's disliked; I'd rather be the baddie than let that happen between them. And I'll feel better, because they have lives that are going to continue, they need each other, they're going to need the strength that each can give.

323

Often they'll both attack me, siding with each other and say, *'We* don't need you anyway!' And I say, 'You're right! Don't call me again, man.'

A glimpse of a midget in a red bathrobe, and then Ben Williams brings the elevator to a shaky halt almost level with the floor above. Some of these hotels become as familiar as home.

There's a lot of shouting going on.

14

The briefing in the coffee shop is indeed brief and to the point. People listen attentively. One of the speakers is a svelte-looking young man, just like the detectives one sees in cop shows, who has been flown in specially to deliver a short address on the tactics used by a section of the demonstrators expected today.

Beware of Coke cans, this expert warns, speaking from personal experience. Used as missiles, they're heavy and have enough edges to inflict nasty head injuries. Opened cans, he adds, are also used, as the liquid from them has a blinding effect when it splashes over a helmet visor.

Beware of demonstrators carrying rolled newspapers, he warns. The newspapers have been known to be hiding lengths of pipe.

Beware of the apparently innocuous poles used to hold placards aloft, he warns. These are sometimes disguised weapons, easily detached for use by demonstrators skilled in the martial art of kendo.

Another of the main speakers is Jack Lipton, the man behind the whole rather delicate operation. How embarrassing it would be, were the KKK leader to be injured because a police department, run by a Jew who claims to be above petty bigotry, had failed to afford him adequate protection. But Jack Lipton, who volunteered to plan the strategy and to compile all the detailed check-lists, appears quietly confident. And so does Chief Kolender, as he listens from the sidelines.

The remarkable thing is, of course, that Jack Lipton's rank is only that of agent; in most other police departments, he'd simply be taking orders today. But Chief Kolender believes in recognizing enthusiasm and ability irrespective of rank, and in lowering such a responsibility to the lowest possible level. 'It's what,' he says 'makes people feel good about themselves, and good about their jobs.'

What's more, he's willing to stake his future on it.

15

The four-fifteen in the hotel is in fact a confrontation between two separate families, one Mexican and one black, living in adjoining rooms, and is being pursued most vigorously by the womenfolk on either side.

Ben Williams listens and listens, first to one faction and then to the other. The most noticeable thing about his style of policing is the way he'll listen to people, letting them have their say, rarely interrupting.

> He should feel in command, that I'm listening. Many times, I will resolve a situation, but if they think about it, they'll find I said nothing – *nothing*.

'Well?' demands the Mexican matron in red, having reached the point where she expects a verdict in her favour.

'I believe everything you've told me,' Ben Williams says to her.

Then, to the black matron in green, he says, 'I believe everything you've told me.'

'But if you believe *me*,' protests the matron in red, 'how can you believe *her*?'

'No problem.'

'Well, who's wrong?'

'Me.'

'How's that?' asks the matron in green.

Ben Williams smiles. 'It's you've *both* got me going, damn it!'

They have to laugh, and they do it together.

Only a minute or so later, Ben Williams is back in the elevator, coaxing it to begin a weary descent.

> Before the police force, people banded together for protection, they used their big brothers. Now we're the big brothers. 'There

he is! Go to him! Hey, now I feel better!' The individual feels better, feels safe, knowing his big brothers are always out here when he needs them.

But we're not. My God, if something went down right now, he could lose his life – *fifty* people could lose their lives before I could get there.

But ask the people standing at a bus stop, 'How many police are there in this area?' And they'll say, 'Oh, about sixty?' When they see a police car, they don't look at the driver, and we're back and forth, back and forth. They're thinking, 'Hmm, there's another, that's the fifth one.' It's me again! In fact there are probably ten.

I told the lieutenant the other day, 'It's a good façade we keep up.' If we lose it – Oh God, *watch* out.

16

The clock in the mobile command post, now parked behind the State Building, a short distance from the county courthouse downtown, gives the time as 5:45 p.m.

Captain Walker and Lieutenant Chassam are both here, bent on turning the evening's work into a thundering anti-climax. But just in case things don't go as planned, and Captain Walker has been over that plan again and again with Agent Lipton, a trestle table has been set up for the paperwork involved in processing scores of prisoners, and there are bunches of nylon cuffs festooned here and there, so that arresting officers can take their own handcuffs back into the fray again.

It was in fact originally planned that Tom Metzger should be spirited into the courthouse through a private entrance, but the local press has reported him as saying, 'I don't want to give the impression of being carted around in a box by the police.'

This, the only alternative, is costing thousands of dollars in overtime. 'Some of these people,' says Chief Kolender, referring to the demonstrators, 'have the same propensity for violence as the Klan – I have to do what is necessary to protect the people on both sides, regardless of their politics.'

High on the surrounding rooftops, silhouetted figures keep watch. The reserve riot squad mills round the command post. Over on the other side of the street, SWAT officers are on standby beside their 'bread truck'.

A young officer jokingly practices the robotlike step he learned earlier this afternoon, which will be used if the riot squads have to advance against the demonstrators. First a hard, stamping pace forward, and then the other foot comes forward, scraping slowly and loudly over the asphalt. Stamp-scrape, stamp-scrape; mechanical, inexorable, menacing.

Down the street, according to the radio in the mobile command post, about sixty demonstrators, belonging to the Committee Against Racism and the Progressive Labor Party, are chanting and waving placards outside the courthouse entrance.

One of the placards reads: DEATH TO THE KKK AND ALL FASCISTS.

17

Back and forth, back and forth, it is inevitable that Ben Williams passes the four-hundred block on Market every day, just as he is passing it now, hastening to give cover to a unit making a hot stop on a reported stolen vehicle.

That shooting. I took it kinda hard. It was an emotional thing for me, seeing me actually hurt someone. You get to see a shrink now, to make sure you're okay.

I think it's cultural, by the way – this empathy! It's inbred in blacks, this feeling of caring, this deep undying devotion to 'the other'. I've read books on how blacks react to death, to injury, to the suffering of another, and how we handle it. I don't see this same empathy in other cultures.

And I don't like it, in that it makes me feel I'm acting in a role, and I don't like that role. It bugs the *hell* out of me to know that I'm looked upon to react a certain way.

I prefer being alone. If I have a partner that's black, I enjoy the shift, we can talk over a situation, make the best use of our knowledge. But with a white partner, you're guessing. How is he going to react to this? How is he going to behave?

Say we go to a family disturbance. I'm being guided by my 'Anglo personality', because how much I can rely on him in the future, depends on how I talk to these people. With a black officer, I can drop the façade, and I have a different way with black people. With a white officer, I won't alienate him by remaining in his eyes 'professional' – he has a completely different perspective of me. What he wants is someone who's comical, a clown.

Ben Williams is anything but a clown. I detest being a spectacle. I'm not here for your entertainment. I'm here to do a job. The way I do my job, however, often isn't the way you'd do it, because of your white eyes, your white mind.

The hot stop goes smoothly. The young white arresting officer thanks Ben Williams for his assistance, appreciative of how cordial he has been in sharing the know-how he has picked up over almost a decade. Not all veteran officers are as generous.

Then back up toward the Plaza again, toward Broadway.

18

Three blocks west along Broadway from the Plaza, outside the San Diego County Courthouse, the demonstrators attract the attention of a passerby, and he pauses to watch them, presumably unaware of the concentrated police presence in the area, because the riot squads are being kept back out of sight.

His idle curiosity proves his undoing. He becomes the first arrest of the operation when Sergeant Glen Crawford, head of the Gang Detail, arrests him for carrying a concealed weapon – to wit, a handgun.

He is also the first prisoner to reach the mobile command post, although nobody supposes for a moment that his being armed has any connection with the bedsheet back on Broadway that proclaims, 'Death to the Klan'. It's simply a case of being in the wrong place at exactly the wrong time.

Inside the courthouse, police officers and sheriff's deputies continue their waiting. The tension is mounting, but so is their overtime, and on top of that, they have the demonstrators outnumbered by almost two to one.

19

Three blocks back along Broadway, Ben Williams locks a skinny, mean-faced drunk into the rear of his unit, and then opens his driver's door. 'The people I serve . . .' he sighs, glancing back at some winos on the Plaza, who have watched this arrest with happy interest.

'Don't put me back in jail, man,' his prisoner whines. 'Write me a ticket or somethin'.'

For once, Ben Williams does not appear to be listening.

> He and his brother, they jackroll. They're violent. The drunks are afraid of them. Every incident in which they're involved, I take a report and give it to Homicide. I'm hoping Homicide will tire of my reports, that they will act on them. They're going to injure someone real bad.

The time, he notes for his report, is seven-fifteen.

20

And that's when it happens. A windowless blue van, hardly more dignified than a box, approaches the Union Street entrance to the County Courthouse.

Two lines of riot-equipped police officers emerge from the building, forming a corridor to the edge of the sidewalk. They face outward, holding their riot batons horizontally at arm's length in front of them, ready to block any blows or missiles.

The blue van skids to a halt.

Tom Metzger, stony-faced, wearing a bulletproof vest, leaves the van with his bodyguards packed tightly around him.

'Death to the Klan!' yell demonstrators, surging forward against the police lines.

For a few seconds, it does seem like a riot, as placard sticks batter down on riot batons and cans of soft drink come raining in. One of the cans strikes Metzger a glancing blow on the side of the head, but he is unhurt and keeps moving.

Then he's gone, safe inside the building, and after a few scuffles, during which several arrests are made, it's all over bar the shouting.

'Fascists! Fascist pigs! Death to the Klan!'

An officer with a bullhorn warns that this is now an unlawful assembly, on the grounds that missiles have been thrown, and that anyone remaining in the vicinity will be automatically arrested just for being there.

The riot lines begin advancing on the demonstrators, menacingly enough to drive them up Broadway without much further incident, and within a matter of minutes the dispersal is complete.

A fact confirmed when the Sheriff's Department helicopter, which has been hovering overhead, lifts away, taking with it the last hint of the dramatic.

And when the time comes for Metzger to leave the courthouse again, nobody really notices who isn't paid to notice.

'Hey, Eduardo, how was it?' asks Lieutenant Chassam, as one of the veterans of Union Street returns to the command post.

It couldn't have been too bad. Jaunty, smiling, his riot baton tucked under one arm like a vaudeville cane, Sergeant Juarez looks ready to shout out, *'La Placa rifa!'*

But then that would be only properly understood back in the barrio.

21

Chief Kolender appears no less ebullient as he crosses the patio under a starry sky to attend the debriefing in the coffee shop at nine-thirty.

Four officers hurt, none seriously. The worst injury being a bruised rib, which Sergeant Glen Crawford, of the Gang Detail, received while arresting a stonethrower.

No other reported casualties.

Six arrests.

Metzger intact.

It was very well done. The officers showed restraint. There was some black guy right at their noses, calling them motherfucker and raising hell, but they didn't flinch. He was obviously trying to get knocked on his butt. I was there, although I personally did not say a word. I've had that job, and I know how it can be when you do all the work, and then somebody comes and starts shooting his mouth off. That's bullshit. I was there because, as Chief of Police, it's nice to go for morale and all that sort of thing. In fact, I made an arrest! They say we've got a complaint of police brutality; I say we've got a suspect. I just helped collar him, that's all – no big

330

deal. The only time we took action was when they started throwing that crap.

Now he wants to shake Agent Lipton by the hand, and tell everyone that he is well pleased with the evening's work.

> I believe shit goes down hill, pal, and my job is to set a tone. To set an example, and to attempt to formulate an attitude that pervades the department. An attitude based, not only on the philosophies that I have, but also on what the government of this city wants. They want a well-trained, humanistic police department, and that's exactly what I'm trying to give them.

22

And soon it will be time for Ben Williams to pocket his brass key-ring and take the bus home.

Gradually, his unit makes its way down the long slope of San Diego, heading for the station on West Market.

He isn't in any hurry.

> I love police work. I love it. I'm the big brother – even to the slobbering drunk, yuh? I'm a goodie – *and* a baddie.
>
> It's the challenge. All of it. It's good to walk an alley, shake doors. Your heart is just racing, poundin', and you hear *everything*. It's like the rollercoaster ride!
>
> But it changes. It's not the same ride. It's not the same line. The curve that was here yesterday, isn't here today. I feel an immediate satisfaction and reward.
>
> *I've walked the alley.*

Afterword

This book was not the result of a carefully laid plan to write about a particular police department. My commission was simply to research the American equivalent of my first major attempt at non-fiction, *Spike Island: Portrait of a British Police Division*, and the choice of law-enforcement agency was left to me.

Easier said than done from the other side of the Atlantic, and to further complicate matters, I felt it essential to insist on the same 'terms of reference' I had been granted in Liverpool by the Merseyside Police for *Spike Island*: unrestricted access, permission to make free use of a tape-recorder, sufficient time to extend my research well beyond the superficial level of 'first impressions', and the right to prepare a manuscript which would not be subject to editorial interference.

I began with metropolitan police departments to which I had introductions of a sort, approaching them one at a time as courtesy demanded. The reason most commonly given for turning me down was that pressure of work made it impossible for the police department concerned to have an outsider in its midst for more than a few days. Another stock response was breathtaking in its moral superiority: 'We do not cooperate with publications that have a profit motive.' Just try, no matter how serious your intent as a writer, to find an answer to that – they're a canny lot, police officers.

So I decided I needed help. The United States Embassy in London was asked if it could assist me in my search, given its infinitely greater resources. It could and did (although not without experiencing much the same difficulties I had done), and eventually, after a last-minute change of mind by the St Louis Police Department, I received news that I was welcome in San Diego, any time I liked.

335

I had my travel agent point me in the right direction, and left.

It wasn't sheer exasperation. I had been around policing for far too long to give in as easily. It was something far less defensible: a strong hunch that providence had finally dealt me the right card in the pack.

I was met at San Diego airport by Mrs Jeanne Brace, president of the local International Hospitality Council, and given an immediate tour of the city. This gracious gentle-woman, who wore a rose-scented perfume that for once expressed a personality with precision, could not do enough to make me feel at home. Hotel accommodation, a typewriter, everything I could possibly need, were promptly arranged, and it was only at this stage that I fully realized how much I owed to her already. Mrs Brace, having heard of my search through the Voluntary Visitors Division of the International Communication Agency in Washington, had called up Chief Bill Kolender, a family friend, and had somehow talked him into agreeing to give the go-ahead.

I say 'somehow' because the following morning Chief Kolender said to me from behind his large desk: 'Just what was it you wanted to do here in San Diego?' Seven thousand miles from Oxford, and very reluctant to leave on the next plane home again, I took a deep breath before describing the type of documentary-style book I intended to write, and was decidedly uneasy about listing my requirements regarding tape–recorders, free access, no editorial interference, and being allowed as much time as possible to conduct my research. 'Oh, okay,' he said affably, quite unperturbed, and that's about all there was to it.

The officer delegated to make the arrangements for my research was Lieutenant Charles E. Ellison III of Patrol Administra-tion, who had in his charge matter as various as the Gang Detail and Community Relations. A former U.S. Marine, now in his forties, he had a shaven head, wore gold-rimmed aviator-style glasses, and carried a snub-nosed revolver in a holster clipped to his waistband. Beside his desk leaned a gigan-tic sack of popcorn, and on his wall was a John Wayne poster.

We started the day with another tour of the city, only this

336

time seeing it through a police windshield: 'This area, Fifth and Island, used to be really wild. Most of the pimps and the prostitutes are sleeping right now – we don't really have a redlight district.' We called in at the police academy, where I met an ex-British bobby in process of becoming a cop. So much was the same, he said – and so much was different.

I nodded. Lieutenant Ellison had just been telling me about how, while in charge of the Juvenile Unit, he had helped to introduce the idea of having social workers assigned to the department to deal with cases like dirty homes which didn't involve any actual criminal activity, but were causes for concern all the same. 'You mean they share the same office, where the interrogations are held and everything?' I had asked. 'Sure,' he'd replied, apparently a little puzzled.

It was just that I'd no previous experience of detectives willing to have other professionals working literally alongside them, witnesses to everything that went on – least of all social workers for whom, at best, a cheerful if wary contempt was generally reserved.

And from that moment on, I felt certain of my hunch. Here indeed was a police department worth investigating, if only because, in the process, I might be able to satisfy some of my own curiosity as to the hows and whys of such a radical departure from conventional police attitudes.

But two precautions had to be taken before I actually joined Second Watch, Central Division, both of which were directly related to an advertisement appearing in magazines on San Diego's newsstands at the time. The advertisement, inserted by Handgun Control, Inc., carried this stark piece of information above a chunky revolver, painted with the Stars and Stripes:

LAST YEAR, HANDGUNS KILLED
48 PEOPLE IN JAPAN
8 IN GREAT BRITAIN
34 IN SWITZERLAND
52 IN CANADA
58 IN ISRAEL
21 IN SWEDEN
42 IN WEST GERMANY
10,728 IN THE UNITED STATES

337

Lieutenant Ellison went to considerable lengths to find an insurance company prepared to offer me hospital cover, and finally I paid out $60 or so for a short-term policy. I was also issued with a bullet-proof vest, the back half of which I soon abandoned because it was so uncomfortable in the heat (I'm not sure I'd still have done this had I known that the medical insurance company would be writing to me later in the year, when I was safely back home in England, to say that, on review, my policy application had been refused).

That done, I started accompanying officers on patrol, and of course the fact they were armed was one of those differences to which the ex-British bobby had been referring. I can't pretend this seemed strange to me: I'd grown up in a land where the police were always armed, and as a crime reporter in South Africa, I had sometimes been armed myself.

What I did find novel, however, after the many shifts I'd spent with Merseyside officers on the streets of Liverpool, was the *indirect* influence that being armed seemed to have. People were so obedient; an officer could tell three youths to stand in a semi-circle, while he turned his back to talk to a fourth, and they would remain there. In Liverpool, they'd have vanished even before that back was properly turned. Then again, when dealing with a hostile group, just having that handgun in its holster seemed to have a restraining effect; what in Liverpool could have turned into a brawl, because an officer had been pushed in the chest, stayed a strictly verbal exchange on the streets of San Diego. Female officers, I noted, were certainly treated with greater respect than chivalry alone could account for, because I had witnessed the limits of chivalry when British policewomen, who patrol completely unarmed, carrying not even a small baton, encounter aggressive defiance.

As a matter of fact, my initial failure to realize how comparatively *un*physical San Diego policing could be, meant that I made rather a fool of myself to begin with. I was used to engaging the interest of patrol sergeants by asking them how many injuries their squads (or 'sections') suffered in a week, and to have them recount with doleful glee the problems they faced in making up for the number of walking wounded. But when I asked the same question in California, the response tended to be, 'Huh?' The reason for this soon became apparent. Take a bar fight. In Liverpool, the bobby could expect to become involved in that fight, and to be attacked by onlookers as well, before subduing his prisoner – more often than not without drawing his truncheon, the use of which would be judged as either 'provocative' or 'soft', depending on his sergeant's disposition. And God help him if he applied any sort of hold that affected his prisoner's breathing or circulation. In San Diego, on the other hand, the cop could expect onlookers to mind their own business, and if he had any difficulty in making the arrest, he would simply use the 'choke hold', rendering the subject instantly unconscious.

In time, these observations merely underscored what must seem an obvious contrast between being a British bobby and working as an American cop: the former goes out on the streets hoping not to get hurt; the latter, in hope of not being killed. For me, the more surprising differences lay in lesser things.

I was astonished, for example, by how comparatively little colorful language San Diego police officers used, whether in public or in private among themselves. Where a Liverpudlian bobby would be 'effin' and 'blindin', stringing together profoundly vivid epithets from a vast vocabulary of references to matters sexual, political, lavatorial and philosophical, his San Diegan counterpart seemed content to restrict himself chiefly to the word 'ass' in its limited number of permutations. Granted, an occasional 'scumbag' could be heard, but for the most part 'asshole' was judged sufficiently dismissive.*

I was equally taken aback by how often offenders failed to make any attempt to evade arrest by leaving the scene while they had a chance. In Liverpool, flight and fight had been the norm, even among quite elderly delinquents. But in San Diego, time and again suspects would just remain where they were, in a state of apathy not necessarily drink- or drug-related, and wait while they were pointed out to the officer answering the call. Weird, I thought, and nobody was able to explain this to me – not even the prisoners themselves.

*While on the subject of words, I should perhaps add that 'baton' (not 'night-stick') and 'handie-talkie' (not 'walkie-talkie') are correct San Diego PD terminology.

Then there were all those things that were much the same. Admittedly, officers in San Diego did not seem haunted by the thought of complaints being made against them by the public, and had no need to dread having to notify relatives of sudden deaths, as bobbies do, but they would actually repeat, almost word for word, sentences that had already appeared in *Spike Island*: 'Patrol is hours and hours of nothing, punctuated by split-seconds of terror.'

A universal truth of sorts, which probably first appeared in yet another book somewhere.

And this of course presented a major problem when, several months later, I began work on *Cop World*: the split-seconds were relatively easy to write about, the hard bit was going to be attempting to show that the 'nothing' could be, in an unsensational way, often just as diverting.

But first I had more than 150 hours of tape to transcribe. God, what a horrible experience. I swore a great deal, much of the time at myself for not making more of an interview, interruptions by drunks, battered victims and irate prisoners notwithstanding. I cursed very loudly indeed when all too often Communications obliterated a vital quote with some blaring radio message that was in itself the height of inanity. I sat silent and numbed when I discovered that a group of tapes had been garbled by I know not what, although a technically-minded friend suggested some brush with a magnetic field, possibly at an airport.

The loss of these recordings was a disappointment made all the more bitter by the fact *Spike Island* had had its casualties, and I'd tried to take every precaution against a repeat performance. But there it was, and I had to reconcile myself to making do without George, Art, Vicki, Ed and Joe, Rulette, Jack, Max and Ed, Mark, Chet, Bob, Rob . . . Even so, each would still be making a valuable contribution to the book by having provided me with a much more complete picture to work from.

And so I began on the manuscript, taking certain liberties with clock and calendar, but always striving to ensure that nothing was juxtaposed gratuitously. This wasn't easy and took time, an enormous amount of time, but at last the final page left my typewriter.

What a lot of people had helped me reach that stage, and it's only right that I pause now and thank as many of them as possible. I will not grade my gratitude, for each in his or her way stinted nothing, and so I'll use instead a listing that is roughly categorized, occasionally alphabetical. My profound thanks go:

To Pat Kavanagh, my agent, and to Peter Matson, her associate in America; to my editors at Pantheon Books, Andre Schiffrin and Dan Cullen; to my editors at Macmillan London Limited, Lord Hardinge of Penshurst and Hilary Hale; to Sonny Mehta of Pan Books.

To Anthea L. Buckeridge, of the International Communication Agency, U.S. Embassy, London; to Ursula Mahin, of the Voluntary Visitors Division I.C.A., Washington D.C., to Jeanne Brace and her husband, Clayton; to Arthur Maling of Chicago; to Richard Jackson.

To Chief William B. Kolender; to Inspector M. C. Guaderrama, Patrol; to Lieutenant Ellison; to Bill Robinson, Public Information Officer; to all the officers of the San Diego Police Department who helped me in my research, and in particular those who gave me permission to use their words in this book.

To my family – Lorly, James, Alistair and Kirsten – who once again bore the brunt of a seemingly endless task; to Bert Lockwood, Christina Rose, Don Wall, Eddie Farrell, Jim Whittington, Joan Kahn, Joe Josephs, Monica Horn, Olov Svedelid, Robin Hutton, Sam Ellis, Sandra Skillen, Tony Fogarty and Wendy Robinson; to Ken Howard of A.D. Peters & Co.; and to Don Mills of the National Westminster Bank, whose wisdom and steady nerve never wavered.

The job done, I had the manuscript in the post as soon as possible, but my interest in the San Diego Police Department continued. I heard that Chief Kolender, reputedly still the only Jewish police chief out of 25,000 others in America, had been offered the job of Chief of Police in Washington after the attempted assassination of President Reagan, and that he'd turned it down – just as he'd previously turned down the same high office in Los Angeles.

I was sent news of a decentralization program going ahead, which divided the city into seven command areas, each with its own police station. I received a letter not too long ago that said: 'Things in this city are always changing. The Plaza, with all the hustle and bustle, has all but disappeared. Where the Cabrillo theater stood, is a level pad of earth. Only the fountain and some grass remain. The street people have, for the most part, filtered south into the older part of the city.

'Chief Kolender was an unofficial contender for the Mayor's job – Pete Wilson is now a U.S. Senator – and seemed to have a good chance, but he decided instead to stay on as Chief of Police. Norm Stamper has been designated as Assistant Chief. This is a curious placement for a non-sworn person, but he is totally qualified and permanent appointment seems likely. Now instead of advising, he can direct.

'Sergeant (Eduardo Juarez) has found his niche. He is working with Inspection and Control, looking at policies and procedures throughout the department. (Jean Cummings) is now our first female lieutenant, commanding a patrol unit in the eastern part of the city. Coincidentally, our first black lieutenant is also assigned there.

'Lieutenant (Rae Chassam) has been reassigned as manager of ARJIS, one of the largest computer programs dedicated to crime information. Captain Walker may soon be Commander Walker.

'Some things haven't changed though. People are still stealing from each other, hurting one another and killing one another . . .'

And I have been assured that policing the streets of San Diego hasn't changed either in any essential way since I was there, and isn't likely to, not while those hours and hours still have their moments.

September 4, 1980

Dear Jim,

This is just a short note to let you know I really enjoyed the books. We had an officer shot after you left. A couple of gang members from the Crips set him up. One of them knocked on his passenger window while Steve was sitting in his vehicle. When Steve looked to the passenger side, he felt a gun to the back of his head and heard a 'click'.

342

Scarey, huh? He turned around and grabbed the gun, but it went off in his face. It hit him in the left cheek area. It traveled to the base of the neck and stopped there. He is fine and returns to work tomorrow. That's one lucky fellow.

Your good friend,
Harry O

About the Author

James McClure was born in Johannesburg, South Africa, and grew up in the capital of Natal, Pietermaritzburg, where he worked as a commercial photographer and taught art, history, and English at his former preparatory school. Later, while working for three major newspapers in Natal, he became a specialist in crime and court stories. After emigrating to Great Britain, he worked at the *Scottish Daily Mail*. In 1965 he became deputy editor of the Oxford Times Group of weekly papers, a post he held until 1974, when he resigned to devote more time to writing.

McClure is most familiar to American readers for his novels, of which he has written seven. He won the Crime Writers' Association's Golden Dagger Award for *The Steam Pig*, and their Silver Dagger Award for *Rogue Eagle*.

Spike Island, published by Pantheon in 1980, is McClure's highly acclaimed study of a British police division, and the companion of *Cop World*. His newest novel, *The Artful Egg*, will be published by Pantheon in early 1985.